BIRDING
Florida

HELP US KEEP THIS GUIDE UP TO DATE

Every effort has been made by the author and editors to make this guide as accurate and useful as possible. However, many things can change after a guide is published.

We would appreciate hearing from you concerning your experiences with this guide and how you feel it could be improved and kept up to date. While we may not be able to respond to all comments and suggestions, we'll take them to heart, and we'll also make certain to share them with the author. Please send your comments and suggestions to the following address:

FalconGuides
Reader Response/Editorial Department
246 Goose Lane, Suite 200
Guilford, CT 06437

Thanks for your input!

BIRDING
Florida

A Field Guide to the Birds of Florida

RANDI MINETOR
Photography by NIC MINETOR

GUILFORD, CONNECTICUT

FALCONGUIDES®

An imprint of The Rowman & Littlefield Publishing Group, Inc.
4501 Forbes Blvd., Ste. 200
Lanham, MD 20706
www.rowman.com

Falcon and FalconGuides are registered trademarks and Make Adventure Your Story is a trademark of The Rowman & Littlefield Publishing Group, Inc.
Distributed by NATIONAL BOOK NETWORK

Copyright © 2021 The Rowman & Littlefield Publishing Group, Inc.
Maps by The Rowman & Littlefield Publishing Group, Inc.
Interior photographs by Nic Minetor unless otherwise noted
Parts of a Bird drawing on page 18 by Todd Telander

British Library Cataloguing-in-Publication Information available

Library of Congress Cataloging in Publication Data

Names: Minetor, Randi, author. | Minetor, Nic, photographer.
Title: Birding Florida : a field guide to the birds of Florida / Randi Minetor ; photography by Nic Minetor.
Description: Guilford, Connecticut : FalconGuides, [2021] | Includes bibliographical references and index. | Summary: "A complete guide to birding in Florida. Includes sections on birding technology, equipment, identification techniques, birding 'by ear,' where to view birds, field guides, optics, and other essentials to get birders of all skill levels into the field to identify birds throughout Florida"— Provided by publisher.
Identifiers: LCCN 2020053186 (print) | LCCN 2020053187 (ebook) | ISBN 9781493055159 (paperback) | ISBN 9781493055166 (epub)
Subjects: LCSH: Birds—Florida—Identification. | Bird watching—Florida.
Classification: LCC QL684.F6 M54 2021 (print) | LCC QL684.F6 (ebook) | DDC 598.072/34759—dc23
LC record available at https://lccn.loc.gov/2020053186
LC ebook record available at https://lccn.loc.gov/2020053187

♾TM The paper used in this publication meets the minimum requirements of American National Standard for Information Sciences—Permanence of Paper for Printed Library Materials, ANSI/NISO Z39.48-1992.

CONTENTS

Ground Birds

Birds of Prey

Non-Perching Birds (Nonpasserines)

Perching Birds (Passerines)

ACKNOWLEDGMENTS

In our time researching for this book and photographing birds in Florida, we rediscovered what we have found in every other part of the country: Birders are some of the best people in the world. We don't know the names of most of the people who helped us sort out winter-plumaged shorebirds on Sanibel's beaches or find active red-cockaded woodpecker nests, but we are grateful to every single one of them.

In particular, we must thank the staff members at Florida's many national wildlife refuges, Audubon bird sanctuaries, and state, county, and city parks who pointed us in the right direction for limpkin, painted buntings, nanday parakeets, and dozens of other specialty species.

We are very grateful to birders closer to our upstate New York home whose rare bird alerts and personal guidance led us to birds that did not put in an appearance for us in Florida: Dominic Sherony, Jill Church Heimrich, Robert Buckert, Jules Wagner, Nick Kachala, Willie D'Anna, Josh Ketry, Andy Garland, Kyle Gage, Diane Henderson, Lucretia Grosshans, Shirley Shaw, Bill Howe, Dick Horsey, Greg Lawrence, Pat Martin, Mike Tetlow, Tom and Jeanne Verhulst, Michael Gullo, and Andrew Guthrie. When the COVID-19 pandemic made it impossible for us to return to Florida to finish our photography, Dominic Sherony provided many of his own excellent photos to help us finish this book. He and Mike Tetlow also provided much-needed assistance in reviewing our photos to be sure of all identifications, helping us improve our skills and ensuring this book's quality and accuracy.

Our friends Jane and Richard Patterson walked us up to their neighborhood's burrowing owls in Cape Coral and provided hospitality during our Florida travels; likewise, my lifelong friend Diane Hardy and her husband, Chris, gave us lodging and helped us locate the brown-headed nuthatch pictured in this book. When friends who are not birders muster up enthusiasm for our pursuits, it means everything to us. Thanks so much, guys.

The folks at the Seneca Meadows Landfill in upstate New York did us and the entire region a tremendous favor when they opened their facility to allow birders to see the blue grosbeak that appeared there in May 2020—a rarity for the state, and one that did not show itself to us while we birded Florida.

As always, the team at Falcon Guides has produced a great book: editorial director David Legere, production editor Meredith Dias, copy editor Paulette Baker, cartographer Melissa Baker, layout artist Joanna Beyer, and proofreader Beth Richards. Our brilliant agent, Regina Ryan, continues to keep our publishing careers on track as she has for the past fifteen years, taking extraordinary care of us so we can pursue our passions throughout the region and beyond.

Finally, to the friends and family who support us in all our efforts, we cannot say enough about your generosity of spirit when it comes to our literary endeavors. Ken Horowitz, Rose-Anne Moore, Martin Winer, Bruce Barton, Lisa Jaccoma, Kevin Hyde, Christine Tattersall, Martha and Peter Schermerhorn, Ruth Watson, John King, Cindy Blair, Paula and Rich Landis, Margery Kimbrough (who sewed us masks in camouflage patterns so we could keep birding throughout the pandemic); neighbor Pam Bartemus, and all the others scattered across the country: You make every chapter fun, and there are no words strong enough to express our gratitude.

INTRODUCTION

One of the most exciting states in the country for birding, Florida offers novice and experienced birders alike an adventure you will find nowhere else in the United States. Here northern birding meets tropical paradise, with mixed deciduous (leafy) and coniferous (cone-bearing) woodlands along the Florida Panhandle bumping up against expansive salt marshes, which in turn reach southward to the Gulf of Mexico's white sand beaches. Two extensive coastlines edge the Atlantic Ocean as well as the Gulf, providing some of the most productive beaches and marshes for spotting many species of gulls, terns, shorebirds, long-legged and short wading birds, pelicans, cormorants, grebes, waterfowl, and even some pelagic birds that troll fishing boats not far from shore.

Inland birding provides an equally thrilling experience, with a wide range of southern birds of prey, doves, cuckoos, and a dizzying array of passerines (perching birds). Songbirds including warblers, vireos, tanagers, and orioles gather in trees within and outside of populated areas, while a wide range of wrens, thrushes, kinglets, swallows, flycatchers, and jays make this state their year-round home—and still more migrate through or arrive to spend the summer. Moving southward, the wonders of birding in and around Miami, Fort Myers, and the Keys reveal themselves, with some of the area's most colorful and exotic species populating city parks, neighborhood squares, and residential backyards.

Whether you've recently turned to birding as a new hobby or you've been watching and seeking out birds for decades, you'll find treasure in Florida—an unending variety of both dependable and unexpected species to keep you busy for a morning, a vacation, a season, or a lifetime.

Geography and Habitats

In its 65,755 square miles of landmass—none of it more than 345 feet above sea level—Florida holds an unusually diverse variety of habitats for resident and migrating birds. Two distinctly different coastlines, saltwater and freshwater marshes, northern successional forests, open farmland and plains, islands and keys, and America's most famous "river of grass" all offer opportunities for dependable sightings of much-sought-after birds.

The Coasts

Some 1,350 miles of Atlantic Ocean and Gulf coastline offer birders a remarkable opportunity to find nearly every species that frequents the nation's eastern seaboard. While beaches can be crowded with tourists and residents throughout much of the year, a number of areas protected specifically for birds and marine life offer spectacular birding without the crush of people seeking sun, sand, and surf.

Nowhere on Florida's Atlantic coast will you find more bird species than on Canaveral National Seashore and the adjacent Merritt Island National Wildlife Refuge. Here on Florida's Space Coast, long-legged waders including great blue, tricolored, and little blue herons; great, snowy, and cattle egrets; reddish egret, black-crowned and yellow-crowned night-herons, glossy and white ibis, anhinga, wood stork, and roseate spoonbill all linger in various seasons, and clapper and Virginia rails, American and least bittern, and sora also wander out from between tall reeds to give birders occasional but satisfying glimpses. The Canaveral beach provides views of Forster's, Caspian, sandwich, and royal terns throughout the year, and common and least terns during the migration and breeding seasons. Black skimmer and American oystercatcher are usually found in this birder's paradise as well. In Merritt Island's wooded area near the visitor center, painted buntings come to feeders and white-eyed vireo, orange-crowned and pine warblers, blue-headed vireo, and blue-gray gnatcatcher are all residents. This park is also the easiest place in the state to find Florida scrub-jay, the only bird that is found exclusively in Florida—try the area around the Canaveral Seashore pay station, the shrubs along the Black Point Wildlife Drive, or the aptly named Scrub Trail.

The Atlantic coastline becomes densely populated south of Cocoa Beach, but across the FL 913 causeway in Miami, two significant ocean parks provide some significant birding. Crandon Park and Bill Baggs Cape Florida State Park offer the chance to see shorebirds including the endangered piping plover, as well as semipalmated plover, ruddy turnstone, sanderling, least and spotted sandpipers, willet, and many of the long-legged waders sought by visiting birders. This park can be the place to begin racking up a list of exotic species sightings, including Egyptian goose; Indian peafowl; white-eyed, mitred, blue-crowned, yellow-chevroned, or monk parakeet; orange-winged parrot; and common myna. Vagrant birds from the Caribbean islands often blow into this park during major storms, so keep an eye out for western spindalis and Bahama mockingbird if you happen to find yourself here post-hurricane. At Bill Baggs Park, sightings of magnificent frigatebird, gray kingbird, Louisiana waterthrush, all kinds of migrating warblers, and smooth-billed ani are not only possible but common. The wading birds, gulls, and terns are here as well, and you are likely to come across Eurasian collared dove and common ground dove among the mourning doves on this point.

On the Gulf of Mexico coast (we haven't skipped the Everglades—see their section below), birders come from all over the world to visit J. N. Ding Darling National Wildlife Refuge on Sanibel Island. Not only will you find every long-legged wader in Florida here, but the refuge's driving route takes birders through subtropical woodland that rings with birdsong. The elusive and highly prized mangrove cuckoo resides here, occasionally giving birders great looks in early to mid-morning as it sits calmly in a tree over the wetland. This is a great place to find the magnificent frigatebird soaring overhead, and black-and-white, prothonotary, yellow-throated, and prairie warblers are all known to nest here. Watch the skies for swallow-tailed kite and red-shouldered hawk along with the more usual turkey vultures.

If you happen to be on Sanibel Island during the spring migration, there is no better place to position yourself than at Point Ybel Lighthouse Beach Park. This migrant stopover site attracts just about every species of warbler, vireo, tanager, swallow, and thrush passing through on its way north, with peak viewing time during the last two weeks of April and the first week of May. Here you may find Swainson's, Kentucky, and yellow-throated warblers, which breed in the eastern-central United States and don't make their way much farther north.

For close-up views of shorebirds, Fort De Soto Park, at the very end of the island causeway off the southern coast of St. Petersburg, provides the kind of superlative birding that brings people here from all over the country. This is where to go for Wilson's and snowy plovers, as well as piping, black-bellied, and semipalmated plovers; willet; ruddy turnstone; sanderlings by the hundreds; least, semipalmated, spotted, pectoral, and western sandpipers; short-billed dowitcher; dunlin; and all the long-legged waders. Clapper rail puts in regular appearances here, as do American avocet and marbled godwit. The palm trees along the park road provide the easiest place in Florida to see nanday parakeet, a large black-headed, bright green bird from South America that established a colony in this park decades ago.

Dozens of parks along the Gulf coast provide places to see shorebirds, terns, gulls, and wading birds, but be sure to plan some time on the Panhandle to visit St. Marks National Wildlife Refuge. South of Tallahassee, this magnificent park's salt marshes are one of the few places in Florida where you may glimpse American flamingo, a bird nearly extirpated from the state by the aggressive activity of the fashion industry a century or more ago. Flamingo feathers were once a staple on ladies' hats and other finery, so the birds were hunted nearly to extinction and now are seen largely in captivity (visit Walt Disney World to be assured a sighting, even though captive birds are not considered "countable" by the American Birding Association). Every so often, however, one shows up here at St. Marks— perhaps an escaped bird from a private collection, or maybe one of the last remaining wild ones. White-faced ibis, a bird more commonly found in Louisiana and parts west, also makes winter visits to this refuge. The woods here can be filled with warblers and vireos, both during migration and throughout the summer, and all manner of shorebirds and other water-loving birds dominate the mudflats and marshes. Pay a visit to the lighthouse area for views of many seabirds.

The Everglades

With so many high-rise hotels and apartment buildings per square mile of coastline, it's hard to imagine that much of Florida's southern acreage once consisted of tall grasses and a natural ecosystem that filtered and refreshed its own water supply throughout the year. Today, a fraction of the "real Florida" remains in Everglades National Park, a 1.5-million acre expanse that preserves the land in its original state. This protected wilderness gives visitors a view into an utterly unique phenomenon, the only one of its kind in the world.

Here, at the confluence of salt- and freshwater, a bounty of ancient and comparatively new forms of life nourish one another by supplying the organic materials they need to thrive. A spongy substance called periphyton forms the base of this food chain, blanketing wide stretches of land and providing sustenance to plants, microorganisms, and larger animals, and holding the moisture this river of grass needs to survive throughout the dry seasons. It's a remarkable natural achievement, created entirely through the evolution of plant matter and microscopic life, and massive efforts by the National Park Service, the State of Florida, and other organizations are in place to preserve it just as it has been for eons.

Even so, the Everglades are under attack. Municipal water systems syphoned off the delicate balance between moisture and plant life, endangering the ecosystem's survival. The release of Burmese pythons and other invasive species by well-meaning but careless individuals have created an infestation of huge snakes that multiply prolifically and devour small animals and birds. Rabbits, raccoons, groundhogs, shrews, mice, and other small mammals have all but disappeared in the face of this destructive force; birds have the advantage of flight, so while the snakes have indeed decimated their populations, many bird species are holding their own. It's still easy to see all the wading birds and specialties like purple gallinule, anhinga, swallow-tailed kite, short-tailed hawk, black vulture, black-crowned night-heron, wood stork, roseate spoonbill, American and least bitterns, white-crowned pigeon, and a wide range of passerines here in the park. Begin your explo- ration at Anhinga Trail, a wonderful paved path and boardwalk that gives you up-close access to many birds as they pick their way through lily pads or perch on tree branches. You'll see plenty of alligators here as well. My word to the wise is simple: Don't bother them, and they won't bother you.

Extend your Everglades visit by making your way down the park road with stops at Long Pine Key Campground, where you have an excellent chance of encountering common ground dove, gray kingbird, brown-headed nuthatch, and other woodland specialties; and Paurotis Pond, where long-legged birds, birds of prey, ducks and duck-like birds, and even king rail often gather toward sunset. The road ends at Flamingo, a well-known birding paradise with all kinds of sightings on and near Florida Bay as well as in the surrounding woodland.

Just north of the park, additional protected areas preserve wetlands that play a role in the Everglades' ability to maintain its own ecosystem. Big Cypress National Preserve and Everglades and Francis S. Taylor Wildlife Management Area provide additional oppor- tunities to bird in this important wilderness area. Mississippi kite, snail kite, and all the wading birds are often spotted in these areas, and roseate spoonbill and wood stork both nest here. Keep in mind that hunting is permitted at specific times of the year, however, so check the schedule and wear blaze orange if your birding trip coincides with hunting season.

The North-Central Wetlands

With so much of its land at or nearly at sea level, much of Florida has a wetland compo- nent of one kind or another. Freshwater marshes surround Newnans Lake in Gainesville and Lake Apopka farther south, providing excellent opportunities to spot limpkin, whimbrel, mottled duck, black-bellied whistling duck, gray-headed swamphen, bitterns, rails, sandhill crane, American avocet, and a wide variety of others. The mix of northern and southern foliage in this region can yield just about any woodland or scrub-loving bird species as well, making birding here especially diverse and exciting.

Sweetwater Wetland Park provides one of the most delightful birding habitats in the state, a walkable mix of paved trail and boardwalk through wetland and woodland habitat. Here black-bellied whistling ducks gather in small flocks or sit in trees, purple gallinule and gray-headed swamphen fraternize with common gallinule and American coot, and limpkin are easy to spot among the other tall wading birds. Not far down the road, Orlando

Wetlands Park provides an equally enchanting experience, with the possibility of mottled duck, American bittern, barred owl, and wood stork in the mix.

Lake Apopka Wildlife Drive is open only on Friday, Saturday, and Sunday from 7 a.m. to 3 p.m., but if you manage to synchronize your schedule with this availability, you will have a remarkable experience. Not only are all the waders and many of Florida's shorebird species easy to see here, but this is one of the best places in Florida to find fulvous whistling duck. Expect to spend at least 2 hours driving the one-way, 11-mile loop, with the assumption that you will make many stops to scan the pools for a wide variety of species. Follow your drive with a walk through Lake Apopka's North Shore's 2.6-mile Loop Trail for warblers, tanagers, sparrows, blackbirds, orioles, towhees, finches, and more.

Exotics

If you live in Miami or have visited before, you may be well aware of the abundance of exotic bird species—birds whose normal range would not include North America or, in many cases, the Western Hemisphere—that roam the city, especially in the western and southern suburbs. Whether these colonies of chattery, gregarious, charismatic birds grew from a few escaped pets, a failed pet store owner's mass release, escapes from private collections in botanical gardens, or from some other mysterious source has been cause for considerable speculation among birders for generations. Today, as many as seventy-two species of exotic parrots and parakeets have been spotted in the Miami area, according to a USDA report, as well as an estimated twenty-two species of exotic waterfowl, and communities around Fort Myers and Naples on Florida's west coast have their own established flocks as well.

We have included some of these birds in this book, based on the recommendations of the American Birding Association (ABA) and their accepted records of breeding populations. The hot spots we have provided for these birds may lead to sightings of additional species, as many parrots and parakeets enjoy the same kinds of habitats and may vie for their own territory in fairly limited surroundings. Exotic waterfowl seem relatively content to share city ponds with other species, so there is less conflict there. Spotting many of these birds is virtually inevitable in south Florida, so if you see something unexpected, take note—it may turn out to be a life bird you can "count" according to ABA guidelines.

Where are these magical areas filled with parakeets, parrots, macaws, and mynas? The vicinity of West Kendall Baptist Hospital in Kendall provides a veritable parrot roost, with several species usually spotted there at a time. Neighborhoods in Miami Springs have individual populations of parrots and parakeets, and city parks in that area play host to an ever-changing array of bright green birds. Other places to check include Ocean Bank at 788-700 FL 953 in Miami, the Mutineer Restaurant retention pond in Florida City, the Tamarac Exotic Duck Pond in a suburb of Fort Lauderdale, and the Fairchild Tropical Botanic Garden in Coral Gables. If you are a golfer, you may run into flocks of parrots and parakeets on courses in Boca Raton and West Palm Beach; if shopping is more your jam, the retention ponds and groves of trees around shopping plazas in south Florida often attract parakeet colonies and exotic waterfowl. Crandon Park and Fort De Soto Park, both mentioned earlier, also have exotic bird populations.

Optics and How to Choose Them

If you are new to birding and have not yet acquired your own binoculars or decided on the need for a spotting scope, we offer some basic guidance:

1. Yes, you need binoculars. Birds rarely land close enough to give you a good, satisfying look, especially if you're examining an unfamiliar wing pattern, an alternate seasonal plumage, or details you've never seen in person before. Binoculars are key to your enjoyment of the birds, but which binoculars are right for you? Here are the most important elements to understand when purchasing a pair for your birding enjoyment:

- **Look for the magnification and diameter formula,** usually stamped on the focus knob. For example, it may say 7×35, 8×42, or 10×40. The first number indicates the number of times the binoculars magnify the image of the bird—so if the first number is "8," it means you will see the bird at eight times its normal size. You may believe, then, that a magnification of 10 or more would be the best for your purposes, but before you leap to buy such a pair, try it out in person. You may find that 10× binoculars are too heavy to hold still, making the additional magnification an expensive waste. Many birders are most comfortable with a factor of 8.
- **The diameter number** (35, 40, 42, or 50) tells you how much light comes through the large end of the binoculars. The number is the diameter of the lens itself, and the larger it is, the brighter and clearer the image will be when it reaches your eye. Binoculars with a larger diameter are especially good in low-light situations, like when you're trying to see the mating dance of the American woodcock at dusk or you're attempting to spot a barn owl calling in a dim forest.
- **The secret is the multicoating.** Why are your grandfather's 10×50 binoculars, purchased in the 1960s, not nearly as good for birding as a modern pair at 7×35? Optics technology has come a long way over the past fifty years, eliminating distortions like

the blue-and-yellow fringe around objects you may see through your granddad's pair. "Fully multicoated" means every piece of glass inside and out—as many as eighteen surfaces—is layered with coatings that reduce glare, distortion, fringing, and other issues that can keep you from seeing a bird clearly.

- **Get past the sticker shock.** Cheap binoculars are not going to cut it in the field, so if you're a committed birder and want the best experience possible, you're going to have to spend a little money. There's good news on this front, however: Several top manufacturers have developed excellent binoculars at a price point of about $250, so you don't need to stretch for a top-of-the-line pair in the $1,200 range to have perfectly serviceable optics.

2. Do you need a spotting scope? It's a valid question, especially if you're new to birding, and one you need to answer in your own time. To get an idea of the possibilities a scope opens up for you, participate in a field trip with your local birding association and look through several of the scopes other birders use. Remember how you felt the first time you saw a bird through a good pair of binoculars? The leap from binoculars to a scope is equally dramatic. If you do decide to purchase your own scope, keep in mind that the tripod is every bit as important as the magnification and diameter—on a windy day or when you're standing on a busy boardwalk, you'll be glad you chose a slightly heavier, more stable tripod that keeps your scope from vibrating.

Bird Classifications

The American Ornithological Society and the American Birding Association have teams of experts who have spent years determining the exact biological category each bird belongs in, what family of birds it belongs to within that category, and what its taxonomic (Latin) name should be. This is critically important work for our scientific understanding of birds, their evolution, and the discovery of new species through DNA analysis and other methods.

Bird taxonomy informed this book, but we also relied on our own field experience, gathered through more than thirty-five years of birding, and our use of a wide range of field guides. In this book we have endeavored to group birds within their taxonomic families, but also in a manner that will make it easy to compare one bird to another for purposes of identification. So you'll find all the pelagic species grouped together, as well as all the wading birds, all the swimming birds, the birds of prey, and so on. This enhances the usability of this guide, allowing you to focus on studying the bird's field marks in relation to others in the same general habitat.

Seasonal Plumage and Other Mysteries

As if the process of identifying each bird were not confounding enough, most birds lose their bright breeding plumage once the mating season is over. All birds molt at least once a year, dropping their old feathers and replacing them with new ones, but not all of them change the look of their plumage from one season to the next. When they do, it can result in considerable frustration for birders struggling to identify individuals in a mixed flock of what the 1980 Peterson *Field Guide to the Birds* famously dubbed "confusing fall warblers."

To help you sort out the field marks (or lack of them) when the birds make it the hardest to do so, we have provided detailed descriptions of nonbreeding plumage for each of the birds that make this transition. Many fall warblers look nearly identical in their nonbreeding plumage, with perhaps a single feature that differs, so you can make careful comparisons of the descriptions to determine which species you may be seeing. Remember that the bird's habitat, food choices, song, and behavior are still the guiding factors to its identification, especially when the plumage provides few clues.

Many waterfowl go through two periods of molt each year, based on their nesting and breeding schedule. Male ducks lose their bright feathers soon after nesting, changing over to a drab appearance called "eclipse" plumage as early as the last week of June. This is particularly evident in wood ducks, which go from a coat of many colors to a brown mantle with a white patch at the throat. In early winter, when other species of birds are still cloaked for fall, male wood ducks and other waterfowl regain their stunning plumage in preparation for attracting their mate.

Birding by Ear

One of the most important skills you need to bird in any area of the world is an ability to identify birds by song. It's not as difficult as you may think—the more you listen in the field and practice with recordings, the clearer it will become that each bird has a distinctly different way of expressing itself.

We have provided phonetic transcriptions of each bird's song or call in this book, with popular phrases and mnemonics to help you learn some of the most common and familiar calls. That being said, there is no substitute for a good smartphone app that puts every bird's song in your pocket. Some apps serve as an adjunct to field guides (or are part of a field guide app, such as iBird Pro, National Geographic Birds, Sibley eGuide, Audubon Birds Pro, and Peterson Birds), so you can choose a bird and listen to all the variations of its song. Others actually teach you how to tell one bird song from another and how to remember each song. Highly recommended teaching apps include Larkwire, Chirp!, and iKnowBirdSongs; each is available for a onetime fee. Many of these apps use songs from the Macaulay Library at the Cornell Laboratory of Ornithology, one of the most respected and extensive resources for bird information in North America.

If you are daunted by the idea of learning bird songs, let us say this: You will be amazed at how much time it saves you in the field. Start by learning the ten most common birds in your own backyard—for example, house sparrow, northern cardinal, common grackle, blue jay, northern mockingbird, American robin, Carolina chickadee, red-winged blackbird, mourning dove, Carolina wren. Each of these birds has a distinctive song, making this sampler an excellent starting point in learning what makes one song different from another. With these ten (or ten others you choose) firmly in your mind, you'll be able to identify these birds in the field whether you actually see them or not, allowing you to apply more of your time and effort to finding more unusual birds on each field trip.

Rare, Endangered, and Extirpated Species

Setting expectations in advance will help you come home from any birding excursion with the satisfaction that you saw what you came to see. That's why we need to be up-front about the birds that are very difficult to see in Florida, as well as the birds that were once, but are no longer, part of the landscape.

The Florida Fish and Wildlife Conservation (FWC) Commission lists five species that once lived in Florida and are now extinct: passenger pigeon (the last known individual in the world died in 1914), ivory-billed woodpecker (2004), Carolina parakeet (1910), Bachman's warbler (1988), and Eskimo curlew (1987). Others that were once reported here fairly regularly are rarely seen in Florida at all, so a single sighting can become a regional bird event—whooping crane is an example of this.

In addition to the extinct birds, the US government classifies these five Florida birds as federally endangered: Cape Sable seaside sparrow, Everglade snail kite, Florida grasshopper sparrow, Kirtland's warbler, and red-cockaded woodpecker. Six others are considered federally threatened, meaning they are likely to become endangered in the foreseeable future: crested caracara, Florida scrub-jay, piping plover, roseate tern, red knot, and wood stork.

FWC also has its own current list of species that are endangered or of special concern at the state level. Sightings of these are possible, and this book provides the most likely places to find them, but they may be difficult to locate even in their accustomed hot spots.

- **State threatened species:** Least tern, snowy plover, American kestrel, white-crowned pigeon
- **State species of special concern:** American oystercatcher, black skimmer, brown pelican, burrowing owl, limpkin, little blue heron, marsh wren, osprey, reddish egret, roseate spoonbill, seaside sparrow, snowy egret, tricolored heron, white ibis

Why are these birds—some of which are fairly common in other parts of the country—becoming scarce in Florida? Audubon Florida sees human development and agriculture as the two main reasons for their decline. Habitat has become scarce, concentrating birds in specific areas that contain protected lands for their survival. "The remaining habitat, in many cases, is affected by human disturbance," says Audubon Florida in an article on its website. "Whether resting on a mangrove island or nesting on a barrier island beach, these birds need their space, which is increasingly difficult to find."

The effects of the changing climate also have had an impact in this region, and forecasts by scientists paint an alarming picture. With warmer air temperatures throughout the year, shorter cold seasons, more rain, more severe storms, and rising sea levels, climate change "is changing the fundamental way ecosystems work," a 2017 Audubon report says. Warmer winters, the report goes on, "cause shifts in the way that marine food webs work, which will cascade through the environment and affect fish populations, and in turn, fish-eating birds."

Audubon Florida lists "seawater intrusion, erosion, droughts, and storms" as just a few of the impacts of climate change on bird habitat. South Florida is especially vulnerable, with 6 inches of seawater rise expected by 2030 and 2 feet more by 2060. This will obliterate beaches, salt marshes, and other ocean-adjacent habitat, and will force salt water into freshwater aquifers, affecting the state's water supply. Stormwater from more intense and frequent storms will inundate coastal wetlands and the Everglades, disrupting the natural ecosystem balance there. The consequences are obvious: Loss of salt marsh habitat along the coastline can leave shorebirds, waterfowl, and long-legged waders with nowhere to nest and feed, while the increased storm activity can flood marshes, washing away nests and drowning tiny organisms that live in shallow water and serve as food to wading birds. It's a frightening picture, but the truth is that bird populations are under siege.

There's another side of climate change for birders, however. Major storms, changes in habitat, and shifts in food availability bring rare sightings of birds from other parts of the United States and the Caribbean islands to Florida's shores and forests. Lark sparrow, a bird of the western states, makes regular appearances along the Atlantic coastline—so often, in fact, that we included it in this book. Western spindalis, Bahama mockingbird, and tropical kingbird are found fairly often after major storms. Cinnamon teal, also included in these pages, is an annual visitor, and birds like bridled tern and neotropic cormorant find their way to Florida on occasion.

If you live in Florida or are planning a trip here in the near future, check the rare bird alert lists for each state compiled by the American Birding Association at birding.aba.org. Here you'll find quick links to all the discussions on the birding mailing lists across the country. Birders love to share information, so you are likely to find detailed directions to specific sightings.

Birding Ethics in the Age of Social Media

While your life list is your own and you have the option of counting whatever bird sightings you choose, some aspects of birding ethically are not optional. The American Birding Association provides this Code of Birding Ethics, and you will find that the vast majority of birders you meet follow this to the letter.

American Birding Association Code of Birding Ethics

Reproduced with permission. For more information about the American Birding Association, visit aba.org.

1. **Promote the welfare of birds and their environment.**

    1(a) Support the protection of important bird habitat.

    1(b) Avoid stressing birds or exposing them to danger, exercise restraint and caution during observation, photography, sound recording, or filming.

    - Limit the use of recordings and other methods of attracting birds, and never use such methods in heavily birded areas or for attracting any species that is Threatened, Endangered, of Special Concern, or is rare in your local area.

    - Keep well back from nests and nesting colonies, roosts, display areas, and important feeding sites. In such sensitive areas, if there is a need for extended observation, photography, filming, or recording, try to use a blind or hide, and take advantage of natural cover.

    - Use artificial light sparingly for filming or photography, especially for close-ups.

    1(c) Before advertising the presence of a rare bird, evaluate the potential for disturbance to the bird, its surroundings, and other people in the area, and proceed only if access can be controlled, disturbance minimized, and permission has been obtained from private landowners. The nesting sites of rare birds should be divulged only to the proper conservation authorities.

1(d) Stay on roads, trails, and paths where they exist; otherwise, keep habitat disturbance to a minimum.

2. Respect the law, and the rights of others.

2(a) Do not enter private property without the owner's explicit permission.

2(b) Follow all laws, rules, and regulations governing use of roads and public areas, both at home and abroad.

2(c) Practice common courtesy in contacts with other people. Your exemplary behavior will generate goodwill with birders and non-birders alike.

3. Ensure that feeders, nest structures, and other artificial bird environments are safe.

3(a) Keep dispensers, water, and food clean and free of decay or disease. It is important to feed birds continually during harsh weather.

3(b) Maintain and clean nest structures regularly.

3(c) If you are attracting birds to an area, ensure the birds are not exposed to predation from cats and other domestic animals or dangers posed by artificial hazards.

4. Group birding, whether organized or impromptu, requires special care.

Each individual in the group, in addition to the obligations spelled out in Items 1 and 2, has responsibilities as a Group Member:

4(a) Respect the interests, rights, and skills of fellow birders, as well as people participating in other legitimate outdoor activities. Freely share your knowledge and experience, except where code 1(c) applies. Be especially helpful to beginning birders.

4(b) If you witness unethical birding behavior, assess the situation and intervene if you think it prudent. When interceding, inform the person(s) of the inappropriate action and attempt, within reason, to have it stopped. If the behavior continues, document it and notify appropriate individuals or organizations.

Group Leader Responsibilities [amateur and professional trips and tours]:

4(c) Be an exemplary ethical role model for the group. Teach through word and example.

4(d) Keep groups to a size that limits impact on the environment and does not interfere with others using the same area.

4(e) Ensure everyone in the group knows of and practices this code.

4(f) Learn about and inform the group of any special circumstances applicable to the areas being visited (e.g., no audio playback allowed).

4(g) Acknowledge that professional tour companies bear a special responsibility to place the welfare of birds and the benefits of public knowledge ahead of the company's commercial interests. Ideally, leaders should keep track of tour sightings, document unusual occurrences, and submit records to appropriate organizations.

Why follow this code? Naturally, it's good for the birds, even if it means you don't have the opportunity to get a good look at a rarity or add a bird to your life list. There's another facet we must take into consideration in the age of social media, however: Infractions can be photographed or recorded, and your peccadillo in the field can become a matter of indelible public record.

A vivid example of this took place in September 2017, when a crowd of birders in Norwich, England, on a "twitch"—a hunt for a rare bird sighted and staked out by other birders—actually trespassed and damaged a fence in an attempt to frighten and flush a rare grasshopper sparrow into the open. This process of "organized flushing" is frowned upon and considered unethical in birding circles all over the world, but some birders consider this an acceptable practice. The rare sparrow, most likely already exhausted from somehow finding itself in unfamiliar territory thousands of miles from its accustomed home, may suffer even more from this disruption as it tries to rest and feed. Impatient birders, however, neglect to take the bird's welfare into consideration in their zeal to catch a glimpse of it and add it to their life lists.

This particular group of birders clashed with wardens on the property, however, and one individual began recording video of the exchange. The resulting 8-minute tantrum, as remarkably patient wardens attempted to reason with the agitated birders, now lives on Twitter, YouTube, and on author James Common's *Birders Behaving Badly* blog (https:// commonbynature.co.uk/2017/09/21/birders-behaving-badly/) for folks like us to see from half a world away. Whether or not these birders ever actually saw the sparrow is not noted, but their faces, voices, and words will linger on the internet for many years, and they no doubt took some grief from others in their own community for placing their own chance at a rare bird sighting over someone's private property, basic civility, and—most important for our purposes—the health and safety of the bird.

The moral is simple: Behave yourself in the field, and put the bird's survival before your zeal to check off a sighting or get a great photo. It's the right thing to do for the birds, and it will keep you from getting a bad reputation that lives forever online.

HOW TO USE THIS GUIDE

On each page you'll find photographs and details that will help you identify the birds you see, and determine the best places to find them.

Field marks: In addition to the photos, we have listed the features that differentiate this bird from others. These descriptions begin with a breeding male and are followed by breeding female and any changes for nonbreeding plumage.

Size: The bird's approximate length (L) or height (H) (for tall wading birds like great blue heron) and wingspan (WS) can be important to its identification.

Similar species: Misidentifications are easy to make, as every birder knows. We've simplified the process of elimination by providing the key field marks that may indicate the bird in your sights is not what you think it is.

Season: The time of year you are most likely to see this bird.

Habitat: Birds wander, but they tend to stay close to their nesting sites and to the areas in which they can find food. We provide the most likely habitat for each.

Food source: This will help you determine whether the bird you seek can find its food in the place you're looking. If you don't see evergreen trees with cones, for example, you're not likely to find crossbills.

Nest: Many of the birds in this book do not nest and breed in Florida. For the ones that do, we've provided the probable nest location—in a tree above 50 feet, for example, or on the ground among reeds and tall grasses.

Call: Nothing beats a recording of an actual birdcall, but the phonetic transcriptions you find here may help you match the kind of call you're hearing so that you can narrow down the possibilities for identification. If male and female have different calls, both are provided.

Hot spots: Here you'll find three to six places in Florida where the bird has been seen season after season or year after year. To determine these hot spots, we toured Florida and visited hundreds of birding locations while completing the photography for this book, using our personal experience to determine which places yielded the most sightings and provided a high-quality experience in general. We rejected some sites because they were on private or restricted property, they did not provide a safe place to leave a vehicle, or there was no clear path to the birding location.

I also applied science to the task. I used the sightings reported by tens of thousands of birders in eBird, the crowdsourced database developed and managed by the Cornell

Laboratory of Ornithology at Cornell University. Rather than delving back through decades of sightings to find where a bird may have been seen historically, I used data collected over the past three years—providing you with the most up-to-date information about where each bird has been seen most recently and consistently. I looked not only for a long list of sightings of a specific species—these, after all, could all be a single bird seen by a large group on one day—but also for year-after-year sightings of that species, a sign that this hot spot drew the desired species consistently.

You will see that many of the hot spots are cited repeatedly: for example, Fort De Soto Park, St. Marks National Wildlife Refuge, Lake Apopka Wildlife Drive, Sweetwater Wetlands Park, Merritt Island National Wildlife Refuge, Everglades National Park, J. N. Ding Darling National Wildlife Refuge, and many others. We hope this emphasis speaks to the obvious point: These are the best places to bird to find the greatest number of species in one place. Make note of these as you plan your exploration of Florida.

Each of these hot spots includes the nearest town or city, the state, and GPS coordinates for the entrance or location. (Please note: GPS coordinates *do not* mean, "Stand here and you'll see this bird." They are simply provided to make certain you reach the right wildlife refuge, forest, beach, lake, or parking area.)

Range map: This map shows the season and areas of Florida in which the bird is usually seen.

Map Key

Winter
Migration (spring or fall)
Summer
Year-round

Birders well know that no sighting is guaranteed. Birds have minds of their own, and they can decide to move hours or seconds before you arrive; they also may choose a new place to rest, feed, and raise their young from one year to the next. We have provided information about the type of habitat each bird prefers so that you can search in suitable places if the birds reject a particular beach, a salt marsh disappears as the sea level rises, or a section of forest does not produce a hardy cone crop in a given year.

PARTS OF A BIRD

We have used plain English terms throughout the descriptions in this book, but this illustration will help you determine which area we mean.

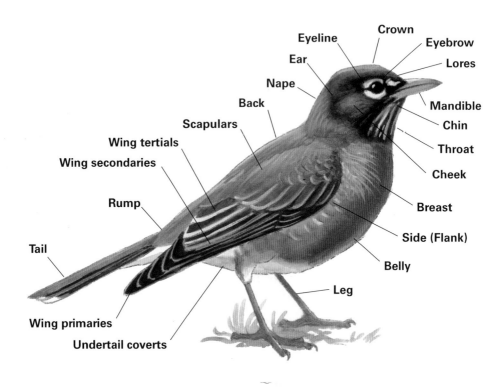

LOON

COMMON LOON
Gavia immer

This loon seeks the Florida coast's open water in winter and wanders into the Gainesville area during migration.

Field marks: Black head, black bill, red eye, pinstriped collar ending in a black band, striking checkerboard pattern on back, white breast. Nonbreeding plumage is slate gray with a white eye ring and collar-like white notch around neck.

Size: L: 26"–32", WS: 41"–52"

Similar species: Red-throated loon is smaller and grayer, with thin bill and more white on face (and is not usually seen in Florida). Double-crested cormorant is all black with a yellow bill.

Season: Winter and early spring

Habitat: Coastal waters, lakes and other open water

Food source: Fish

Nest: In secluded spots along lakeshores with easy access to water (not in Florida)

Call: Plaintive trill that has become synonymous with wilderness: a tremolo of ten or twelve beats in quick succession; also a yodeling call: *woooWAHwha, woooWAHwah*

Hot spots: Bill Baggs Cape Florida State Park, Key Biscayne, 25.6733 / -80.1582; Sebastian Inlet State Park, North Beach, 27.8611424 / -80.4495764; Cedar Keys National Wildlife Refuge, 29.1354114 / -83.0340372; Anclote Gulf Park, Anclote, 28.1922058 / -82.7866387; Fort De Soto Park, St. Petersburg, 27.6327266 / -82.718157

GREBES

HORNED GREBE
Podiceps auritus

This bird's white face and throat make it a dapper winter visitor.

Field marks: Winter adult has short, whitish bill, black cap, white face, red eye, white neck, streaked sides, and black back. Breeding adult has rufous neck and sides; bright yellow, triangular patch on sides of head.

Size: L: 13"–15", WS: 18"

Similar species: Red-necked grebe is larger and drabber in winter, and is not commonly found in Florida. Eared grebe is smaller with a peaked head, and is very unusual on the eastern shore.

Season: Winter, early spring

Habitat: Open ocean; often viewable from shore

Food source: Insects, fish, small sea animals

Nest: On a rock or on floating plant matter in water (not in Florida)

Call: Silent in winter; high, squeaky, descending laugh, ending in a series of low notes

Hot spots: Canaveral National Seashore (Apollo Beach), Titusville, 28.85798 / -80.7765913; St. Marks National Wildlife Refuge (lighthouse area), Port Leon, 30.0751008 / -84.180218; Fort Island Gulf Beach, Crystal River, 28.908602 / -82.69082; Courtney Campbell Causeway, Clearwater, 27.9632485 / -82.6800583; Fort De Soto Park, St. Petersburg, 27.6327266 / -82.718157

PIED-BILLED GREBE
Podilymbus podiceps

The region's smallest grebe prefers brackish waters in winter, with scattered individuals on freshwater lakes and ponds in summer.

Field marks: Tan overall with a darker grayish back; distinctive thick bill turns white with a black band in breeding season.

Size: L: 13", WS: 16"

Similar species: Horned grebe is larger and more strikingly marked, with a longer neck.

Season: Winter, with a few individuals in warmer months

Habitat: Ponds, lakes, marshes in secluded areas

Food source: Crayfish and other small crustaceans, small fish

Nest: Well hidden among marshland reeds, usually where water is 1 foot deep or more

Call: Rising bark with evenly spaced syllables: *wa-wa-wa-wa- Whu, Whu, Whu, Whu*, slowing down until it trails off

Hot spots: Any pond, marsh, or small lake at a low elevation may host this common grebe throughout the winter, and they often appear among mixed flocks of overwintering waterfowl in Atlantic and Gulf waters just offshore. The calm water between beaches and barrier islands often contains these grebes, as do large open marshes in central Florida.

WATERFOWL

MUTE SWAN
Cygnus olor

This introduced Eurasian species established residency in Florida on ponds in cities and suburbs, often at shopping centers.

Field marks: All white bird; curved neck, orange bill with a black knob on top.

Size: L: 55"–61", WS: 84"–94"

Similar species: Tundra swan has a straight neck, black bill with yellow spot at its base, and is not usually found in Florida. Trumpeter swan is larger and has an all-black bill.

Season: Year-round

Habitat: Freshwater ponds and lakes, saltwater bays

Food source: Aquatic plants

Nest: Mounds of grass and reeds not far from water

Call: Often silent, but can vocalize using hisses and short barks

Hot spots: Lake Morton, Lakeland, 28.0375919 / -81.9539738; Lake Eola Park, Orlando, 28.5441162 / -81.3731575; Tamarac Exotic Duck Pond, Lauderhill, 26.1916997 / -80.2488828; Coconut Point Mall, Estero, 26.4081205 / -81.8049659; Longboat Key Club Golf Course, Longboat Key, 27.3344126 / -82.5915241

TRUMPETER SWAN
Cygnus buccinator

America's largest waterfowl species resides in specific city and county park ponds in central and south Florida.

Field marks: White overall with long, generally straight neck, long black bill with single yellow line along lower section, always black at base; black eye, black legs and feet. Juvenile is grayish; may have pink in bill, but still with a black base.

Size: L: 60", WS: 80"

Similar species: Tundra swan is smaller and has bright yellow at the base of the bill; generally does not appear in Florida. Mute swan is of similar size and often holds its neck in an S shape; its bill is mostly bright orange.

Season: Year-round in selected ponds; scattered individuals in winter

Habitat: Ponds in city and county parks

Food source: Aquatic plants, some fish eggs and small fish

Nest: A mound of grasses on an existing muskrat house or small island, a short distance from shore

Call: *Ooh-OOH*, not unlike a muted trumpet

Hot spots: Saint David Catholic Church Pond, Davie, 26.0722603 / -80.2504331; Eagle Lake Park, Clearwater, 27.934209 / -82.7651167; Lake Eola Park, Orlando, 28.5441162 / -81.3731575

CANADA GOOSE
Branta canadensis

This northern bird's winter range now extends into northeastern and central Florida.

Field marks: Brown body, lighter brown breast, black neck, black head with white band around throat and cheeks, gray bill, white vent.

Size: L: 25"–43" (considerable variation), WS: 75"

Similar species: Brant is smaller and lacks white panel on face. Greater white-fronted goose has pink bill and legs, white patch on face at edge of bill, and is lighter colored overall. Cackling goose is smaller with a shorter neck and is not generally found in Florida.

Season: Winter, with some year-round populations on inland lakes and ponds

Habitat: Any body of water near grasses or farm fields

Food source: Grass, human crops (rice, corn)

Nest: A pile of sticks and grasses in a field or lawn near water

Call: *Honk-a-honk, honk-a-honk* when taking flight or communicating in a flock

Hot spots: Largo Central Park Nature Preserve, Largo, 27.9158428 / -82.7751357; Blue Cypress Park, Jacksonville, 30.3757545 / -81.6088961; Freedom Point Ponds and CCRC Area, The Villages, 28.9490933 / -81.9616748; Big Talbot Island State Park—Spoonbill Pond, Jacksonville, 30.5101704 / -81.4585671; Lake Elberta, Tallahassee, 30.4297796 / -84.3005751

SNOW GOOSE
Chen caerulescens

Two phases display very different plumage: white in adulthood, and the dark juvenile "blue goose."

Field marks: White face and body, pink bill and legs, black wing primaries.

Size: L: 25"–31", WS: 53"

Similar species: Ross's goose is smaller with a diminutive bill. Mute swan is larger with a longer, curved neck and orange and black bill.

Season: Winter

Habitat: Open fields and wetlands

Food source: Aquatic plants, young crop seedlings, wild rice and millet, some berries

Nest: On the ground in the Arctic tundra

Call: A loud *honk*, higher-pitched than a Canada goose

Hot spots: Individuals have put in appearances along the Atlantic and Gulf coasts over the past several years. A single bird overwintered at the Myakka River State Park boat ramp in Myakka City, 27.2657309 / -82.2901297, in 2020. Earl R. Maize Recreation Area in Feather Sound, 27.9018246 / -82.6603603, hosted an individual snow goose for two weeks in January 2020. Sweetwater Wetlands Park in Gainesville, 29.6151026 / -82.3254061, received a visit from a snow goose for several days around Christmas 2017.

GREATER WHITE-FRONTED GOOSE
Anser albifrons

The white band around the bill and bright orange legs make this occasional visitor easy to spot in a mixed flock.

Field marks: Grayish tones overall with darker banding across the belly, dark head with white band on face at the base of the bill, pink bill, white tail coverts, white band on end of tail, bright orange legs.

Size: L: 26"–34", WS: 42"–60"

Similar species: Canada goose has white patch on head and black neck.

Season: Uncommon winter guest

Habitat: Open fields and marshes

Food source: Plants

Nest: On the Russian and Siberian tundra

Call: Laughing three-note call: *but-a-WAH, but-a-WAH*

Hot spots: St. Marks National Wildlife Refuge, St. Marks, 30.1515653 / -84.1473314; Freedom Point Ponds and CCRC Area, The Villages, 28.9490933 / -81.9616748; Key West Golf Club, Key West, 24.5771388 / -81.7457271

EGYPTIAN GOOSE
Alopochen aegyptiaca

An exotic species from northern Africa, this goose has established a healthy population in central and south Florida.

Field marks: White face and neck with wide red ring around the eye, pink bill with black tip, mottled brown head and nape, pale tan breast, grayish sides and underside, darker brown back, wide white patch on brown/black wings, pink legs and feet. Female similar.

Size: L: 25"–29", WS: 15"

Similar species: Black-bellied whistling duck has an all-gray head, a bright red bill, and black sides. Fulvous whistling duck is more uniformly tan from head to breast.

Season: Year-round

Habitat: Ponds near mowed lawns, in residential or commercial areas

Food source: Seeds, plant stems, leaves, grasses

Nest: In a hole in a mature tree, usually in a park

Call: Rapid, barking *quack*, or a reedy *honk* in flight

Hot spots: Kendall-Baptist Hospital Area, Miami, 25.68765 / -80.33864; Plantation Preserve, Plantation, 26.1156777 / -80.2391624; Palm Lake Park, North River Shores, 27.2232556 / -80.266698; Topeekeegee Yugnee Park, Hollywood, 26.0373118 / -80.1716566; Tamarac Exotic Duck Pond, Lauderhill, 26.1916997 / -80.2488828

BLACK-BELLIED WHISTLING DUCK
Dendrocygnus autumnalis

These distinctive ducks travel in flocks and often roost together in trees.

Field marks: Gray head with noticeable peak, white eye ring, bright red bill, gray neck, tawny breast and back, black wings with prominent white stripe, black underside, pink legs and feet.

Size: L: 20"–22", WS: 30"

Similar species: Fulvous whistling duck has a buff head and breast and no white wing stripe. Egyptian goose has a white face and bold red eye ring.

Season: Year-round

Habitat: Marshes with large bodies of water, open fields

Food source: Aquatic plants, grasses, farm grains, some insects and snails

Nest: In a tree or thicket; sometimes on the ground

Call: A high, squeaky chatter or a distinctive whistle: *dih-doo-WHEE-di-WEE-duh*

Hot spots: These widespread and numerous ducks can be seen on virtually any inland body of water in Florida. Here are some places where large flocks gather: Sweetwater Wetlands Park, Gainesville, 29.6151026 / -82.3254061; Lake Apopka North Shore, Astatula, 28.6740878 / -81.7059258; Lake Meredith Bike Path, Plantation, 27.0629077 / -82.3756358; West Regional WTF Wetlands, Vero Beach, 27.6131434 / -80.5052376; Lake Istokpoga, Windy Point Park and Boat Ramp, Sylvan Shores, 27.3068077 / -81.3127971

FULVOUS WHISTLING DUCK
Dendrocygna bicolor

Not as common as its black-bellied cousin, this duck is partial to flooded rice fields and pastures.

Field marks: Rust head, breast, and underside with thin black eye line, gray-blue bill, gooselike neck, black back and wings with rusty striping, black underside of wings, white striped flanks, white stripe on tail, gray legs.

Size: L: 19", WS: 26"

Similar species: Black-bellied whistling duck has a gray head and pink bill; large white stripe on wings.

Season: Year-round

Habitat: Shallow freshwater marshes, flooded farm fields (especially rice) and meadows

Food source: Seeds of aquatic plants, small invertebrates

Nest: On the ground, usually in reeds or grasses in rice fields

Call: High-pitched *kit-TEE*

Hot spots: Lake Apopka North Shore, Astatula, 28.6740878 / -81.7059258; T. M. Goodwin Waterfowl Management Area, Palm Bay, 27.8452341 / -80.7252359; Sem-Chi Rice Mill, Wellington, 26.6668727 / -80.4574621; Harney Pond Canal Recreation Area, Lakeport, 26.995414 / -81.0675573; Stormwater Treatment Area 1W, Wellington, 26.6762842 / -80.4273806

MUSCOVY DUCK
Cairina moschata

A large, bulky duck that dominates ponds, the Muscovy often confuses birders with its many plumages.

Field marks: Purebred duck is iridescent black overall with an obvious crest, bumpy featherless facial skin around the bill, a yellow bill with a black stripe, white wing patch barely visible in sitting duck, and black legs. Domestic variations include mottled white plumage and bright red skin on the face and around the bill.

Size: L: 30"–32", WS: 48"; female smaller at 25"–26"

Similar species: Black scoter is smaller and is not found on inland ponds. Double-crested cormorant has a long neck and bill and is more often found on Atlantic and Gulf coastlines.

Season: Year-round

Habitat: Wild ducks frequent forests, while domestic varieties gather on city and suburban ponds, at shopping mall water features, and other places where they can get food from humans.

Food source: Aquatic plants, insect, spiders, small crustaceans, fish, small reptiles. Domestic varieties will eat seed, bread, and other things strewn by people.

Nest: In tree cavities or nest boxes

Call: Generally silent, sometimes uttering a single bark

Hot spots: This widespread duck appears on city and suburban ponds throughout the state, in varied plumages that result from interbreeding with domestic ducks. Watch for the distinctive bumpy facial skin, either black in purebred ducks or red in other plumages.

WOOD DUCK
Aix sponsa

One of America's most colorful ducks; the male's facial markings and green cap are particularly distinctive.

Field marks: Male has green cap with crest at back of head, dark face with white outlines, ruddy breast, yellow flanks, green back, long tail with rusty undertail coverts. Female has white oval around eye, gray head and back, brown to buff flanks with contrasting spots. *Eclipse plumage:* Male turns gray-brown with green cap, red eye, gray face with white streaks, whitish throat, green wash on back and wings, gray breast and flanks.

Size: L: 17"–20", WS: 30"

Similar species: Harlequin duck is dark blue overall with a white spot on face and rusty flanks; rarely seen in Florida. Mallard male has a bright green head, pale back, and a shorter tail.

Season: Year-round

Habitat: Ponds and lakes sheltered by trees; wetlands with high grasses

Food source: Plants, insects, small aquatic animals, amphibians

Nest: In a tree cavity or nest box

Call: Female has a *whir-up, whir-up* repeated call; male has a high-pitched whistle.

Hot spots: This very common duck can be found in pairs or small flocks on virtually every pond in the region north of the Everglades, especially ponds that are surrounded by trees or tall reeds and grasses.

MALLARD
Anas platyrhynchos

The most common dabbling duck in the United States, the mallard is found in virtually every lake, pond, or large puddle.

Field marks: Male has green head, yellow bill, white collar, rusty breast, pale brown body, black and white tail. Female is uniformly brown with a paler head and black crown and line through the eye, orange bill with a dark center spot, blue speculum on wings with a white outline, and orange legs.

Size: L: 20"–26", WS: 35"

Similar species: American black duck is darker overall with a lighter head and no wing speculum. Northern shoveler has much longer gray bill, a white breast, and rusty flanks. Ring-necked duck has navy blue head, gray bill with a white outline, and black back.

Season: Year-round

Habitat: Open water from small ponds and wetlands to large lakes, usually close to shore. Mallards also feed in farm fields and other open land areas.

Food source: Insects, freshwater invertebrates, worms, seeds, crop leavings, aquatic plants

Nest: On the ground in grassland, marshes, and near lakes and ponds

Call: The stereotypical *quek, quek, quek*

Hot spots: Mallards can be found in or near any body of water in wild places or in coexistence with humans. Ponds in mall parking areas, housing developments, and schoolyards all host mallards, as do harbors, piers, and parks where people feed them (*not* recommended).

AMERICAN BLACK DUCK
Anas rubripes

Find this dark-plumage dabbling duck in north Florida salt marshes.

Field marks: Dark brown overall with a somewhat lighter head and gray-streaked throat, a purple speculum with a black border. Female has a gray-green bill; male's bill is yellow.

Size: L: 22"–25", WS: 35"

Similar species: Female mallard is lighter overall, has an orange bill and legs, and has a white border around its blue speculum.

Season: Year-round

Habitat: Salt marshes, some inland ponds

Food source: Aquatic plants, seeds, insects, crustaceans, amphibians

Nest: Near water, on the ground or among tall grasses

Call: *Quack, quack,* but in a lower voice than a mallard

Hot spots: National Wildlife Refuge, St. Marks, 30.1515653 / -84.1473314; Perdue Pond Wildlife Area, Jacksonville, 30.4753134 / -81.6148527

GADWALL
Mareca strepera

The male's black rump and gray bill set this duck apart from other dabblers.

Field marks: Male is a drab brown duck with a gray head and sloping forehead, reddish scapulars on wings, black rump and undertail coverts, yellow legs, and gray bill in breeding plumage. In nonbreeding season, the male becomes uniformly mottled brown with a gray head. Female is a mottled brown with white secondaries and a yellow bill.

Size: L: 19"–23", WS: 31"–36"

Similar species: Mallard female has blue speculum. American black duck has purple speculum.

Season: Winter

Habitat: Large ponds and small lakes with tall reeds and aquatic plants

Food source: Pond vegetation, tiny water animals

Nest: In prairies near water; midwestern United States and farther north

Call: Female *quack* is higher-pitched than a mallard; male emits a narrow *mepp.*

Hot spots: St. Marks National Wildlife Refuge, St. Marks, 30.1515653 / -84.1473314; Paynes Prairie Preserve State Park, Gainesville, 29.6068756 / -82.3031116; Lake Apopka Wildlife Drive, Apopka, 28.6691082 / -81.5574338; Estero Bay Preserve State Park, Winkler Point, Fort Meyers, 26.4800134 / -81.898452; Green Cay Wetlands & Nature Center, Boynton Beach, 26.4861584 / -80.1607561

NORTHERN PINTAIL
Anas acuta

The long tail and dapper brown and white neck make this large duck distinctive.

Field marks: Brown head, white breast with a white stripe up each side to the head, gray body, black undertail coverts; long, black "pin" tail. Female is light brown with mottling through the wings and body and a dark gray bill.

Size: L: 20"–25", WS: 30"–35"

Similar species: Long-tailed duck has a white head, short neck, and pink bill ring.

Season: Winter

Habitat: Ponds, marshes, and waterways in marshes

Food source: Seeds and grains, insects, small crustaceans

Nest: On the ground near freshwater or brackish marshes and lakes (not in Florida)

Call: Male call a high whistled *eeowee*; female call a chattered *quack*

Hot spots: St. Marks National Wildlife Refuge, St. Marks, 30.1515653 / -84.1473314; Merritt Island National Wildlife Refuge, Titusville, 28.6411839 / -80.7774067; Orlando Wetlands Park, Orlando, 28.5753263 / -80.9966826; Lake Apopka Wildlife Drive, Apopka, 28.6691082 / -81.5574338; Myakka River State Park, Myakka City, 27.2405033 / -82.3148167

AMERICAN WIGEON
Mareca americana

Find this striking dabbler on ponds with abundant food at the surface.

Field marks: Male's head has a bright green stripe from lores to nape and a white or cream cap; rufous flanks and underside, pinkish back, black wing tips, white undertail coverts, and black rump and tail. Female is mottled rufous from back to underside, with a mottled gray head. Both have light blue bill with black tip, white wing patch with a green speculum. Nonbreeding adult male resembles female.

Size: L: 19"–23", WS: 30"–33"

Similar species: Eurasian wigeon has rufous head instead of green.

Season: Winter

Habitat: Ponds, lakes, and marshes

Food source: Leaves of many kinds of aquatic plants

Nest: Wigeons breed in the Midwest, Great Lakes, and Canada.

Call: Male call a high-pitched *whew-woo-wee*; female a barking *quack*

Hot spots: Robinson Preserve South, Bradenton, 27.5095641 / -82.6649941; Paynes Prairie Preserve State Park, Gainesville, 29.6068756 / -82.3031116; St. Marks National Wildlife Refuge (lighthouse area), Port Leon, 30.0751008 / -84.180; Perdue Pond Wildlife Area, Jacksonville, 30.4753134 / -81.6148527; Lake Apopka Wildlife Drive, Apopka, 28.6691082 / -81.5574338

NORTHERN SHOVELER
Spatula clypeata

This duck's outsize bill makes it easy to identify in any season.

Field marks: Breeding male has green head, long gray bill, white breast and undertail coverts, rufous flanks, black tail. Nonbreeding male has gray head, yellow bill, gray breast, and rufous flanks. Female is mottled brown with large yellow bill.

Size: L: 17"–20", WS: 27"–30"

Similar species: Mallard has much smaller yellow bill.

Season: Winter

Habitat: Marshes, both fresh- and saltwater; also lakes and ponds in flat areas

Food source: Aquatic insects and tiny animals; pond vegetation

Nest: In high vegetation; midwestern United States and Canada

Call: Male call a low *chuk-chuk*; female a nasal *chik-chik*

Hot spots: St. Marks National Wildlife Refuge (lighthouse area), Port Leon, 30.0751008 / -84.180; Paynes Prairie Preserve State Park, Gainesville, 29.6068756 / -82.3031116; Freedom Point Ponds and CCRC Area, The Villages, 28.9490933 / -81.9616748; Lake Apopka Wildlife Drive, Apopka, 28.6691082 / -81.5574338; Merritt Island National Wildlife Refuge, Titusville, 28.6411839 / -80.7774067

BLUE-WINGED TEAL
Spatula discors

One of the nation's smallest ducks overwinters in large flocks on Florida's lakes and ponds.

Field marks: Male has blue head with white crescent before the gray bill, spotted brown body, white patch at hip, blue wing patch with white border, green speculum (both usually visible only in flight). Female is grayish brown with a distinct lighter pattern, dark line through the eye, white at base of bill and at throat.

Size: L: 15"–16", WS: 23"–30"

Similar species: Green-winged teal has bold green and rufous head, solid gray flanks.

Season: Winter; some small flocks remain year-round

Habitat: Shallow ponds and wetlands

Food source: Plants, seeds

Nest: On the ground in tall grass, near water

Call: Male call a high-pitched *chee, chee;* female a midrange *quack*

Hot spots: St. Marks National Wildlife Refuge (lighthouse area), Port Leon, 30.0751008 / -84.180; Paynes Prairie Preserve State Park, Gainesville, 29.6068756 / -82.3031116; Freedom Point Ponds and CCRC Area, The Villages, 28.9490933 / -81.9616748; Lake Apopka Wildlife Drive, Apopka, 28.6691082 / -81.5574338; Merritt Island National Wildlife Refuge, Titusville, 28.6411839 / -80.7774067

CINNAMON TEAL
Spatula cyanoptera

This striking western duck occasionally visits Florida, mingling with large flocks of winter teal.

Field marks: Adult male is a bright rust color overall with a dark gray bill, black back, black tail; wings are dark with a pale blue shoulder and white underwing. Females are buff overall with a longer dark bill, dull blue wing patch, and white underwing. Nonbreeding male resembles female, but with a somewhat more rusty color.

Size: L: 15"–17", WS 22"

Similar species: Eurasian wigeon has a rust-colored head but with a cream cap and a gray back; rarely seen in Florida.

Season: Winter

Habitat: Shallow ponds, wetlands, marshes

Food source: Aquatic plants, insects, small invertebrates, seeds

Nest: In marsh grasses less than 2 feet tall (not in Florida)

Call: Male has a rattling call like wooden beads clacking against one another. Female's call is a low, harsh *quack*.

Hot spots: Lake Apopka North Shore, Astatula, 28.6740878 / -81.7059258; Merritt Island National Wildlife Refuge, Black Point Wildlife Drive, Titusville, 28.6575241 / -80.7545391; Celery Fields, Fruitville, 27.3282173 / -82.4340248; Tamarac Exotic Duck Pond, Lauderhill, 26.1916997 / -80.2488828

GREEN-WINGED TEAL
Anas crecca

America's smallest duck sports a bold facial pattern in breeding plumage.

Field marks: Breeding male has a rufous head with a green band from the eye to the back of the head, gray wings and flanks with a white bar on forward flank. Nonbreeding male is brown overall with visible green speculum. Female is mottled brown overall with a buff streak at the tail; green speculum is visible at rest.

Size: L: 12"–15", WS: 21"–25"

Similar species: Blue-winged teal has a blue head with a white crescent at the base of the bill, blue wing patch.

Season: Winter

Habitat: Lakes, ponds, and wetlands

Food source: Seeds, grasses, aquatic insects, small crustaceans

Nest: In a depression on the ground, some distance from water; Canada and the northern United States west of New England

Call: Brief, staccato whistles from male; laughing *haw-haw* quack from female

Hot spots: St. Marks National Wildlife Refuge, St. Marks, 30.1515653 / -84.1473314; T. M. Goodwin Waterfowl Management Area, Palm Bay, 27.8452341 / -80.7252359; Merritt Island National Wildlife Refuge, Titusville, 28.6411839 / -80.7774067; West Regional WTF Wetlands, Vero Beach, 27.6131434 / -80.5052376; Research Road, Everglades National Park, 25.3712306 / -80.6889582

MOTTLED DUCK
Anas fulvigula

A year-round resident, this dabbling duck's yellow bill helps differentiate it from a female mallard.

Field marks: Male is a warm brown overall with buff streaks and a lighter head, a yellow bill with a black spot at the lower base, and orange legs and feet. Female is lighter overall but very similar.

Size: L: 21"–23", WS: 30"

Similar species: Female mallard has an orange bill with a dark center spot, and a blue speculum with bold white border. American black duck is darker overall with a drab greenish bill.

Season: Year-round

Habitat: Ponds, marshes, freshwater pools, stormwater collection areas

Food source: Plants, rice, small crustaceans, insects, small fish

Nest: On the ground or in short vegetation, usually near water

Call: A raspy, repeated *cra-a-b*; female call is a low *quack*

Hot spots: Any flooded field, wetland, or pond is likely to have mottled ducks, especially as you travel south through Florida. Most likely are the stormwater collection areas in the northern Everglades, as well as ponds and the "river of grass" in Everglades National Park.

CANVASBACK
Aythya valisineria

Identify this large diving duck by its red head, white back, and the slant of its forehead.

Field marks: Red head sloping forward to the dark bill, black breast, white back and flanks, black rear. Female has tan head with sloping forehead, white line through the eye, light body, tan rear.

Size: L: 19"–24", WS: 30"–36"

Similar species: Redhead is smaller and has darker back, rounded head, light blue bill with black tip.

Season: Winter

Habitat: Lakes, bays, and marshes

Food source: Seeds, tubers, and roots of aquatic plants, especially the sago pondweed; some snails and insect larvae

Nest: In areas of marsh vegetation, anchored to tall reeds and grasses; areas of the American Midwest and West and western Canada

Call: Male call a short *coo*, which can sound like a cackle when flocks call at once; female a harsher *kiih*

Hot spots: St. Marks National Wildlife Refuge (lighthouse area), Port Leon, 30.0751008 / -84.180; Crowder Road Landing, Lake Jackson, Tallahassee, 30.507019 / -84.313385; Lake Apopka Wildlife Drive, Apopka, 28.6691082 / -81.5574338; Merritt Island National Wildlife Refuge, Titusville, 28.6411839 / -80.7774067; Tom Renick Park, Ormond-by-the-Sea, 29.3314127 / -81.0578893

REDHEAD
Aythya americana

The smaller of the redheaded ducks, often found in large flocks during migration.

Field marks: Rounded red head, black breast and rear, gray body, bluish bill with a black tip. Female is brown, often with a whitish area around the bill; bill is dark gray, tipped in black.

Size: L: 18"–22", WS: 30"–34"

Similar species: Canvasback is larger and has dark bill, sloping forehead, and white back.

Season: Winter

Habitat: Saltwater bays, freshwater lakes

Food source: Seeds and roots of aquatic plants, small fish, mollusks, insects

Nest: Near water in tall reeds and grasses; prairies in the American and Canadian west

Call: Male call a *wuh-whooa*, arcing upward before descending; female a harder *queh*, like a quack

Hot spots: St. Marks National Wildlife Refuge (lighthouse area), Port Leon, 30.0751008 / -84.180; Crowder Road Landing, Lake Jackson, Tallahassee, 30.507019 / -84.313385; Lake Apopka Wildlife Drive, Apopka, 28.6691082 / -81.5574338; Merritt Island National Wildlife Refuge, Titusville, 28.6411839 / -80.7774067; Tom Renick Park, Ormond-by-the-Sea, 29.3314127 / -81.0578893

RING-NECKED DUCK
Aythya collaris

You'll have to look closely to find the reddish-brown "ring" around this duck's neck.

Field marks: Note the peaked back of the head. Dark purple head, yellow eye, gray bill with white ring and black tip, black back, light gray flanks with a white bar extending upward, black rear. Female is brown overall, with a white line through the eye, a white area just before the bill, and a gray bill with a black tip.

Size: L: 14"–18", WS: 24"–30"

Similar species: Greater scaup has a dark head with a greenish hue. Lesser scaup has a peaked head, no white on the bill, whiter sides, and a lighter back.

Season: Winter

Habitat: Freshwater ponds, marshes, bogs with considerable vegetation

Food source: Pondweed seeds and tubers, other aquatic plants, mollusks, waterborne insects and invertebrates

Nest: Among marsh plants, directly over water

Call: Brief whistled note from male; sharp, repeated *quack* from female

Hot spots: Topsail Hill Preserve State Park, Miramar Beach, 30.370076 / -86.2967277; St. Marks National Wildlife Refuge (lighthouse area), Port Leon, 30.0751008 / -84.180; Alligator Lake Recreation Area, Lake City, 30.1685045 / -82.6204491; Paynes Prairie Preserve State Park, Gainesville, 29.6068756 / -82.3031116; Duck Ponds, Tierra Verde, 27.6679269 / -82.7264071

GREATER SCAUP
Aythya marila

This steeply declining diving duck may be difficult to find among the more numerous lesser scaup.

Field marks: Round, dark head, appearing greenish in the right light (it can also appear dark blue or purple); yellow eye, light blue bill, gray back, white sides, dark rear. Female is uniformly brown with a gray bill and a white facial patch at base of bill.

Size: L: 17.5"–18", WS: 28"–30"

Similar species: Lesser scaup is smaller, has a dark blue head (though it can appear green), and its head comes to a point at the top rear.

Season: Winter, with some individuals remaining in spring on the Gulf coast

Habitat: Ocean coastline; some inland lakes

Food source: Aquatic plants and seeds, mollusks, snails, small crustaceans, insects

Nest: On the ground in areas of tall grass, usually where water cannot reach it

Call: Descending *kuck-oo* from male; rapid, low *quack* from female

Hot spots: Alligator Point, Panacea, 29.8937866 / -84.3737608; St. Marks National Wildlife Refuge, St. Marks, 30.1515653 / -84.1473314; Cedar Keys National Wildlife Refuge, 29.1354114 / -83.0340372; Merritt Island National Wildlife Refuge, Titusville, 28.6411839 / -80.7774067; Tom Renick Park, Ormond-by-the-Sea, 29.3314127 / -81.0578893

LESSER SCAUP
Aythya affinis

Look for large flocks of this diving duck over the winter.

Field marks: Dark head appears glossy navy blue in the right light; the pointed peak at the top rear is the best indication of a lesser (rather than greater) scaup. Yellow eye, gray bill, black breast and rear, gray back, white flanks.

Size: L: 16"–18", WS: 24"–30"

Similar species: Greater scaup is slightly larger, with a rounded head (no peak) that may appear greenish in sunlight.

Season: Winter

Habitat: Ocean bays, lakes, estuaries

Food source: Aquatic invertebrates

Nest: On the ground in areas of high grasses and sedges, on dry land or near lakes; western United States prairies and marshes

Call: Male call a bubbly series of high-pitched *piffs*; female a hoarse, repeated *quick*

Hot spots: Canaveral National Seashore (Apollo Beach), Titusville, 28.85798 / -80.7765913; Fort Island Gulf Beach, Crystal River, 28.908602 / -82.69082; Merritt Island National Wildlife Refuge, Titusville, 28.6411839 / -80.7774067; Jetty Park, Port Canaveral, 28.4064535 / -80.5924523; Cedar Keys National Wildlife Refuge, 29.1354114 / -83.0340372

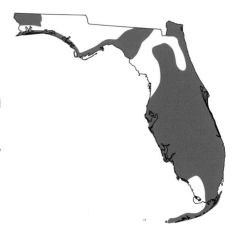

COMMON EIDER
Somateria mollissima

A rare but regular winter visitor along the Atlantic coastline, this duck of northern waters is virtually unmistakable in Florida.

Field marks: Pie slice–shaped head with black cap, white face, steeply sloping forehead, olive greenish bill (yellow in *borealis*), white back, black flanks and underparts, black tail. Female is cinnamon brown with a gray bill; barred throughout the back and flanks.

Size: L: 24"–27", WS: 36"–40"

Similar species: King eider is smaller and has a gray-blue hood and distinctive yellow and orange bill; virtually never found in Florida.

Season: Winter; occasionally in spring

Habitat: Open ocean, saltwater bays and harbors

Food source: Shellfish

Nest: On the ground near water in New England and on the Canadian coast

Call: Male and female call a raspy, continuous *kor-kor-kor*, male also a rising *wha-woo*

Hot spots: Canaveral National Seashore (Apollo Beach), Titusville, 28.85798 / -80.7765913; Rodney S. Ketcham Park, Port Canaveral, 28.4077841 / -80.6305504; Jetty Park, Port Canaveral, 28.4064535 / -80.5924523

LONG-TAILED DUCK
Clangula hyemalis

This luxuriously plumaged diving duck from up north puts in an appearance in Florida just about every winter.

Field marks: Winter male has white cap, gray face, black bill with bright pink stripe, black spot between head and neck, white neck and breast, white cape of feathers across back, black and brown flanks, dark wings, white rump, long black tail curling or pointing upward. Female has white head with black smudge, greenish bill, chestnut brown body, white rump, short tail.

Size: L: 16"–22", WS: 26"–30"

Similar species: Northern pintail has a long neck, brown face, dark gray bill.

Season: Winter

Habitat: Ocean inlets near shore

Food source: Invertebrates found near the surface or at the bottom of the ocean

Nest: On the ground near water in northern Canada

Call: Male call is *oh, oh-a-doo-a-lee*; female is *git, git, git*.

Hot spots: Canaveral National Seashore (Apollo Beach), Titusville, 28.85798 / -80.7765913; Merritt Island National Wildlife Refuge, Titusville, 28.6411839 / -80.7774067; Jetty Park, Port Canaveral, 28.4064535 / -80.5924523; Lake Apopka North Shore, Astatula, 28.6740878 / -81.7059258

SURF SCOTER
Melanitta perspicillata

This occasional visitor appears in Atlantic or Gulf waters in winter and early spring.

Field marks: Male has a black body and head, white patch on back of head, bright orange and white bill with a black spot on each side. Female is uniformly dark brown with a black cap, a white facial patch, and a white patch before the bill.

Size: L: 17"–21", WS: 30"–34"

Similar species: Black scoter lacks white head patch and orange on bill. White-winged scoter is browner, with a white wing patch.

Season: Winter, early spring

Habitat: Atlantic and gulf coastlines

Food source: Small fish, mollusks, crustaceans, water insects, underwater plants

Nest: In the Arctic from Alaska to northern Labrador

Call: A squeaky *buk, buk,* often with wing sounds; soft, repetitive *whudda-whudda-whudda*

Hot spots: Bald Point State Park, Bald Point, 29.9377826 / -84.3381304; Shoreline Park, Gulf Breeze, 30.3527 / -87.1758; Lowdermilk Park Beach, Naples, 26.1630071 / -81.8102932; San Carlos Bay/Bunche Beach Preserve, Fort Myers, 26.476174 / -81.9673795; Canaveral National Seashore, Titusville, 28.85798 / -80.7765913

BLACK SCOTER
Melanitta americana

The darkest scoter overall, with a smaller, flashy yellow bill, this diving duck prefers salt water almost exclusively in winter.

Field marks: Male has black head and body, bill with bright yellow knob and grayish tip. Female is dark brown with a white cheek patch and light area before the bill.

Size: L: 17"–20", WS: 30"–34"

Similar species: Surf scoter has white head patch and orange on the bill. White-winged scoter has white wing patch, white crescent below the eye, and is browner overall.

Season: Primarily winter, sometimes in spring

Habitat: Oceans and large saltwater bays

Food source: Mollusks, small fish, crustaceans, algae, underwater plants

Nest: Disguised in a crack between rocks or behind a grass hummock; the Arctic from Alaska to Labrador

Call: Descending whistle: *peeuu, peeuu*, on the water or in flight

Hot spots: Bald Point State Park, Bald Point, 29.9377826 / -84.3381304; St. Marks National Wildlife Refuge, St. Marks, 30.1515653 / -84.1473314; Canaveral National Seashore (Apollo Beach), Titusville, 28.85798 / -80.7765913; Tomoka State Park, Ormond Beach, 29.3283378 / -81.0756335; Lowdermilk Park Beach, Naples, 26.1630071 / -81.8102932

WHITE-WINGED SCOTER
Melanitta deglandi

The largest of the scoters makes occasional appearances just offshore in Atlantic and Gulf waters.

Field marks: Male has dark brown body and head, orange bill with a gray knob and tip, white crescent under the eye, white wing patch. Female is lighter brown with a black cap, two white patches on the head, and white wing patch.

Size: L: 19"–24", WS: 33"–40"

Similar species: Black scoter and surf scoter lack the white wing patch and eye crescent.

Season: Winter

Habitat: Open ocean and coastal bays in winter

Food source: Mollusks, small fish, crustaceans, water insects, underwater plants

Nest: On the ground in a crevice near water; Alaska and northern Canada

Call: A soft, single *churp*. A flock will chatter continuously during takeoff.

Hot spots: Tom Renick Park, Ormond-by-the-Sea, 29.3314127 / -81.0578893; Jetty Park, Port Canaveral, 28.4064535 / -80.5924523; Emerson Point Preserve, Palmetto, 27.5320111 / -82.6256604; Bald Point State Park, Bald Point, 29.9377826 / -84.3381304

COMMON GOLDENEYE
Bucephala clangula

An occasional winter visitor to northern and central Florida, this diving duck breeds in northern Maine and Canada.

Field marks: Male has dark green head, "golden" eye, round white cheek patch, white flanks, black and white back with thin black barring over white, black rear end. Female has brown head, mostly black bill with yellow tip, gray body and wings, white wing patch.

Size: L: 17"–20", WS: 25"–30"

Similar species: Barrow's goldeneye (rarely seen in Florida) has a flatter head and more defined black barring on back, with a black leading line at the shoulder.

Season: Winter

Habitat: Ocean bays, estuaries, inlets, lakes, ponds

Food source: Mollusks, crustaceans, water insects, small fish, plants in waterways

Nest: In tree cavities in the northern states, usually near a lake or pond

Call: A high *jip-jeet* or a guttural grunt, accompanied by wing whistles in flight

Hot spots: Bald Point State Park, Bald Point, 29.9377826 / -84.3381304; St. Marks National Wildlife Refuge (lighthouse area), Port Leon, 30.0751008 / -84.180; Cedar Key, 29.1354114 / -83.0340372; Seminole Town Center Pond, Sanford, 28.8088904 / -81.3358415

BUFFLEHEAD
Bucephala albeola

North America's smallest diving duck overwinters in ponds, lakes, and bays throughout northern and central Florida.

Field marks: Male has large white area on back of the black head, small bill, black back, white flanks and underside, gray tail. Nonbreeding male loses much of the white area on the head, retaining a patch on each side. Female is all brown with a darker back and head, white oval patch on each side of the head.

Size: L: 13"–14", WS: 21"–24"

Similar species: Hooded merganser is much larger and has a thin black bill, as well as rusty flanks and distinctive white striping.

Season: Winter

Habitat: Ponds, lakes, inlets, some open ocean

Food source: Insects, mollusks, crustaceans, some seeds found underwater

Nest: In cavities, often those left behind by northern flickers

Call: A single syllable *quah*, or a continuous *qua-qua-qua* during breeding season

Hot spots: Pond at St. Marks National Wildlife Refuge Headquarters, Port Leon, 30.089658 / -84.1659272; Fort Island Gulf Beach, Crystal River, 28.908602 / -82.69082; William E. Dunn Water Reclamation Facility, Palm Harbor, 28.1080422 / -82.7675414; Merritt Island National Wildlife Refuge, Titusville, 28.6411839 / -80.7774067; Lake Apopka Wildlife Drive, Apopka, 28.6691082 / -81.5574338

HOODED MERGANSER
Lophodytes cucullatus

The showiest of the mergansers is also the smallest.

Field marks: Male has black head with large white crest it raises during breeding season, thin bill, black back and chest with unique white striping, rusty flanks. Female is all brown with a reddish-brown crest, yellow bill, and long tail held upward. Nonbreeding adult (July–September) is brown overall with no crest.

Size: L: 17"–19", WS: 24"–26"

Similar species: Bufflehead is much smaller and black overall with a thicker, gray bill.

Season: Winter

Habitat: Ponds and streams in wooded areas; swamps and marshes

Food source: Crayfish and other crustaceans, insects, small fish, snails, small amphibians, underwater plants and seeds

Nest: Ten to 20 feet above ground in a hollow tree, often near water (not in Florida)

Call: A deep, rolling, descending croak, like a frog; females utter a grunting *quack*.

Hot spots: This widespread duck can be found on virtually any lake or pond throughout Florida, especially from central Florida northward. Water treatment plants, shopping center retention ponds, and wildlife refuges are most likely to host these ducks throughout the winter.

RED-BREASTED MERGANSER
Mergus serrator

The duck with the ragged crest and long, red bill turns up at coastal ponds and inlets in winter and early spring.

Field marks: Male has dark greenish-black head, ragged crest, long red bill, white collar, reddish-brown breast, black and white back, gray flanks. Female and nonbreeding male are virtually identical, with reddish-brown heads and gray bodies.

Size: L: 20"–26", WS: 30"–34"

Similar species: Hooded merganser has a large white patch on the neatly shaped crest.

Season: Winter and early spring

Habitat: Salt water in winter; inland lakes and ponds in spring

Food source: Primarily fish, but will eat water insects, worms, small amphibians, and crustaceans

Nest: In a hidden hole in the ground or a brush pile; the north country from the Great Lakes to Alaska

Call: A soft *wuh, wuh-wuh* from the male; a quacking call from the female

Hot spots: Just about any coastal viewpoint will have its pair or small group of mergansers. Here are some of the most dependable winter lookouts: St. Marks National Wildlife Refuge (lighthouse area), Port Leon, 30.0751008 / -84.180; Bayport Park, Spring Hill, 28.5342292 / -82.650066; Duck Ponds, Tierra Verde, 27.6679269 / -82.7264071; Pelican Island National Wildlife Refuge, North Beach, 27.8128126 / -80.4324961; Merritt Island National Wildlife Refuge, Titusville, 28.6411839 / -80.7774067

RUDDY DUCK
Oxyura jamaicensis

The bright blue bill, black cap, and rufous body make the male stand out from rafts of ducks during spring migration.

Field marks: Male in breeding plumage has a white face, large black cap covering the top third of the head, bright blue bill, rufous body with tail often pointed upward, white belly visible in flight. Female is brown overall with a darker cap and a dark line across the white cheek. Nonbreeding male is grayish brown overall but retains the white cheeks and black cap; bill is gray.

Size: L: 15", WS: 19"–23"

Similar species: Nothing compares in breeding plumage. Nonbreeding black scoter is larger and drabber overall, with less white on the face.

Season: Winter

Habitat: Freshwater ponds, lakes, and marshes

Food source: Aquatic vegetation, algae, water insects, crustaceans, mollusks

Nest: Floating among reeds in ponds or marshes; western United States and Canada

Call: A low, guttural call like a wet belch

Hot spots: Apalachicola River Wildlife and Environmental Area, Sand Beach Tower, Eastpoint, 29.783593 / -84.910848; Paynes Prairie Preserve State Park, Gainesville, 29.6068756 / -82.3031116; Lake Apopka Wildlife Drive, Apopka, 28.6691082 / -81.5574338; Lake Mirror, Lakeland, 28.044069 / -81.9518495; Canaveral National Seashore, Titusville, 28.85798 / -80.7765913

DUCK-LIKE BIRDS

COMMON GALLINULE
Gallinula galeata

The candy-corn bill and laughing cackle make this sleekly patterned bird (formerly known as common moorhen) distinctive and unmistakable in local marshes.

Field marks: Brown above and bluish gray below with a large white area on the tail, white flank stripe between the gray sides and brown wings. The bill is bright red with a yellow tip, with considerable variation among birds of different ages.

Size: L: 13"–15", WS: 21"–23"

Similar species: American coot is all black with a white bill.

Season: Year-round

Habitat: Freshwater ponds, streams, and marshes with tall reeds

Food source: Water plants and seeds, small invertebrates

Nest: On stems or branches of plants along the edge of water

Call: Falsetto *huh-huh, huh, huh-huh* in a nonrhythmic pattern, like a cartoon laugh

Hot spots: Every pond and marsh has its own population of common gallinule, making them one of the most common waterfowl in the state. Look for them along the edges of canals, retention ponds, and anywhere else where reeds and other tall aquatic plants provide shelter and cover.

AMERICAN COOT
Fulica americana

Large flocks of these all-black birds gather in marshes and ponds throughout the winter.

Field marks: All black with small white stripes on the tail, white bill, greenish-yellow legs. Adults have a red spot at the top of the bill.

Size: L: 15", WS: 24"–26"

Similar species: Common gallinule has a red and yellow bill.

Season: Winter throughout the state, with localized individuals year-round in canals and mall retention ponds

Habitat: Saltwater inlets, bays, and marshes; freshwater ponds and wetlands

Food source: Water plants, many small aquatic animals, occasionally bird eggs

Nest: On a pallet of plant materials anchored to reeds in a marsh or wetland. Most migrate to western United States and Canada to breed, but some remain in Florida.

Call: A midrange clucking: *pukka, pukka, pukka*; more abbreviated as an alarm call

Hot spots: In winter, coots gather by the hundreds in wildlife refuges, freshwater ponds, and along both the Atlantic and Gulf coasts, often in flocks of 1,500 or more. A visit to any sizable body of water is certain to yield sightings of this distinctive bird.

PURPLE GALLINULE
Porphyrio martinica

Strikingly iridescent, this colorful, ground-foraging marsh bird more than lives up to its name.

Field marks: Adult has bright blue-to-purple head, neck, breast, and underside; light blue forehead shield, bright orange-red bill with yellow tip, greenish back and wings, white undertail coverts, black tail, bright yellow legs with yellow, three-toed feet. Juvenile has light brown head and neck, brown bill, white breast and underside, light brown flanks, greenish back and wings, yellow legs, white undertail, greenish tail.

Size: L: 13"–14", WS: 22"

Similar species: Common gallinule has a similar bill but is gray and dark brown overall with a white flank stripe below the wings. Gray-headed swamphen has a bright red bill and forehead shield and a gray face and throat, as well as a purple back, purple and turquoise wings, and orange legs.

Season: Year-round

Habitat: Freshwater marshes with tall grasses for cover and floating plants (water lilies and such) for nesting

Food source: Water lilies, leaves and tubers of other aquatic plants, some insects, snails, small fish, frogs

Nest: In vegetation above water or on the water's surface

Call: Low, descending *kuck-kuck-kuck-kuck-kuck*, with a higher-pitched *kick-kick-kick* in flight

Hot spots: Sweetwater Wetlands Park, Gainesville, 29.6151026 / -82.3254061; Newtown Park, Winter Garden, 28.5772006 / -81.5865755; Orlando Wetlands Park, Orlando, 28.5753263 / -80.9966826; T. M. Goodwin Waterfowl Management Area, Palm Bay, 27.8452341 / -80.7252359; Everglades National Park, Anhinga Trail, Homestead, 25.3820583 / -80.6069362

GRAY-HEADED SWAMPHEN
Porphyrio poliocephalus

Introduced from southeastern Asia, this exotic member of the gallinule family frequents mall retention ponds and some south Florida wetlands.

Field marks: Gray head and throat, red eye, red forehead shield and bill, turquoise throat and breast, purple back and tail, turquoise side and wings, purple dividing line between breast and sides, white under tail, orange legs and feet.

Size: L: 15"–17", WS: 35"

Similar species: Purple gallinule has purple head, pale blue forehead shield, orange and yellow bill, yellow legs and feet, greenish wings and back.

Season: Year-round

Habitat: Marshes, edges of lakes and slow-moving rivers, canals and retention ponds with tall reeds

Food source: Grasses and other vegetation, small fish, small aquatic animals, offerings from humans

Nest: Among reeds and grasses near water

Call: A harsh note resembling a sneeze, as well as a squeaky, toy-horn *kee*

Hot spots: T. M. Goodwin Waterfowl Management Area, Palm Bay, 27.8452341 / -80.7252359; Wellington Environmental Preserve, Wellington, 26.6293528 / -80.3059387; Harney Pond Canal Recreation Area, Lakeport, 26.995414 / -81.0675573; Dolphin Mall, Sweetwater, 25.783585 / -80.3782082; Harns Marsh, Buckingham, 26.6496729 / -81.6869336

PELAGIC BIRDS: SHEARWATER, STORM-PETREL, GANNET, AND JAEGERS

DOMINIC SHERONY

AUDUBON'S SHEARWATER

Puffinus lherminieri

The smallest North American shearwater prefers the warm waters off Florida's Atlantic coast.

Field marks: Very dark mantle with tapered wings, black cap that descends below eye, white spot in front of eye, black tail with dark undertail. White cheeks, throat, breast, and underside.

Size: L: 12"–13", WS: 27"

Similar species: Great shearwater is half again larger with longer, scalier wings and a scaly back.

Season: Spring and summer

Habitat: Open ocean

Food source: Fish, squid

Nest: On islands in colonies of many birds

Call: Generally silent at sea; colonies of birds emit an elongated *squaaaa.*

Hot spots: Rarely seen from shore, shearwaters are more often spotted on pelagic boat trips in April and May. The Space Coast Birding and Wildlife Festival in Titusville offers an annual pelagic trip. The Yankee Fleet in Key West, Wes Biggs Florida Nature Tours, and several private guides also take birders out into the Atlantic Ocean and Gulf of Mexico for pelagic bird sightings. Visit surfbirds.com/Pelagic/ecoast.html.

© SHUTTERSTOCK.COM/AGAMI PHOTO AGENCY

WILSON'S STORM-PETREL
Oceanites oceanicus

A large white patch at the base of the squared-off tail provides the best field mark for this common pelagic bird.

Field marks: Dark brown above with pale wing patch, square tail, white stripe across rump; yellow feet may show beyond tail. Watch for skimming and hovering behavior over water.

Size: L: 7.25", WS: 18"

Similar species: Leach's storm-petrel is slightly larger, browner, and has a forked tail; rarely seen in Florida.

Season: Summer

Habitat: Open ocean

Food source: Tiny crustaceans and fish

Nest: On islands in Antarctica and southern South America

Call: Usually silent at sea

Hot spots: Storm-petrels are a common sight on pelagic boat trips in June. The Marine Science Center in Ponce Inlet sponsors pelagic trips off the state's east coast; find more information at marinesciencecenter .com. The Yankee Fleet in Key West, Wes Biggs Florida Nature Tours, and several private guides also take birders out into the Atlantic Ocean and Gulf of Mexico for pelagic bird sightings. Visit surfbirds.com/ Pelagic/ecoast.html for more information.

NORTHERN GANNET
Morus bassanus

Watch for this bird's all-white body, black wing tips, and dramatic diving plunge into the sea as it feeds.

Field marks: Adult is all white with striking black wing tips and long, straight wings, white tail, and silvery bill. Juveniles have a dark mantle, white upper tail coverts, and dark underwing in their first year, paling to dark underwing patches in second year.

Size: L: 37", WS: 72"

Similar species: Masked booby, the closest species in appearance, has a pronounced black mask across the eyes and at the base of the bill, and wide black patches on its wing primaries and secondaries. Gannets are much larger than any local gulls or snow geese and have a longer bill and more tapered, angular wings than swans.

Season: Winter and spring migration

Habitat: Open ocean

Food source: Fish and squid that swim close to the water's surface

Nest: Breeds in colonies on flat cliff ledges in the northern Atlantic Ocean

Call: Silent at sea; repetitive *kruk-kruk-kruk* in breeding colonies

Hot spots: Gannets are seen frequently on the horizon from beaches all along Florida's Atlantic coast. To see them at closer range, take a pelagic boat tour or a trip to Dry Tortugas National Park aboard one of the tour boats that departs from Key West in April: drytortugas.com/key-west-ferry/

SHUTTERSTOCK.COM/MINDSTORM

MASKED BOOBY
Sula dactylatra

This strikingly black and white bird is a Key West/Dry Tortugas specialty.

Field marks: Large, white head and body, black mask across eyes and at base of bill, light yellow-to-pink bill, black primary and secondary wing feathers, black tail, gray feet. Juvenile has a brown head, neck, and throat; gray bill, brown wings, white underside.

Size: L: 31"–32", WS: 62"

Similar species: Northern gannet lacks black mask, has yellowish band across back of head, and has white wings with black wing tips. Brown booby has a brown head, neck, and throat; brown wings.

Season: Year-round, but more easily seen in late spring/summer during breeding season

Habitat: Open ocean; in colonies on islands off the coast of Key West and in the Dry Tortugas

Food source: Fish, squid

Nest: In a scrape on the ground, often near a cliff

Call: Silent at sea; young may give a *chuk, chuk* from shore.

Hot spots: Garden Key, Dry Tortugas National Park, 24.6276 / -82.8728; Hospital Key, Dry Tortugas National Park, 24.6473 / -82.8522; Middle Key, Dry Tortugas National Park, 24.6493 / -82.8275; Key West National Wildlife Refuge, Key West, 24.5330692 / -82.0074463

DOMINIC SHERONY

BROWN BOOBY
Sula leucogaster

The smaller of Florida's two *Sula* species is easily identified by its sloping forehead and solid brown head.

Field marks: Brown head, neck, and throat; long, light yellow bill; bright white breast and underside, brown back and wings, brown tail. Juvenile is uniformly brown with a gray-brown bill.

Size: L: 29"–31", WS: 57"

Similar species: Juvenile masked booby has a bright white breast and underside, and white between the head and back.

Season: Year-round

Habitat: Open ocean; jetties and piers where brown pelicans and gulls roost

Food source: Fish and squid

Nest: On flat terrain, often using whatever materials are close by

Call: Scratchy *kerr-ack-ack* from females; otherwise mostly silent

Hot spots: Tom Renick Park, Ormond-by-the-Sea, 29.3314127 / -81.0578893; Jetty Park, Port Canaveral, 28.4064535 / -80.5924523; Dr. Von D. Mizell–Eula Johnson State Park, Hollywood, 26.0711624 / -80.1124978; Garden Key, Dry Tortugas National Park, 24.6276 / -82.8728; Lassing Park, St. Petersburg, 27.7513228 / -82.6299119

POMARINE JAEGER
Stercorarius pomarinus

Heavier and larger than parasitic jaeger, this bird appears darker overall.

Field marks: Heavy head, neck, and bill; yellow bill with black tip, black cap that extends down past bill, dark mantle (white wing patches on juveniles, white nape on light adults), white breast with distinct vertical streaking on sides.

Size: L: 21"–23", WS: 52"

Similar species: Parasitic jaeger is smaller, has rufous areas, has a slimmer, dark bill, and lacks the twisted tail feathers.

Season: Winter

Habitat: Open ocean

Food source: Rodents, birds, eggs, carrion, marine invertebrates

Nest: On the tundra along the Arctic Ocean in western North America

Call: Short single bark; rarely heard at sea

Hot spots: Tom Renick Park, Ormond-by-the-Sea, 29.3314127 / -81.0578893; Canaveral National Seashore (Apollo Beach), Titusville, 28.85798 / -80.7765913; Boynton Beach Inlet Park, Ocean Ridge, 26.5446541 / -80.0426102; Fort De Soto Park, St. Petersburg, 27.6327266 / -82.718157; on boat trips to the Dry Tortugas in early spring

© SHUTTERSTOCK.COM/MARTIN PELANEK

PARASITIC JAEGER
Stercorarius parasiticus

An uncommon pelagic bird in Atlantic waters with a slim body and short, pointy center tail feathers.

Field marks: Adult has dark brown cap descending over the eye, ivory neck, barring across the nape; dark mantle with rusty wash, white breast, gray to brown undertail coverts; pointed middle tail feathers. Juvenile may be easiest to distinguish from other jaegers by its all-over rufous wash.

Size: L: 17"–19", WS: 46"

Similar species: Pomarine jaeger is larger and stockier, with longer, twisted center tail feathers and dark brown undertail coverts. Juvenile pomarine jaegers are darker brown.

Season: Winter

Habitat: Open water within a few miles of shore; often viewed from beaches or in estuaries

Food source: Birds, eggs, small rodents, some fish

Nest: On tundra or islands above the Arctic Circle

Call: Mostly silent during migration; a single harsh *chuh* note when vocal

Hot spots: Tom Renick Park, Ormond-by-the-Sea, 29.3314127 / -81.0578893; Canaveral National Seashore (Apollo Beach), Titusville, 28.85798 / -80.7765913; Boynton Beach Inlet Park, Ocean Ridge, 26.5446541 / -80.0426102; Fort De Soto Park, St. Petersburg, 27.6327266 / -82.718157; on boat trips to the Dry Tortugas in early spring

PELICANS, FRIGATEBIRD, CORMORANT, AND ANHINGA

AMERICAN WHITE PELICAN
Pelecanus erythrorhynchos

A large white bird with a big pouch under its bill, this pelican is found on islands in freshwater lakes.

Field marks: White overall; long orange bill, orange legs and feet, black primary wing feathers.

Size: L: 62"–72", WS: 108"

Similar species: Northern gannet has black primaries, a tan cap, and a gray bill.

Season: Winter and early spring

Habitat: Islands in freshwater lakes and ponds

Food source: Fish

Nest: On islands, building low mounds of mud and debris

Call: A throaty croak

Hot spots: Any inland body of water is likely to provide a winter home to a few individuals or to flocks of hundreds of white pelicans, so you don't need to travel far out of your way to find them. They also may make appearances closer to the coast, sometimes in the same places you usually find brown pelicans. Causeway parks, the Intracoastal Waterway, and many man-made ponds and water features may attract these "snowbirds."

BROWN PELICAN
Pelecanus occidentalis

The unmistakable denizen of Florida's seashores gathers in flocks at every port, bridge, and pier.

Field marks: Adult has yellow head in breeding season with dark brown nape and neck (white in nonbreeding), and huge gray-to-brown bill with underhanging pocket for catching and transporting fish. Gray-brown back and wings, dark brown breast and underside, brown legs and feet. Juvenile has brown head and neck and whitish underside. Plunging dive while catching fish helps in identifying these birds over water.

Size: L: 50"–53", WS: 79"–80"

Similar species: American white pelican is all white with black trailing edge of wings and is not found at the seashore. Double-crested cormorant is smaller and all black with a bright yellow-orange bill.

Season: Year-round

Habitat: Open ocean and ocean shores

Food source: Fish

Nest: On the ground among thick vegetation or in a shrubby area; sometimes in an exposed treetop

Call: Mostly silent; young emit a low growl/groan in the nest

Hot spots: Any trip to the Atlantic Ocean or Gulf of Mexico will yield brown pelicans. Watch bridge and causeway railings, posts at piers and wharves, and beaches for groups of pelicans. A scan of the ocean from any beach will reveal pelicans skimming just above the water as they watch for fish, and then executing their complex, twisting dive maneuver to catch them. These birds also frequent large lakes farther inland.

MAGNIFICENT FRIGATEBIRD
Fregata magnificens

With an immense wingspan and deeply forked tail, this bird soars over seaside lands; the male's bright red breast allows for instant identification.

Field marks: Adults have black head, long gray bill hooked downward at the end, long black wings with distinct angle, very long tail with deep fork, usually held closed in flight. Breeding male has bright red throat and breast, which inflates for courtship display. Female has white breast, shoulders, and underside; juvenile has white head, throat, and breast; whitish stripe on wings.

Size: L: 38"–42", WS: 90"

Similar species: Double-crested cormorant is all black and smaller, with a longer neck and bright yellow-orange bill. Brown pelican has white/yellow area on head, massive bill with underhanging pouch, and short wedge tail.

Season: Year-round

Habitat: Seashores, almost always in the air

Food source: Fish and squid, some crustaceans

Nest: In colonies on islands in low shrubs and trees

Call: Usually silent at sea, with an occasional scratchy, guttural call on approach. Males make a hollow, clattery sound as part of mating rituals.

Hot spots: Fort Zachary Taylor Historic State Park, Key West, 24.5463 / -81.8106; Marathon Government Center, Marathon, 24.711388 / -81.09767; Bill Baggs Cape Florida State Park, Key Biscayne, 25.6733 / -80.1582; Marco Island, 25.9412201 / -81.7159653; J. N. Ding Darling National Wildlife Refuge, Sanibel, 26.4540529 / -82.1155071

DOUBLE-CRESTED CORMORANT
Phalacrocorax auritus

Very common seabird on ocean shores and large freshwater lakes.

Field marks: Black overall; orange lores, gray bill; white tufts on crown during breeding. Juveniles have pale or tan throat and underside.

Size: L: 32"–33", WS: 50"–54"

Similar species: Neotropic cormorant is smaller, and breeding birds have a white V at the base of the bill.

Season: Year-round

Habitat: Open water, especially along the ocean shore; also found inland at large lakes and flowing rivers

Food source: Fish, crustaceans

Nest: In rocky or sandy areas along ocean, lake, or river shoreline

Call: Mostly silent, with some grunting during nesting

Hot spots: Virtually every beach wall, rocky outcropping, offshore island, and sandbar has its own complement of double-crested cormorants, and many large inland lakes and reservoirs provide homes to these large dark birds as well. You do not need a special hot spot to find one—just go to any beach or shoreline overlook and scan the horizon. Cormorants sit low in the water, making them look similar to loons, so check carefully for the bright orange-yellow bill to make the identification.

71

ANHINGA
Anhinga anhinga

The lacy white mantle over black wings, long neck, and very long tail make anhingas fairly easy to identify.

Field marks: Adults are black overall with a long, bright yellow bill, longer tail than a cormorant, and a white wash over black wings. Juveniles have a cream to light brown head, neck, throat, and upper breast.

Size: L: 34"–36", WS: 45"

Similar species: Double-crested and neotropic cormorants are smaller and have shorter necks and tails and a shorter bill.

Season: Year-round

Habitat: Slow-moving freshwater, including shallow rivers, streams, drainage canals, and the Everglades

Food source: Mostly small fish

Nest: In the crotch of a tree near water

Call: Usually silent except during nesting, when they may croak to one another with a dry, rattling sound.

Hot spots: Anhingas appear just about everywhere in Florida, spreading their wings to dry on the edges of natural and man-made ponds, rivers, canals, and streams, and along bridges, piers, berms, dikes, and structures in water treatment areas. Their large size and idiosyncratic stance make them easy to spot among the egrets, herons, and other large waterbirds.

GULLS AND TERNS

BONAPARTE'S GULL
Chroicocephalus philadelphia

You'll find this gull on ocean beaches in flocks, especially during winter.

Field marks: Breeding adult has black hood ending high on the back of the neck, partial white eye ring, black bill; white body, gray wings with black tips, white tail with black tip. Nonbreeding adult has white head, dark spot at ear.

Size: L: 12"–14", WS: 33"–35"

Similar species: Little gull has more extensive hood, red bill with black tip.

Season: Winter

Habitat: Marshes, rivers, large lakes, beaches

Food source: Aquatic insects, plant matter

Nest: Near water; western Alaska and northern Canada

Call: Short, burry *keeo, keeo, keeo* in flight; staccato *kee-kee-kee* in groups

Hot spots: Huguenot Memorial City Park, Jacksonville, 30.4112444 / -81.4206594; Tom Renick Park, Ormond-by-the-Sea, 29.3314127 / -81.0578893; North Jetty Park, Venice, 27.1135693 / -82.4675176; John's Pass, Treasure Island, 27.7819866 / -82.7840424; Mashes Sands County Park, Panacea, 29.973171 / -84.3438435

LAUGHING GULL
Leucophaeus atricilla

Named for its cackling call, this black-headed gull is one of the most widespread gull species in Florida.

Field marks: Breeding adult has black head extending to the neck, partial white eye ring, heavy red bill that droops slightly at the end; white body, dark wings, white tail with black band at the end, black legs. Nonbreeding adult has white head streaked in gray at the back, black bill.

Size: L: 16"–17", WS: 40"–42"

Similar species: Little gull is smaller, has a slim bill, and has a dark underwing. Bonaparte's gull is smaller and has a thin black bill and light gray wings.

Season: Year-round

Habitat: Ocean beaches, salt marshes, large and small lakes

Food source: Insects and invertebrates, shellfish, berries, human trash

Nest: On the ground in a salt marsh, hidden among grasses

Call: Repeated *kyah, kyah*, increasing in speed until it sounds like a human laugh

Hot spots: Laughing gulls are prevalent from the southern tip of the Keys all the way to Jacksonville and St. Marks National Wildlife Refuge in the Panhandle. Their year-round presence, especially on beaches, makes them easy to find for vacationers as well as residents.

RING-BILLED GULL
Larus delawarensis

The most common gull in America, this scavenger turns up in flocks in parking lots, in mowed grassy areas, and at your outdoor restaurant table.

Field marks: Breeding adult has white head and body; yellow bill with black ring near the tip, gray wings, black wing tips, yellow legs. Juveniles have varying degrees of brown streaking over the head, body, and wings; pink bill with black tip, pink legs.

Size: L: 17.5"–19", WS: 47"–48"

Similar species: Herring gull is larger and has a yellow bill with a red spot. Laughing gull has a black hood in breeding season, and has darker wings year-round.

Season: Year-round

Habitat: Ocean beaches, lagoons, inlets, marshes, parks, parking lots, landfills

Food source: Human discards, fish, rodents, eggs and chicks from other birds' nests

Nest: In a depression on the ground; in colonies on an island or other protected area

Call: Piercing *keey-oh, keey-oh*, or a harsh, high-pitched barking call

Hot spots: You will see these ubiquitous birds every time you visit the beach, go to a supermarket or park, or venture into any wilderness area that contains a lake or large pond. Ring-billed gulls often stand in large flocks in parking areas waiting for food scraps to drop from unsuspecting humans' vehicles.

HERRING GULL
Larus argentatus

More numerous on the Atlantic side of the state, this common gull confuses birders with its many plumage variations.

Field marks: Breeding adult has white head and breast, yellow eye, heavy yellow bill with red spot on lower mandible; gray wings with black tips, white tail, pink legs. Nonbreeding adult is similar but with brown streaking on the head and neck. Juveniles in first and second winter have extensive brown mottling over the head, breast, underside, tail, and wings, with black wing tips and a dark brown band at the end of the tail. Extent of streaking will vary from one bird to the next.

Size: L: 24"–26", WS: 55"–58"

Similar species: Great black-backed gull is larger with black wings. Lesser black-backed gull is slightly smaller and has darker gray wings and yellow legs. Ring-billed gull is smaller and has a yellow bill with a black ring.

Season: Primarily winter

Habitat: Ocean beaches, islands, large lakes, rivers

Food source: Fish, aquatic invertebrates, shellfish, carrion, other birds, human discards

Nest: On the ground on the beach or an island not far from shore

Call: A squeal followed by a high *hyah-hyah-hyah-hyah*, not unlike a human laugh. Other calls include a long whistle ending in a high-pitched squeal.

Hot spots: Frank Rendon Park, Daytona Beach Shores, 29.1803062 / -80.9837973; Lighthouse Point Park and Jetty, Ponce Inlet, 29.077 / -80.9211; John D. MacArthur Beach State Park, North Palm Beach, 26.8204 / -80.0388; Gasparilla Island State Park, Boca Grande, 26.7174771 / -82.2609043; Bald Point State Park, Bald Point, 29.9377826 / -84.3381304

LESSER BLACK-BACKED GULL
Larus fuscus

If a dark-backed gull looks too small to be a herring gull, check for the yellow legs—that's the most easily distinguishable characteristic of a lesser black-backed gull (pictured here on the left, with a herring gull on the right for comparison).

Field marks: Breeding adult has a white head and body, yellow bill with red spot on lower mandible; dark gray wings, black primaries with white spots, bright yellow legs. Nonbreeding adult has dark, dense streaks on the head and neck. Juvenile is gray and brown streaked overall with darker streaks on wings, black bill, pinkish legs.

Size: L: 21"–22", WS: 54"

Similar species: Great black-backed gull is larger, with truly black wings and pink legs. Herring gull is larger and lighter-colored overall, pink legs.

Season: Winter

Habitat: Ocean and gulf coasts

Food source: Invertebrates, insects, fish, shellfish, small birds and mammals, bird eggs, carrion

Nest: On the ground near water; northern Europe

Call: Single-note *gaw, gaw, gaw*; also an *arr-arr-arr-arr* alarm call

Hot spots: Port Orange Causeway Park, Port Orange, 29.147495 / -80.9769201; Barge Canal, North Banana River Drive, Merritt Island, 28.4085296 / -80.6628549; Fort Pierce Inlet State Park, Fort Pierce, 27.4748466 / -80.2935362; Hollywood Beach, Hollywood, 26.0144629 / -80.1154912; Suncoast Seabird Sanctuary, Redington Shores, 27.8364529 / -82.8373781

GREAT BLACK-BACKED GULL
Larus marinus

The largest local gull stands out from a mixed flock because of its height and true-black wings.

Field marks: Adult has white head and body, yellow bill with red lower mandible spot, black wings with large white spots on primaries, pinkish legs. Juvenile has darkly streaked head and body, mottled black and white wings, large black bill, pale pink legs. Streaking fades over the course of three winters.

Size: L: 28"–31", WS: 62"–65"

Similar species: Lesser black-backed gull is smaller with yellow legs; wings are dark gray rather than black. Herring gull is smaller and has gray wings.

Season: Winter, with some individuals year-round on the northern Florida ocean coast

Habitat: Ocean coast, tidal wetlands, bays and inlets

Food source: An aggressive scavenger; fish, mollusks, crustaceans, small mammals, insects, bird eggs and chicks, berries, human discards

Nest: Tucked in among rocks on a cliff face or other rocky outcropping

Call: Deeper-throated than other gulls; an alto moan, leading to a series of *ay-yah, ay-yah, ay-yah* syllables in various combinations

Hot spots: You'll find one or two of these large gulls among flocks of ring-billed, herring, and laughing gulls on virtually every ocean beach in northern and central Florida, but they are more sparsely seen on the Gulf side. With their black backs and wings, bright yellow bills, and several inches more height than the gulls around them, great black-backs make it fairly easy to sort them out from the crowd of gray-winged varieties.

SOOTY TERN
Onychoprion fuscatus

Striking with its bright white and deep black plumage, this bird comes ashore only to nest.

Field marks: Black cap extending to black eye, black nape, bright white forehead to gray bill, white body, black wings with white notch at shoulder, black tail, black legs. Juvenile is all brown-black with white spots on wings, white underside.

Size: L: 16", WS: 32"

Similar species: Bridled tern is slightly smaller and has dark grayish wings; tail extends beyond wingtips when standing.

Season: Spring and early summer

Habitat: Sandy islands off the Keys; open ocean in the tropics

Food source: Small fish, squid

Nest: A scrape on the ground, usually in open area

Call: High-pitched *kah-wah* in flight; constant chatter in colonies

Hot spots: Dry Tortugas National Park, 24.6344 / -82.8699; pelagic trips around the Florida Keys, otherwise undependable along Florida coast, with sporadic single sightings from shore

DOMINIC SHERONY

© SHUTTERSTOCK.COM/CHRISTOPHER UNSWORTH

BRIDLED TERN
Onychoprion anaethetus

Grayer-winged and longer-tailed than sooty tern, this bird can be hard to distinguish from a sooty on open water.

Field marks: Black cap with thin black line through the eye, white forehead extending to black bill; white breast and underside, dark gray wings, white tail slightly longer than wings, black legs. Juveniles lack the black cap but have a smudgy line through the eye.

Size: L: 14"–16", WS 30"

Similar species: Sooty tern has darker wings, and young are all black. Sooty tern's tail is shorter.

Season: Spring and summer

Habitat: Open tropical ocean, usually staying close to shore

Food source: Fish and squid, some small crustaceans

Nest: Under a ledge or tucked between rocks on small islands, sometimes with terns of other species

Call: Single bark from adults in colonies; otherwise silent

Hot spots: Dry Tortugas National Park, 24.6344 / -82.8699; pelagic trips around the Florida Keys, otherwise undependable along Florida coast, with sporadic single sightings from shore

CASPIAN TERN
Hydroprogne caspia

The oversize, boldly red bill on the largest local tern is the key to its identification.

Field marks: White head with black cap past its eye, large red bill with dark gray tip, pale gray wings with dark primaries, black legs. Nonbreeding adult has streaky gray cap.

Size: L: 20"–23", WS: 50"–53"

Similar species: Royal tern is smaller and has thinner orange-red bill. Common tern is much smaller and has thinner black cap.

Season: Winter; summer in south Florida

Habitat: Ocean shore, lakes and rivers with gravel shores

Food source: Fish, occasional crustaceans

Nest: In the sand on ocean and lake beaches; northeastern Atlantic Ocean, central Canada, western United States, and Pacific coast

Call: A single raspy croak

Hot spots: St. Marks National Wildlife Refuge, St. Marks, 30.1515653 / -84.1473314; Fred Howard County Park, Tarpon Springs, 28.1532114 / -82.7937412; San Carlos Bay/Bunche Beach Preserve, Fort Myers, 26.476174 / -81.9673795; Parrish Park/ Max Brewer Causeway, Titusville, 28.6237063 / -80.794487; Fort Matanzas National Monument, Crescent Beach, 29.7150991 / -81.233517

ROYAL TERN
Thalasseus maximus

Smaller and sleeker than the Caspian tern, this tern has a slimmer red bill and a more-pronounced crest.

Field marks: Breeding adult has white head with black cap and pointed crest on back of head, red-orange bill, pale gray wings with black tips, white tail, black legs. Nonbreeding adult's white forehead tapers to black shading; black line from eye to crest. Juvenile's bill is more yellow, with white forehead, black shading on back of head, mottled wings, yellow legs.

Size: L: 18"–20", WS: 40"–42"

Similar species: Caspian tern is larger and has heavier bill. Common tern has a red bill with a black tip; red legs in breeding plumage.

Season: Winter; summer in south Florida

Habitat: Ocean beaches, saltwater bays and inlets

Food source: Fish, water invertebrates

Nest: On coastal islands, in a hollow dug in the sand

Call: Single note *cur-rick*; also very high, short trill

Hot spots: Just about any beach will have its share of royal terns. Here are some places where they gather in flocks: Marco Island, Tiger Tail Beach, 25.948098 / -81.74456; Fred Howard County Park, Tarpon Springs, 28.1532114 / -82.79374; Boca Chica Beach, Key West, 24.5631321 / -81.6773723; Crandon Park, Key Biscayne, 25.7089712 / -80.1536322; Hightower Beach Park, Satellite Beach, 28.1942452 / -80.5943903

COMMON TERN
Sterna hirundo

Small, slender, and strong with a forked tail like a barn swallow, this northern tern passes through on its way to breeding grounds in New England and the Canada coast.

Field marks: Breeding adult has a white head, light gray body, black cap that narrows toward the back of the neck, red bill with black tip, pale gray wings that extend past the tail, deeply forked tail, dark primaries visible on underwing, red legs. Nonbreeding adult has black cap on back of head, exposing white forehead; black bill, dark "shoulder" on wing, black legs. Juvenile birds have gray wings streaked with white, limited black cap with white forehead, black bill and legs.

Size: L: 12"–15", WS: 30"–31"

Similar species: Tail of Forster's tern extends past the wings. Roseate tern has a black bill and a long tail.

Season: Spring and fall migration, with occasional summer sightings

Habitat: Beaches and inlets

Food source: Fish, mollusks, squid, crustaceans, some insects

Nest: On the ground on a beach, in seaweed or gravel just above the high-tide line (not in Florida)

Call: A gravelly *kee-yur*, a single chip note in flight

Hot spots: Dr. Von D. Mizell–Eula Johnson State Park, Hollywood, 26.0711624 / -80.1124978; Marco Island, Tiger Tail Beach, 25.948098 / -81.74456; San Carlos Bay/Bunche Beach Preserve, Fort Myers, 26.476174 / -81.9673795; St. Marks National Wildlife Refuge, St. Marks, 30.1515653 / -84.1473314; Huguenot Memorial City Park, Jacksonville, 30.4112444 / -81.4206594

FORSTER'S TERN
Sterna forsteri

Telling Forster's and common terns apart can be tricky. Generally, Forster's is slightly larger, and breeding birds have no gray or black on the primaries.

Field marks: Breeding adult has black cap extending to the nape, orange bill with black tip, white body, pale gray wings with white primaries, deeply forked white tail, orange legs. Nonbreeding bird has white head with large black spot just behind the eye, darker wing primaries.

Size: L: 13"–15", WS: 30"–31"

Similar species: Common tern is smaller, retains most of its black cap in nonbreeding plumage, and has a redder bill.

Season: Winter, with small flocks staying through the migration into summer

Habitat: Ocean shoreline, salt marshes

Food source: Fish, tadpoles, mollusks, crustaceans

Nest: Built on a foundation of dead plants in salt marshes

Call: High-pitched *keek, keek, keek*; lower, rapid clicking or chucking sound

Hot spots: Any ocean or gulf beach may yield Forster's sightings, but these spots regularly receive larger flocks throughout the winter: Cedar Key, 29.1354114 / -83.0340372; Honeymoon Island State Park, Dunedin, 28.0706 / -82.8314; Stump Pass Beach State Park, Manasota Key, 26.9022934 / -82.346805; Jetty Park, Port Canaveral, 28.4064535 / -80.5924523; Fort Matanzas National Monument, Crescent Beach, 29.7150991 / -81.233517

© SHUTTERSTOCK.COM/NOAH STRYCKER

ROSEATE TERN
Sterna dougallii

A red and black–billed tern with a rounded head, this bird gets its name from the pale pink wash it gains on its underparts during breeding season.

Field marks: Breeding adult has white head with black cap, thin black bill, white breast with pale pink tint, pale gray wings, white primaries, deeply forked white tail extending beyond the wing tips, red legs. Nonbreeding bird has white forehead, darker primaries, and no pink wash.

Size: L: 12.5"–15.5", WS: 29"

Similar species: No other tern has the pink tint during breeding season. Common tern has a red bill with a black tip and darker primaries year-round.

Season: Summer

Habitat: Ocean beaches and islands, salt marshes

Food source: Fish

Nest: On the ground in a salt marsh with grass cover

Call: Single, repeated *chi-wek, chi-wek* note; also a crackling *cha* note in flight

Hot spots: Roseate terns sometimes are spotted from beaches in central and south Florida, but the most dependable locations for them are all in the Keys: Marathon Government Center, Marathon, 24.711388 / -81.09767; Fort Zachary Taylor Historic State Park, Key West, 24.5463 / -81.8106; Garden Key, Dry Tortugas National Park, 24.6276 / -82.8728

LEAST TERN
Sternula antillarum

North America's smallest tern is distinctive with its aggressive diving style, white forehead, and yellow bill.

Field marks: Breeding adult has white head and body, black cap, white forehead, yellow bill, pale gray wings, two dark gray primaries, white tail with short V shape, yellow legs. Nonbreeding bird has black bill, light primaries; black cap recedes to middle of head.

Size: L: 8"–9", WS: 20"

Similar species: All other terns are larger; only least tern has a yellow bill and legs.

Season: Summer

Habitat: Sandy beaches and sandbars

Food source: Fish, shrimp

Nest: In the sand on a beach

Call: Single, repeated note: *chik, chik, chik;* faster and squeakier when used as an alarm

Hot spots: Virtually any beach will produce sightings of least tern in season. These sites often serve as seasonal feeding grounds for larger flocks: Dr. Von D. Mizell–Eula Johnson State Park, Hollywood, 26.0711624 / -80.1124978; Crandon Park, Key Biscayne, 25.7089712 / -80.1536322; Gulf Islands National Seashore, Fort Pickens, Pensacola Beach, 30.3231 / -87.2829; St. Marks National Wildlife Refuge, Stoney Bayou 1 & Twin Dikes, 30.1257123 / -84.1436863; Fort De Soto Park, St. Petersburg, 27.6327266 / -82.718157

BLACK TERN
Chlidonias niger

This unique tern passes through coastal and inland marshes in spring and fall.

Field marks: Breeding adult has black head and body with a white rear, gray wings, gray back and tail, dark red legs. Nonbreeding bird has white head with black spots at crown and ear, white underside, gray back and wings.

Size: L: 9.5", WS: 22"–24"

Similar species: No other local terns look like this one. White-winged tern, an accidental visitor, is heavier, and the underside of its wings is black and white.

Season: Spring and fall migration

Habitat: Marshes, lakes, ponds, ocean coast

Food source: Fish, shellfish, crayfish, insects

Nest: In colonies farther north, on nests floating on water

Call: Harsh *kyew*; sharp, higher *ip, ip* in flight

Hot spots: Canaveral National Seashore, Titusville, 28.85798 / -80.7765913; Anastasia State Park, St. Augustine, 29.8661797 / -81.2705122; Browns Farm Road, Sixmile Bend, 26.6321916 / -80.5711555; Gandy Beach, Tampa Bay, 27.8715551 / -82.6048279; Gulf Islands National Seashore, Fort Pickens, Pensacola Beach, 30.3231 / -87.2829

GULL-BILLED TERN
Gelochelidon nilotica

Look for the heavy black bill that distinguishes this midsize tern from similar birds.

Field marks: Black cap that covers the eye and forehead, heavy black bill, light gray wings with dark trailing edge at tips, dark tail, black legs. Nonbreeding bird loses the black cap, maintaining a gray patch just behind the eye.

Size: L: 14", WS: 34"

Similar species: Sandwich tern has a black crest and a black bill with a yellow tip. Royal tern has an orange bill.

Season: Summer on the east coast and inland; year-round on the Gulf side

Habitat: Ocean and gulf beaches in summer; salt marshes, stormwater treatment areas and plowed fields in winter

Food source: Fish, small reptiles and aquatic animals

Nest: On sandy beaches

Call: A single *kay-wek*, or a series of rapid, cackled *wa-wa-wa* notes

Hot spots: Huguenot Memorial City Park, Jacksonville, 30.4112444 / -81.4206594; Browns Farm Road, Sixmile Bend, 26.6321916 / -80.5711555; Everglades National Park, Flamingo, 25.1416 / -80.9255; Stormwater Treatment Area 1W, Wellington, 26.6762842 / -80.4273806; Orlando Wetlands Park, Orlando, 28.5753263 / -80.9966826

SANDWICH TERN
Thalasseus sandvicensis

A smaller tern than other year-round residents, this is the only one with a yellowish tip on its black bill.

Field marks: White overall with pale gray wings, black cap with tuft on back of head, black bill with pale yellow-to-white tip, black legs. Nonbreeding bird has a white forehead, black cap recedes to back of the head.

Size: L: 14"–16" WS: 34"

Similar species: Royal tern has an orange bill and grayer wings. Common tern has grayer wings, dark orange bill with black tip, dark wing primaries.

Season: Year-round

Habitat: Ocean beaches, occasionally found inland on lakeshores

Food source: Fish, some invertebrates

Nest: In colonies on ocean beaches, on the ground in a shallow depression

Call: High-pitched single *chee*, or a scratchy, repeated *kur-wik* series between members of a pair

Hot spots: Any beach may provide sandwich tern sightings, but these spots are especially popular with the birds: Gulf Islands National Seashore, Fort Pickens, Pensacola Beach, 30.3231 / -87.2829; Fred Howard County Park, Tarpon Springs, 28.1532114 / -82.79374; Stump Pass Beach State Park, Manasota Key, 26.9022934 / -82.346805; Jetty Park, Port Canaveral, 28.4064535 / -80.5924523; Anastasia State Park, St. Augustine, 29.8661797 / -81.270512

BROWN NODDY
Anous stolidus

This member of the tern family breeds on islands in the Dry Tortugas.

Field marks: Muted brown overall with a darker brown tail, white forehead fading to gray on back of head, dark gray bill slightly longer than other local terns. Juvenile has lighter brown wings.

Size: L: 15"–16", WS: 32"

Similar species: No other local seabird has this solid brown plumage. Black noddy—seen very rarely on Garden Key—is black overall with a more-defined white crown.

Season: Summer; also seen on pelagic trips through spring and fall migration

Habitat: Colonies on islands in open ocean

Food source: Fish

Nest: On islands in the Dry Tortugas, near the ground in a cedar or cactus

Call: Elongated *kurrr*, scooping up at the end

Hot spots: Garden Key, Dry Tortugas National Park, 24.6276 / -82.8728; Hospital Key, Dry Tortugas National Park, 24.6473 / -82.8522; open water on pelagic boat trips between Key West and Dry Tortugas

BLACK SKIMMER
Rynchops niger

With its elongated shape, oversize lower mandible, and spellbinding water-skimming behavior, black skimmer is a favorite among coastal birders.

Field marks: Black mantle from top of head to wing tips, white underside, white forehead, orange and black bill with longer lower mandible, orange legs.

Size: L: 18"–19", WS: 42"–45"

Similar species: American oystercatcher has similar coloring but lacks the pronounced bill configuration.

Season: Year-round, with higher concentrations in winter

Habitat: Sandbars, beaches, salt marshes, estuaries, bays

Food source: Fish, shrimp

Nest: In a depression on the ground, hidden by vegetation

Call: Single note: *duh, duh, duh*; faster in flight or as an alarm

Hot spots: Everglades National Park, Flamingo, 25.1416 / -80.9255; Fort Matanzas National Monument, Crescent Beach, 29.7150991 / -81.233517; Little Talbot Island, Jacksonville, 30.4240678 / -81.4124787; St. Marks National Wildlife Refuge, St. Marks, 30.1515653 / -84.1473314; Fred Howard County Park, Tarpon Springs, 28.1532114 /-82.79374

BITTERNS, HERONS, AND EGRETS

AMERICAN BITTERN
Botaurus lentiginosus

This skulking wader blends seamlessly into reedy marsh backgrounds.

Field marks: Chunky, long-necked brown bird overall with darker brown primaries, buff throat and neck streaked with chestnut, black patch on either side of neck, yellow-green bill and legs.

Size: L: 28"–32", WS: 42"

Similar species: Least bittern is smaller with dark back (when breeding) and yellower color. Black-crowned night-heron has white chest and underside and black cap. Yellow-crowned night-heron has black and white face, yellow crown, long white plumes. Green heron has long black bill, bold chestnut sides, green cap, white throat.

Season: Winter

Habitat: Large freshwater marshes with dense reeds

Food source: Amphibians, fish, small mammals, insects

Nest: Well-hidden among the reeds

Call: Distinctive, repeated *wunk-a-chunk* during breeding season

Hot spots: Stormwater Treatment Area 1E, auto entrance, Wellington, 26.6809958 / -80.3004992; Wakodahatchee Wetlands, Delray Beach, 26.4781984 / -80.144738; Green Cay Wetlands & Nature Center, Boynton Beach, 26.4861584 / -80.1607561; Orlando Wetlands Park, Orlando, 28.5753263 / -80.9966826; Barr Hammock Preserve, Levy Loop Trail, Micanopy, 29.5165735 / -82.3061907

DOMINIC SHERONY

DOMINIC SHERONY

LEAST BITTERN
Ixobrychus exilis

A small, secretive bittern rarely glimpsed in freshwater marshes.

Field marks: Brown overall with a darker back, reddish patch at nape, neck streaked in white and brown, yellow bill and legs.

Size: L: 11"–14", WS: 17"

Similar species: American bittern is twice the size. Green heron has long black bill, bold chestnut sides, green cap, white throat. Virginia rail has gray head, pink bill with white tip, rusty neck and chest, and barred black and white flanks.

Season: Summer north of Orlando; year-round in central and south Florida

Habitat: Wetlands and marshes with dense reeds and cattails

Food source: Fish, small amphibians, slugs, aquatic insects

Nest: Deep in the reeds in nests made of living plants

Call: Low cooing

Hot spots: Green Cay Wetlands & Nature Center, Boynton Beach, 26.4861584 / -80.1607561; Stormwater Treatment Area 1E, auto entrance, Wellington, 26.6809958 / -80.3004992; Celery Fields, Fruitville, 27.3282173 / -82.4340248; Body Hill Nature Park & Lake Maggiore, St. Petersburg, 27.7322367 / -82.6521206; Lake Apopka North Shore, Astatula, 28.6740878 / -81.7059258

GREAT BLUE HERON
Ardea herodias

The tallest of the long-legged waders, this majestic bird stands quietly and waits for prey, then grabs or stabs its target in a split-second attack.

Field marks: Gray-blue with grayish legs, large bill, yellow lower mandible, black crown, long plumes from neck. In flight, legs extend far beyond tail, neck curls in, and darker flight feathers become visible.

Size: H: 46", WS: 72"

Similar species: Tricolored heron has white underbelly. Little blue heron is darker blue and half as tall.

Season: Year-round wherever there is open water

Habitat: Fresh- and saltwater marshes, grasslands, any pond with ample fish

Food source: Fish, small mammals, frogs, birds, insects

Nest: High in trees in colonies (rookeries), often some distance from feeding grounds

Call: Hoarse croaking *bwaaaaah*; alarm is a series of chuffing sounds like *bwaak, bwaak, bwaak.*

Hot spots: The most common tall wading bird in North America, the great blue heron can be seen easily at virtually any inland pond, tidal marsh, and wetland wildlife refuge throughout Florida.

GREAT EGRET
Ardea alba

Florida's tallest egret is a sight to behold. Pure white with a long, curving neck, it's easy to see as it stands motionless and waits for prey to swim by.

Field marks: All white, long yellow-orange bill, black legs and feet.

Size: H: 39", WS: 51"

Similar species: Snowy egret has a black bill with yellow lores, black legs, and yellow feet.

Season: Year-round

Habitat: Salt- and freshwater marshes, mudflats, other wetlands along the Atlantic and Gulf coasts, as well as inland lakes, wetlands, and farm fields

Food source: Fish, frogs, other small wetland creatures

Nest: In colonies, high in trees

Call: Low, squawking *caaaah*, dropping still lower at the end

Hot spots: Numerous and easy to distinguish from other long-legged birds, great egrets can be found virtually everywhere in Florida except for city streets. Check any retention pond or drainage canal in a suburb, at a mall, or in an open area, as well as in open spaces including marshes, fields that routinely flood, and rice fields.

SNOWY EGRET
Egretta thula

This elegant member of the heron family sports long plumes during the breeding season, and its bright yellow feet make it unique among egrets.

Field marks: All white; long white plumes from head and chest during breeding season, slender black bill, yellow lores, black legs with yellow feet.

Size: H: 24", WS: 41"

Similar species: Great egret is significantly larger and has a yellow bill and black feet. Cattle egret is smaller and has shorter bill and black feet (red during breeding).

Season: Year-round

Habitat: Marshes (salt, brackish, and freshwater), ponds, wetlands

Food source: Fish, small crustaceans, worms, frogs, insects

Nest: In colonies, toward the tops of trees or tall shrubs

Call: Croaking *maaaw, morr*; higher pitched than great egret or great blue heron

Hot spots: Any area with water—a pond, lake, slow stream, wetland, flooded field, bay, or gulf—is likely to have its own population of snowy egrets. These colony-loving birds are easy to spot in rows along canals or sharing a tree arched over a lagoon. They gather in wildlife refuges and at all of Florida's national park sites, as well as along causeways on both the Gulf and Atlantic coasts.

TRICOLORED HERON
Egretta tricolor

Smaller than the great blue heron and strikingly marked, this heron is as numerous in Florida as its egret cousins. Find it in the quiet waters of fresh- and saltwater marshes.

Field marks: Steel blue back, wings, neck, and head; streak of white outlined with rusty red down the front of the long neck, white underparts, pink legs (yellow in juveniles), blue-gray bill tipped with black.

Size: H: 26", WS: 36"

Similar species: Great blue heron has blue-gray underparts, heavier yellow bill.

Season: Year-round

Habitat: Coastal marshes, inland freshwater wetlands

Food source: Fish, small crustaceans, insects, frogs

Nest: In colonies with other herons and egrets, high in trees

Call: Nasal, rasping two-syllable *wiwur, wiwur,* alarm call is a continuous grunting.

Hot spots: One of the charms of birding in Florida is the abundance of long-legged wading birds, giving the state a true sense of a tropical paradise. Tricolored herons are as easy to find as great and snowy egrets and great blue herons—virtually any body of water or perpetually wet area will have them. They are most numerous in south Florida, with concentrations in and around the Everglades and at ponds and sloughs from Palm Beach to Fort Myers.

LITTLE BLUE HERON
Egretta caerulea

Often standing still enough to blend with its surroundings, this dark blue and purple bird stays in the shadows while patrolling for prey.

Field marks: Uniformly dark blue with gray legs, light bluish bill. Head and neck may be dark purple in mature adults. Juvenile is pure white with gray bill and greenish legs.

Size: H: 24", WS: 40"

Similar species: Great blue heron is much larger, lighter colored, and has a yellow bill. Tricolored heron is somewhat taller and has white underparts and a white streak down the front of its neck. Cattle egret is smaller, with a shorter neck and darker bill than a juvenile little blue heron.

Season: Year-round

Habitat: Fresh- and saltwater wetlands and marshes, wet fields, estuaries, quiet streambeds, drainage canals along roadsides

Food source: Fish, small crustaceans, dragonflies, frogs

Nest: Short trees, shrubs, usually concealed by vegetation

Call: Series of harsh *mow, mow, mow* croaks in flight; short staccato croaks while stationary. These may vary in length and frequency.

Hot spots: Like the great blue and tricolored herons, the little blue heron is widespread and abundant throughout the state. Many birders find them trolling drainage canals along roadsides or standing quietly on the edges of city and suburban ponds, especially on the outskirts of landscaped apartment complexes and mall parking areas. Keep an eye on the side of the road as you drive the Tamiami Trail or Florida's Turnpike.

REDDISH EGRET
Egretta rufescens

A wader of southern climates, this egret stays close to the coast in shallow saltwater marshes. Its population appears to be declining throughout the region.

Field marks: Rufous head and neck, blue skin around eye, pink bill with black tip, grayish-blue body and wings, gray legs. Juvenile may have pinkish-gray head and neck instead of reddish; some juveniles are pure white with gray legs, but retain the pink and black bill.

Size: L: 29"–31", WS: 46"

Similar species: Little blue heron is smaller and is dark blue overall with a gray-blue bill. Juvenile tricolored heron is more brilliantly rufous, with the reddish color carrying onto the wings.

Season: Year-round

Habitat: Saltwater marshes, bays, estuaries

Food source: Fish

Nest: In mangrove swamps, in a tree just above the water

Call: A series of single, low grunting notes, accompanied by bill clattering during courtship

Hot spots: J. N. Ding Darling National Wildlife Refuge, Sanibel, 26.4540529 / -82.1155071; Merritt Island National Wildlife Refuge, Titusville, 28.6411839 / -80.7774067; Honeymoon Island State Park, Dunedin, 28.0706 / -82.8314; Fort De Soto Park, St. Petersburg, 27.6327266 / -82.718157; Everglades National Park, Snake Bight Canoe Launch/Trail, 25.1633089 / -80.886755

CATTLE EGRET
Bubulcus ibis

This egret gets its name from its relationship with livestock, foraging for insects large animals kick up as they move around a pasture. The bird even stands on animals' backs to catch fleas, flies, and ticks.

Field marks: Short, stocky, short-billed, all-white egret with a yellow bill and black legs and feet. When breeding, this egret develops light orange areas on its head, back, and neck/chest, and its legs turn red.

Size: H: 20", WS: 36"

Similar species: Snowy and great egrets are larger and have bills more than twice the length. Great egret has a long neck. Snowy egret has yellow feet.

Season: Year-round

Habitat: Open fields, often sharing a pasture with cattle, horses, or other large animals.

Food source: Primarily insects, foraged on the ground (or off the backs of cattle)

Nest: In the tops of trees in a swamp or marsh

Call: Flight call is a measured *ruh, ruh*; conversation among groups of birds is a clucking not unlike chickens.

Hot spots: Drive along any highway in Florida and watch the open fields for these abundant birds dotting the landscape. They are often seen actually standing on a cow's back, just as their name would suggest. When there are no cattle, the birds can be seen with their heads down, foraging for insects on mowed lawns or in farm fields.

GREEN HERON
Butorides virescens

A quiet, secretive hunter, the green heron moves slowly among tall grasses at the edges of estuaries or ponds and waits for prey to reveal itself.

Field marks: Dark green back, chestnut neck and head, dark crest, long dark bill, yellow legs. Often seen hunkered down on the edge of a creek or riverbank, then standing with neck extended to full length. Young birds have white streaks on chestnut neck.

Size: H: 18", WS: 26"

Similar species: Night-herons are white, gray, and black, with no chestnut or green areas. American bittern is a lighter brown overall, though neck is similarly streaked. Least bittern is a bright yellow-brown color.

Season: Most often seen in spring and fall

Habitat: Banks of creeks, ponds, and rivers; usually seen low and close to the water

Food source: Primarily fish

Nest: Hidden in a tree from ground level to 30 feet up, usually (but not always) near a water source

Call: A low, throaty *ga-wuh*; a surprisingly high *kyur* alarm call, or a chattering *kuh-kuh-kuh* when something gets too close to the nest

Hot spots: Like the other long-legged waders in Florida, green heron may appear at the edge of any pond, lake, estuary, drainage canal, retention pond, or other still body of water, especially in protected wetlands. Just about any visit to a wildlife refuge or the Everglades will yield at least one green heron sighting.

101

BLACK-CROWNED NIGHT-HERON
Nycticorax nycticorax

Secretive and nocturnal, this heron reveals itself by flying at dusk to its wetland feeding grounds. By day it roosts in trees, often on branches overhanging an open wetland.

Field marks: Stocky bird with black back and crown; gray wings, chest, and neck; white forehead above black bill, red eye, yellow legs. Juveniles have streaky brown chest and underparts, mottled gray and brown back, yellowish bill.

Size: H: 25", WS: 44"

Similar species: Yellow-crowned night-heron has a white crown and cheeks and a longer, thinner neck. Bitterns are browner or more brightly colored (least).

Season: Year-round

Habitat: Salt- and freshwater marshes, ponds, shallow wetlands

Food source: Fish and aquatic animals, shellfish, reptiles, amphibians, insects

Nest: On an island or deep in a swamp, usually in a tree or hidden in cattails

Call: Cackling series of *kwak kwok* syllables when flushed or in flight

Hot spots: St. Marks National Wildlife Refuge, St. Marks, 30.1515653 / -84.1473314; Lake Apopka North Shore, Astatula, 28.6740878 / -81.7059258; Sweetwater Wetlands Park, Gainesville, 29.6151026 / -82.3254061; Circle B Bar Reserve, Lakeland, 27.9959173 / -81.8652327; J. N. Ding Darling National Wildlife Refuge, Sanibel, 26.4540529 / -82.1155071; Everglades National Park, Anhinga Trail, 25.3820583 / -80.6069362

YELLOW-CROWNED NIGHT-HERON
Nyctanassa violacea

The striking facial pattern of this heron, with its bright yellow crown, makes it easy to distinguish from its black-crowned cousin. Despite its name, the yellow-crowned night-heron can be seen easily in the middle of the day.

Field marks: Gray body, wings, and neck with darker gray flight feathers. Adults have a black and white facial pattern with a white cheek and bands of black, a yellow crown, and a plume in breeding season. Juveniles have streakier chest and neck, wings covered in white dots. Yellow legs and red eyes are present in both juveniles and adults. Thick, dark bill is shorter than black-crowned night-heron.

Size: H: 24", WS: 42"

Similar species: Black-crowned night-heron is stockier, has a shorter neck, and lacks the yellow crown. Bitterns are brown.

Season: Year-round in south Florida and along the coasts; summer breeding season inland and farther north

Habitat: Coastal ponds, salt marshes

Food source: Crabs and other small crustaceans, insects, small fish

Nest: High in oak and pine trees near water or low in thick shrubs, often in colonies with other heron species

Call: A single barked syllable: *rowf*

Hot spots: Disappearing Island, New Smyrna Beach, 29.0676462 / -80.9213448; Safety Harbor Waterfront Park, Safety Harbor, 27.9913611 / -82.6845217; Brewer Park, Miller Drive Roost, South Miami, 25.7178837 / -80.2961969; Everglades National Park, Gulf Coast Visitor Center, Everglades City, 25.8452381 / -81.3862064; Ocean Bay Riverside Park, Hutchinson Island South, 27.3381582 / -80.2365983

IBISES, SPOONBILL, AND STORK

GLOSSY IBIS
Plegadis falcinellus

This striking bird's downcurved bill and iridescent feathers set it apart from other long-legged waders.

Field marks: Dark all over but with distinctly iridescent wings and mantle; reddish face, neck, and underparts in breeding season, with thin white lines on face from bill to eye. Face, neck, and underparts dark blue-gray in other seasons. Eye is always dark, and long light brown bill curves downward.

Size: H: 23", WS: 36"

Similar species: Juvenile white ibis has bright pink bill, line of white outer feathers on wings. White-faced ibis has a distinct white border around its eye and bill, and always has a red eye and pink-to-red facial skin. Great blue heron is much larger and blue-gray.

Season: Year-round

Habitat: Marshes, flooded fields

Food source: Insects

Nest: On the ground on an island, or higher in a shrub or tree; may nest in a colony of other herons

Call: Hoarse grunt, sometimes in groups of four grunts

Hot spots: Glossy ibis populations have increased in recent years throughout the state, so virtually any wetland will have its own flock of these birds. In south Florida, flocks can number in the hundreds, especially around stormwater treatment areas and the Everglades.

WHITE IBIS
Eudocimus albus

A long-legged wader with a bright red, decurved bill, this bird of southern marshes makes any flat, open space with a water feature its home.

Field marks: White overall with black wing tips, long bill curving downward, red legs. Juvenile has a brown-black body with a white leading edge of the wing, gray neck and head, yellow-green bill and legs.

Size: H: 22"–26", WS: 42"

Similar species: Glossy ibis is darkly iridescent overall. All egrets have straight yellow or black bills. Juvenile little blue heron has a yellow-green bill and legs.

Season: Year-round

Habitat: Grassy marshes, open ponds and pools

Food source: Insects, crustaceans

Nest: In a tree, above water

Call: Grunting *unk-unk-unk* (male); squealing from female

Hot spots: You won't need a special place to look for white ibis in Florida. One of the most abundant long-legged waders in the state, white ibis turns up in ponds and marshes, along drainage canals and retention pools, in stormwater treatment areas, and in or near virtually every body of shallow water.

DOMINIC SHERONY

WHITE-FACED IBIS
Plegadis chihi

An occasional but regular winter/early spring visitor to Florida, this bird's resemblance to glossy ibis can make it hard to identify.

Field marks: In breeding plumage, rusty iridescent head, neck, and breast; bright white line around pink-to-red facial skin, red eye, long gray bill curved downward; iridescent green wings and tail, reddish underside, bright red legs. Nonbreeding and juvenile: Dark gray head, neck, breast, and underside; white on face disappears, but red eye and facial skin remain.

Size: L: 23"–24", WS 36"

Similar species: Glossy ibis has very similar plumage, but the skin on its face is dark and the white lines on its face in breeding plumage are finer than those on the white-faced ibis.

Season: Winter, sometimes spring migration

Habitat: Wetlands and secluded ponds

Food source: Insects, worms, small crustaceans

Nest: In the thick of marsh cattails and other tall aquatic plants (not in Florida)

Call: A repeated *honk* as it flies out of a wetland; a low, single *whunk* grunt while feeding

Hot spots: No spot in Florida is dependable for white-faced ibis sightings, but these sites have had visits from this bird in more than one recent year: St. Marks National Wildlife Refuge, St. Marks, 30.1515653 / -84.1473314; Home Depot Retention Pond, Gainesville, 29.6567309 / -82.4195838; Lake Apopka North Shore, Astatula, 28.6740878 / -81.7059258

ROSEATE SPOONBILL
Platalea ajaja

The bright pink plumage, long silvery bill, and unusual feeding behavior make this tall wading bird a favorite among birding tourists and Florida residents alike.

Field marks: White head and neck with black vertical band between the head and neck; long light gray bill with a spoon-shaped tip; bright pink wings, back, and underside; darker pink legs with gray knees and feet. Juvenile birds are whiter with a pale pink wash.

Size: L: 32"–34", WS: 50"

Similar species: American flamingo is taller, more uniformly pink, and has a shorter, hooked bill (and is rarely seen outside of captivity). No other tall waders in Florida are pink or have the long bill with the spoon-shaped end.

Season: Year-round in south Florida; some move into central and northern Florida after breeding.

Habitat: Coastal wetlands, shallow ponds, lagoons, mangrove keys

Food source: Small fish, aquatic invertebrates; the bird searches for prey in the mud with its feet and sweeps them up with its spoonbill.

Nest: In colonies in mangrove swamps or other shallow waters, in trees about 15 feet above the water

Call: A low, throaty grunt, often punctuated by clacking its bill

Hot spots: Everglades National Park, Snake Bight Canoe Launch/Trail, 25.1633089 / -80.886755; Francis S. Taylor Wildlife Management Area, Everglades Parkway rest area, Alligator Alley, 26.1469438 / -80.6291342; 28th Street wetlands, St. Petersburg, 27.8720862 / -82.6715183; Lake Apopka Wildlife Drive, Apopka, 28.6691082 / -81.5574338; Guana Tolomato Matanzas National Estuarine Research Reserve, St. Augustine, 30.0074 / -81.3325

WOOD STORK
Mycteria americana

North America's only stork makes Florida one of its central breeding regions.

Field marks: Dark gray, scaly head and neck; long, heavy gray bill that hooks downward at the end; white body and wings with black flight feathers; gray legs. Juvenile has buff head and neck, black mask, pale bill.

Size: L: 40", WS: 61"

Similar species: White ibis is shorter and has bright pink bill. American white pelican has a bright yellow bill, a white head, and a longer neck.

Season: Year-round

Habitat: Shallow wetlands, ponds, and marshes; wetlands with trees during breeding season

Food source: Fish and aquatic invertebrates, sometimes reptiles and small amphibians

Nest: In trees above standing water

Call: Low, hoarse *kick-kick, kick-kick*

Hot spots: T. M. Goodwin Waterfowl Management Area, Palm Bay, 27.8452341 / -80.7252359; Pelican Island National Wildlife Refuge, North Beach, 27.8128126 / -80.432496; Loxahatchee National Wildlife Refuge, Valencia Reserve, 26.4928139 / -80.2168894; Everglades National Park, Paurotis Pond, 25.2813046 / -80.8001782 (also Snake Bight Canoe Launch/Trail); Celery Fields, Fruitville, 27.3282173 / -82.4340248

CRANES

SANDHILL CRANE
Antigone canadensis

Sandhill crane populations in Florida have grown significantly in recent years, making this bird fairly easy to locate.

Field marks: Tall gray bird with a whitish face and red crown, gray bill, some red on the wings; long, black legs.

Size: H: 38"–41", WS: 73"–80"

Similar species: Whooping crane is white with black primary wing feathers. Great blue heron is bluer, has a distinctive head pattern, and is larger. Glossy ibis is darker colored overall, with iridescence, and has a long, curving bill. Limpkin is darker brown with white spots and a longer yellow bill.

Season: Winter throughout the state, permanent resident of the northeastern coast

Habitat: Ponds in flat areas, marshes, farm fields

Food source: Seeds, grains, plants, small mammals, reptiles, amphibians, insects

Nest: On the ground, usually near water

Call: Repetitive, rattling *ooh-ah, ooh-ah, ooh-ah*

Hot spots: Pairs or small groups of sandhills may be found virtually anywhere in central or south Florida. These locations often see large flocks: Ralph V. Chisholm Regional Park, St. Cloud, 28.2782779 / -81.2518787; Myakka River State Park, Myakka City, 27.2405033 / -82.3148167; St. Marks National Wildlife Refuge, St. Marks, 30.1515653 / -84.1473314; Paynes Prairie Preserve State Park, Gainesville, 29.6068756 / -82.3031116; Harns Marsh, Buckingham, 26.6496729 / -81.6869336

WHOOPING CRANE
Grus americana

A handful of these endangered white cranes—the tallest birds in North America—make their way to central Florida each winter from the Northwest Territory of Canada.

Field marks: Very tall, all-white bird with a red crown and malar stripe, yellow and gray bill, black primary wing feathers, and dark legs. Juveniles have faded brown feathers on head, neck, and body, and are generally not seen in Florida.

Size: L: 52"–54", WS: 87"

Similar species: Sandhill crane is gray overall. Great egret is not as tall, has an all-white head and body and a bright yellow bill. Snowy egret is smaller and has a black bill and yellow feet.

Season: Winter

Habitat: Marshes, tidal flats, and open farmland

Food source: Small aquatic invertebrates, frogs, mice, voles, snakes, grains

Nest: In potholes in marshes among aquatic plants, in northern Canada

Call: An elongated, high-pitched *whoop*

Hot spots: There are no absolutely dependable places for whooping crane in Florida, but these areas have had more than one visit from these birds over the past several years: Paynes Prairie Preserve State Park, Gainesville, 29.6068756 / -82.3031116; Tuscawilla Prairie, Micanopy, 29.5003493 / -82.2685432; Joe Overstreet Road and Landing, Kenansville, 27.9426789 / -81.2050366; private farm on Backbone Road, Babson Park, 27.865025 / -81.51752

RAILS

CLAPPER RAIL
Rallus crepitans

Poking its way along the edges of reedy coastal saltwater marshes, the clapper rail is the easiest to see of the rail species.

Field marks: Gray overall with a lighter gray/buff breast, gray face with a black stripe through the red eye, and a black cap. In flight, the rail displays a reddish-brown upper wing and pinkish legs.

Size: L: 14"–15", WS: 19"–20"

Similar species: King rail is more boldly patterned, especially in its black and white–barred underside and bright orange breast and throat. Virginia rail is much smaller.

Season: Year-round

Habitat: Saltwater marshes along the Atlantic and Gulf coasts

Food source: Small crustaceans and fish, frogs, invertebrates, insects

Nest: Hidden in salt marsh reeds and grasses

Call: A rhythmic clicking, like striking two rocks together; female call is more vocal: *kuk-kuk-kuk-kuk* with a descending trill at the end.

Hot spots: Mashes Sands County Park, Panacea, 29.973171 / -84.3438435; Fort Island Gulf Beach, Crystal River, 28.908602 / -82.69082; Merritt Island National Wildlife Refuge, Titusville, 28.6411839 / -80.7774067; Guana Tolomato Matanzas National Estuarine Research Reserve, St. Augustine, 30.0074 / -81.3325; Spanish Pond Trailhead, Jacksonville, 30.3839526 / -81.4953234

KING RAIL
Rallus elegans

Larger and brighter colored than either of the more prevalent rails, king rail makes both brackish and freshwater marshes its home.

Field marks: Rufous head and neck with gray area behind eye, black cap, yellow bill, neatly patterned back, rufous breast and underside to rear flanks, black rear with pronounced white bars. Female is drabber overall.

Size: L: 15", WS: 51"

Similar species: Clapper rail (Atlantic race) is grayer and lacks the bright rufous coloring. Virginia rail is roughly half the size.

Season: Year-round

Habitat: Brackish and freshwater marshes

Food source: Water insects, small crustaceans, frogs, plant seeds, small shellfish

Nest: Hidden among marsh grasses and reeds

Call: Descending series of *chk-chk-chk-chks*

Hot spots: Sweetwater Wetlands Park, Gainesville, 29.6151026 / -82.3254061; Lake Apopka Wildlife Drive, Apopka, 28.6691082 / -81.5574338; Merritt Island National Wildlife Refuge, Titusville, 28.6411839 / -80.7774067; Kissimmee Prairie Preserve State Park, Basinger, 27.5746341 / -81.0228825; Celery Fields, Fruitville, 27.3282173 / -82.4340248

VIRGINIA RAIL
Rallus limicola

Small, shy, and secretive, this reddish rail may reveal itself toward sunset or just before sunrise.

Field marks: Gray face, red eye, black cap, orange-brown bill with black tip; rufous neck, breast, and back; black belly barred with white, pinkish legs; large, three-toed feet.

Size: L: 9"–10", WS: 13"–14"

Similar species: King rail and clapper rail are each nearly twice the size.

Season: Winter

Habitat: Freshwater marshes with tall, dense vegetation

Food source: Duckweed, seeds of water plants, insects, small invertebrates

Nest: In a dry spot among the reeds, grasses, and water plants

Call: A grunting *nn-cha, nn-cha, nn-cha*, descending and gaining in speed; also a squeaky rattle, like two rocks grinding together

Hot spots: Celery Fields, Fruitville, 27.3282173 / -82.4340248; Lake Apopka North Shore, Astatula, 28.6740878 / -81.7059258; St. John's National Wildlife Refuge, Titusville, 28.5587 / -80.8906; Green Cay Wetlands & Nature Center, Boynton Beach, 26.4861584 / -80.1607561; Orlando Wetlands Park, Orlando, 28.5753263 / -80.9966826

SORA
Porzana carolina

The smallest local rail is easy to distinguish from the others because of its shorter yellow bill, black face, and rounded body.

Field marks: Gray head and neck, brown cap, black mask between bill and eye, brown mottled back and wings, brown and rusty underside with white barring, white undertail coverts, yellow legs.

Size: L: 8"–9", WS: 13"–14"

Similar species: Virginia rail is redder with a longer, orange-brown bill and pinkish legs. Black rail is smaller and darker, with a rusty nape, orange eye (in adults), and gray-green legs.

Season: Winter

Habitat: Freshwater marshes

Food source: Small aquatic animals, marsh plant seeds, insects, duckweed

Nest: Basket woven from grass, reeds, and cattails, fastened to adjoining reeds

Call: High *pur-eet, pur-eet, pur-eet* call in spring, but most familiar is a long, descending giggle: *pur-WEET-eet-eet-eet-eet-eet*.

Hot spots: Lake Apopka North Shore, Astatula, 28.6740878 / -81.7059258; Orlando Wetlands Park, Orlando, 28.5753263 / -80.9966826; Merritt Island National Wildlife Refuge, Titusville, 28.6411839 / -80.7774067; Celery Fields, Fruitville, 27.3282173 / -82.4340248; Everglades National Park, Shark Valley Tram Road and Observation Tower, 25.7567969 / -80.7660771

LIMPKIN
Aramus guarauna

This large, brown, white-speckled bird has edged its tropical range northward into most of Florida.

Field marks: Tall as a heron, white and brown–streaked head and neck, brown body with white streaking and spots, long gray bill with yellow at the gape and a hook at the end, gray legs.

Size: L: 25"–29", WS: 40"–48"

Similar species: Young night-herons are smaller with a shorter bill. Sandhill crane is taller and all gray with red facial mask. Great blue heron is taller, blue-gray overall, and has a bright yellow bill and a black plume at the crown.

Season: Year-round

Habitat: Freshwater marshes, swamp forests, canals, shallow ponds

Food source: Primarily apple snails, as well as other snails and mussels

Nest: Near water, usually on top of floating plants and grasses

Call: Long, descending screech; also a shorter, softer but still squeaky *kon, kon*

Hot spots: Center Pointe Lane Pond, Tallahassee, 30.474417 / -84.237235; Sweetwater Wetlands Park, Gainesville, 29.6151026 / -82.3254061; Paynes Prairie Preserve State Park, Gainesville, 29.6068756 / -82.3031116; Emeralda Marsh Conservation Area Wildlife Drive, Lisbon, 28.90279 / -81.79877; Loxahatchee National Wildlife Refuge, Valencia Reserve, 26.4928139 / -80.2168894

PLOVERS

BLACK-BELLIED PLOVER
Pluvialis squatarola

This large plover is easy to spot, with its black face, neck, breast, and underside in breeding plumage; black underwings in any season.

Field marks: Breeding adult has white head with grayish cap; black face, breast, and underside; short black bill, white undertail coverts, mottled gray and white mantle, black legs; black "armpits" visible in flight. Nonbreeding bird has gray head and breast, light gray-to-white underside, mottled gray mantle.

Size: L: 11.5"–13", WS: 25"–29"

Similar species: American golden plover has black undertail coverts, warm tan tone on back and wings.

Season: Spring and fall migration; also winter, with larger flocks in winter

Habitat: Beaches, wetland mudflats, open fields and pastures with standing water and muddy areas

Food source: Small invertebrates

Nest: On open tundra; Arctic region

Call: High-pitched whistled *peeu, peeu-ee*

Hot spots: Any sandy beach on the Atlantic or Gulf coast is likely to have a flock of black-bellied plovers and other mixed shorebirds during spring and fall migration. These often have some of the largest flocks: Dr. Von D. Mizell–Eula Johnson State Park, Hollywood, 26.0711624 / -80.1124978; Merritt Island National Wildlife Refuge, Titusville, 28.6411839 / -80.7774067; Sem-Chi Rice Mill, Wellington, 26.6668727 / -80.4574621; San Carlos Bay/Bunche Beach Preserve, Fort Myers, 26.476174 / -81.9673795; Fort De Soto Park, St. Petersburg, 27.6327266 / -82.718157

AMERICAN GOLDEN-PLOVER
Pluvialis dominica

A relative rarity in Florida, this plover's golden mantle and gray underwings set it off from similar black-bellied plovers in mixed flocks.

Field marks: Warm brown cap; black face, throat, and underside; black undertail coverts, warm brown and black back and wings, gray legs.

Size: L: 10"–11", WS: 22"–26"

Similar species: Black-bellied plover has black and gray mantle, black axillaries (armpits) in flight, and white undertail coverts.

Season: Fall migration

Habitat: Wetlands, open fields and pastures with muddy areas

Food source: Butterflies and other insects, small crustaceans and shelled animals

Nest: On the ground in open tundra; Arctic region

Call: Whistled *pur-eet, pur-eet*

Hot spots: No specific place is reliable for golden-plover sightings, but the bird has appeared in multiple recent years at these locations: Fort De Soto Park, St. Petersburg, 27.6327266 / -82.718157; St. Marks National Wildlife Refuge, St. Marks, 30.1515653 / -84.1473314; Tom Renick Park, Ormond-by-the-Sea, 29.3314127 / -81.0578893; Merritt Island National Wildlife Refuge, Titusville, 28.6411839 / -80.7774067

SNOWY PLOVER
Charadrius nivosus

This pale little plover confines itself to Gulf coast beaches.

Field marks: Breeding bird has buffy brown head and back with black forehead, black eye with black ear patch, black line on side of short neck, black bill; white face, throat, breast, and underside; brown legs. Nonbreeding adult is grayer above with no forehead stripe or ear patch, dark line at neck; white throat, breast, and underside.

Size: L: 6"–6.5", WS: 17"–18"

Similar species: Wilson's plover is darker overall with a black breast band in breeding plumage and a longer, heavier bill. Semipalmated plover is darker with white forehead, orange bill with black tip, and orange legs. Piping plover is lighter overall with a narrow, unbroken dark breastband, an orange bill with black tip, and orange legs.

Season: Winter

Habitat: Gulf coast beaches, coastal plains, barrier islands

Food source: Various invertebrates

Nest: A scrape in open ground lined with pebbles and grasses, usually in a protected area away from foot traffic

Call: A trilled *prrrrt*, sometimes a high-pitched *tur-WEET*

Hot spots: Marco Island, Tiger Tail Beach, 25.948098 / -81.74456; Lovers Key State Park, Bonita Springs, 26.3911316 / -81.8713188; Sanibel Beach, Sanibel Island, 26.4447544 / -82.0266724; Fort De Soto Park, St. Petersburg, 27.6327266 / -82.718157; Honeymoon Island State Park, Dunedin, 28.0706 / -82.8314

WILSON'S PLOVER
Charadrius wilsonia

The heavy bill, longer than in other plovers, helps single out this bird from a plover flock.

Field marks: Medium brown head, back, and wings; orange ear patch over brown cheek, black breastband in breeding plumage (brown in nonbreeding), white face and breast, dull pinkish legs.

Size: L: 7.5"–8", WS: 19"

Similar species: Snowy plover lacks the breastband and is paler overall with a tiny black bill. Semipalmated plover is darker with white forehead, orange bill with black tip, and orange legs. Piping plover is lighter overall with a narrower breastband, an orange bill with black tip, and orange legs.

Season: Year-round

Habitat: Atlantic and Gulf coast beaches, coastal plains, barrier islands

Food source: Invertebrates in sand and water

Nest: A scrape in the sand in a fairly open area, sometimes by the side of the road

Call: *prrr-REET, prrr-REET*, quickly in succession; also a simple *PEET* followed by shorter chirps

Hot spots: Fort De Soto Park, St. Petersburg, 27.6327266 / -82.718157; Anastasia State Park, St. Augustine, 29.8661797 / -81.2705122; Fort Matanzas National Monument, Crescent Beach, 29.7150991 / -81.233517; Merritt Island National Wildlife Refuge, Titusville, 28.6411839 / -80.7774067; Marco Island, Tiger Tail Beach, 25.948098 / -81.74456

PIPING PLOVER
Charadrius melodus

This sand-colored bird earned its endangered species status by laying its eggs in a scrape on busy sandy beaches, making it especially vulnerable to human disturbance.

Field marks: Pale tan and white head with black stripe on forehead, orange bill with black tip, narrow black collar, pale tan back and wings, white underside, yellow legs. Nonbreeding bird has a black bill and a pale tan collar.

Size: L: 7.25", WS: 19"

Similar species: Semipalmated plover is darker brown with a black mask and white forehead.

Season: Winter

Habitat: Atlantic and Gulf beaches

Food source: Insects, small invertebrates

Nest: In a scrape of sand on ocean beach

Call: Low, whistled, elongated *ooo-ee, ooo-ee*, plus tiny, piping *peep* notes

Hot spots: Bald Point State Park, Bald Point, 29.9377826 / -84.3381304; Dunedin Causeway, Dunedin, 28.0521363 / -82.8020668; Fort De Soto Park, St. Petersburg, 27.6327266 / -82.718157; San Carlos Bay/Bunche Beach Preserve, Fort Myers, 26.476174 / -81.9673795; Crandon Park, Key Biscayne, 25.7089712 / -80.1536322

SEMIPALMATED PLOVER
Charadrius semipalmatus

"Semipalms" are numerous in mixed flocks of migrating shorebirds, and their bold facial pattern makes them easy to distinguish.

Field marks: Tan cap, black mask, white forehead and throat, yellow bill with black tip (breeding plumage), black collar, tan back and wings, white underside, yellow legs. Nonbreeding bird has less-pronounced mask, and bill is black on top and yellow below.

Size: L: 7.25", WS: 19"

Similar species: Piping plover is much lighter overall and lacks the dark mask. Killdeer is larger and has two wide black rings around its neck.

Season: Spring and fall migration

Habitat: Ocean beaches, muddy areas in open fields

Food source: Small invertebrates, insect larvae, tiny shellfish

Nest: In a low spot on the ground; Arctic region

Call: A whistled *chee-up, chee-up*

Hot spots: Literally any beach in Florida may host semipalmated plovers and other common shorebirds, so checking the beach or the edges of bays nearest you may be your best strategy (assuming they are not crowded with people enjoying the weather). If you'd like to explore further, the sites listed here are well known for the quantity and variety of shorebirds that stop here during migration: Fred Howard County Park, Tarpon Springs, 28.1532114 / -82.79374; Fort De Soto Park, St. Petersburg, 27.6327266 / -82.718157; San Carlos Bay/Bunche Beach Preserve, Fort Myers, 26.476174 / -81.9673795; Marco Island, Tiger Tail Beach, 25.948098 / -81.74456; Crandon Park, Key Biscayne, 25.7089712 / -80.1536322

KILLDEER
Charadrius vociferus

Nesting on golf courses, in parking lots, and in other human-populated areas, the killdeer feigns a broken wing to lure potential predators away from its nest.

Field marks: Brown or rufous cap, white face with bold markings, two wide black rings across the throat and breast, rufous-brown back and wings, white underside, bright rufous rump; wide, white stripe the length of the wings visible in flight.

Size: L: 9"–10.5", WS: 20"–24"

Similar species: Semipalmated plover is smaller, has a yellow bill, and has only one ring around its neck.

Season: Year-round

Habitat: Large mowed lawns, golf courses, open prairie, farm fields

Food source: Insects and small invertebrates, especially worms and grasshoppers

Nest: In an area with gravel—a field, parking lot, golf course, or roof

Call: A piercing, repeated *kill-DEER, kill-DEER*

Hot spots: Flocks of killdeer are likely to mix with migrating and resident shorebirds on beaches, as well as ground feeders on landscaped properties and in mowed parks all over Florida. These birds are so plentiful and easy to spot that you should have no trouble ticking them off your list.

OYSTERCATCHER

AMERICAN OYSTERCATCHER
Haematopus palliatus

With its clownish features and propensity for chatter, the east coast's oystercatcher makes itself unmistakable on local beaches.

Field marks: Black head and neck, orange eye and long orange bill, white chest and underside, brown back and wings, white stripe on wings visible in flight, white rump, pale yellow legs.

Size: L: 17"–21", WS: 32"

Similar species: Black skimmer has a more tapered body, black back and wings, and a two-toned orange and black bill with a longer lower mandible.

Season: Year-round

Habitat: Ocean beaches

Food source: A variety of shellfish, including oysters

Nest: In a scrape in the sand on ocean beaches

Call: A variety of hurried *peeps*, sung in quick succession; also short, single *peeps*, longer *pee-uy* calls in flight

Hot spots: Alligator Point, Panacea, 29.8937866 / -84.3737608; Cedar Key, 29.1354114 / -83.0340372; Fort De Soto Park, St. Petersburg, 27.6327266 / -82.718157; Snook Islands Natural Area, Lake Worth, 26.6159905 / -80.0461936; Guana Tolomato Matanzas National Estuarine Research Reserve, St. Augustine, 30.0074 / -81.3325

STILT AND AVOCET

BLACK-NECKED STILT
Himantopus mexicanus

The stylishly marked stilt breeds in marshes throughout Florida, especially on the Gulf side.

Field marks: Male is black above from forehead to tail, black and white face; long, slim black bill; white below from face to undertail coverts; black wings; long red legs. Female has a brown-black back.

Size: L: 14"–15", WS: 25"–29"

Similar species: American avocet male has a light brown head and an upcurving bill; nonbreeding female has a grayish-white head.

Season: Summer breeding season

Habitat: Salt- and freshwater marshes

Food source: Small aquatic animals, tadpoles, insects, some seeds

Nest: In marshes from Delaware to Florida

Call: Repeated *kik-kik-kik*, harsher when alarmed

Hot spots: Bystre Lake, Hill 'N Dale, 28.5383481 / -82.3242474; Lake Dan Nature Preserve, Odessa, 28.1584802 / -82.6369393; 28th Street Wetlands, St. Petersburg, 27.8720862 / -82.6715183; Myakka River State Park, Myakka City, 27.2405033 / -82.3148167; Browns Farm Road, Sixmile Bend, 26.6321916 / -80.5711555

AMERICAN AVOCET
Recurvirostra americana

Avocets return to specific marshes along Florida's coastlines each winter.

Field marks: Light brown head, neck, and breast; long, upcurved bill; white body and tail, wide black stripes on back visible in flight, black wings with wide white stripe, gray legs. Nonbreeding female has a grayish-white head.

Size: L: 18"–20", WS: 31"–37"

Similar species: Black-necked stilt has black and white head, red legs.

Season: Winter, although individuals show up during spring and fall migration.

Habitat: Salt- and freshwater marshes

Food source: Aquatic insects, crustaceans, plants

Nest: On a beach or mudflat; midwestern United States

Call: Continuous, high-pitched *mee-tee-meet-meet-meet*

Hot spots: St. Marks National Wildlife Refuge, St. Marks, 30.1515653 / -84.1473314; Myakka River State Park, Myakka City, 27.2405033 / -82.3148167; Everglades National Park, Flamingo, 25.1416 / -80.9255; Merritt Island National Wildlife Refuge, Titusville, 28.6411839 / -80.7774067; Big Talbot Island State Park, Spoonbill Pond, Jacksonville, 30.5101704 / -81.4585671

125

SANDPIPERS AND SNIPE

DOMINIC SHERONY

DOMINIC SHERONY

UPLAND SANDPIPER
Bartramia longicauda

This sandpiper prefers dry fields, pastures, and grasslands, making it distinctly different from all others in the region.

Field marks: Tall sandpiper with a thin neck, large black eye, short yellow bill with a black tip, brown-streaked neck, mottled black and brown back and wings, white underside with black barring on flanks, light yellow legs.

Size: L: 11"–13", WS: 20"–26"

Similar species: Buff-breasted sandpiper has a spotted, light brown breast. Stilt sandpiper is darker overall, with a brown ear patch, dark cap, and longer bill.

Season: Primarily fall migration; spring sightings possible as well

Habitat: Farm fields, grasslands, pastures

Food source: Insects, invertebrates, spiders, snails

Nest: In a hollow spot on the ground

Call: A high-pitched trill rising upward, spiraling into a long descending whistle, often with harmonics

Hot spots: Celery Fields, Fruitville, 27.3282173 / -82.4340248; Browns Farm Road, Sixmile Bend, 26.6321916 / -80.5711555; Joe Overstreet Road and Landing, Kenansville, 27.9426789 / -81.2050366

WHIMBREL
Numenius phaeopus

The East Coast's only regularly occurring curlew is easily identified by its long, downward-curving bill.

Field marks: Tall, grayish brown overall with a streaked neck and mottled back and wings; white underside is heavily barred in brown. Cap has a pale stripe in the center and dark brown stripes on either side; long black bill curves downward.

Size: L: 15"–19", WS: 31"–33"

Similar species: Marbled godwit is browner overall and has an upward-curving bill. Hudsonian godwit has a dark rufous chest and underside and an upward-curving bill. Long-billed curlew has a longer bill and is a rustier color overall.

Season: Winter, with some individuals during spring and fall migration

Habitat: Ocean shoreline, mudflats and marshes near the ocean

Food source: Aquatic invertebrates and crustaceans, small fish, mollusks

Nest: On the ground in a shallow hollow; northwestern Canada and Alaska

Call: A whistling, rising note, followed by a series of staccato notes on the same pitch

Hot spots: Honeymoon Island State Park, Dunedin, 28.0706 / -82.8314; Fort De Soto Park, St. Petersburg, 27.6327266 / -82.718157; Crandon Park, Key Biscayne, 25.7089712 / -80.1536322; Merritt Island National Wildlife Refuge, Titusville, 28.6411839 / -80.7774067; Big Talbot Island State Park, Spoonbill Pond, Jacksonville, 30.5101704 / -81.4585671

LONG-BILLED CURLEW
Numenius americanus

The largest shorebird in North America makes occasional visits to the northern and central Florida coasts.

Field marks: Rusty overall with a brown and rufous mottled back, wings, and tail; bright rufous patches on wings. Long, pink and black bill curves notably downward. Dull pinkish-brown legs

Size: L: 20"–25", WS: 28"–35"

Similar species: Whimbrel is smaller, has a shorter curving bill, and is grayer overall. Hudsonian godwit also has a rufous chest and underside, but it is smaller and its bill curves upward.

Season: Winter

Habitat: Tidal mudflats, open farmland, prairies

Food source: Insects, aquatic crustaceans and invertebrates

Nest: A scrape on the ground amid short vegetation; in America's western plains

Call: A trill followed by elongated, high-pitched *peeer, peeeer, peeeer,* also a high, reedy, two-syllable *wee-eet, wee-eet* to signal a mate

Hot spots: There are no reliable spots in Florida for a long-billed curlew sighting, but these have had stopovers in multiple years: Fred Howard County Park, Tarpon Springs, 28.1532114 / -82.79374; San Carlos Bay/Bunche Beach Preserve, Fort Myers, 26.476174 / -81.9673795; Estero Bay Preserve State Park, Winkler Point, Fort Myers, 26.4800134 / -81.898452; Fred and Idah Schultz Preserve, Gibsonton, 27.8110279 / -82.3913412

DOMINIC SHERONY

HUDSONIAN GODWIT

Limosa haemastica

An infrequent visitor, this godwit is usually seen along the Atlantic or Gulf coast during the spring or fall migration.

Field marks: Male in breeding plumage has gray-streaked face and neck, dark cap; long, pink, upward-curving bill with a black tip; dark wings and back, dark rufous breast and underside; undertail coverts barred in rufous. Black underwing, white rump, and black tail are visible in flight. Nonbreeding bird is gray overall, with whitish underside, black tail.

Size: L: 14"–16", WS: 26"–28"

Similar species: Marbled godwit is browner overall. Whimbrel is browner, has a white underside, and its bill curves downward.

Season: Spring and fall migration, though more commonly seen in fall

Habitat: Shoreline with mud and sand, marshes, farm fields with standing water and muddy areas

Food source: Insects, small aquatic invertebrates, tiny shellfish

Nest: In a depression on the ground; northern Canada tundra

Call: Harsh bark, followed by a rapid series of sharp, high-pitched *ta-twit, ta-twit* calls

Hot spots: This bird may appear in any coastal habitat for a day or two, usually not putting in more than one appearance in the state in a single season. These spots have received more than one visit in recent years: Honeymoon Island State Park, Dunedin, 28.0706 / -82.8314; Merritt Island National Wildlife Refuge, Titusville, 28.6411839 / -80.7774067; Big Talbot Island State Park, Spoonbill Pond, Jacksonville, 30.5101704 / -81.4585671

MARBLED GODWIT
Limosa fedoa

The larger of the two godwits that visit Florida, this bird frequents the coast in winter but puts in summer appearances as well. The inset compares the godwit to the much smaller black-bellied plover.

Field marks: Mottled brown overall, with a long, upward-curving pink bill with a black tip. In nonbreeding plumage, the barring on the underside disappears, revealing a buff-colored breast and flanks.

Size: L: 18"–19", WS: 30"–32"

Similar species: Hudsonian godwit is smaller and has a rufous breast. Whimbrel is grayer overall, and its bill curves downward.

Season: Winter, with some passing through during spring and fall migration; some brief visits in summer

Habitat: Grassland, tidal mudflats, marshes

Food source: Invertebrates, mollusks, crustaceans, insects

Nest: In a hollow on the ground in grasslands

Call: Chattering *raddika-raddika-raddika*; also *whit, ter-whit*

Hot spots: Dunedin Causeway, Dunedin, 28.0521363 / -82.8020668; Big Bend Wildlife Management Area, Hagen's Cove, Perry, 29.7722 / -83.5795; Fred Howard County Park, Tarpon Springs, 28.1532114 / -82.79374; Fort De Soto Park, St. Petersburg, 27.6327266 / -82.718157; Merritt Island National Wildlife Refuge, Titusville, 28.6411839 / -80.7774067

RUDDY TURNSTONE
Arenaria interpres

This boldly patterned member of the sandpiper family stands out from the crowd on beaches and mudflats.

Field marks: Breeding adult has striking black and white facial and breast pattern, russet back with wide white stripe up the middle; russet, black, and white wings; white rump, black end of tail, orange legs. Nonbreeding plumage is mottled gray and brown with a muted breast and head pattern. White underside in all seasons.

Size: L: 9"–10", WS: 18"–21"

Similar species: Killdeer is taller and thinner and has two wide black bands around the neck.

Season: Winter; departs late during migration and returns early in fall

Habitat: Coastal beaches and mudflats

Food source: Mainly insects; some mollusks and crustaceans

Nest: In a hollow on the ground; northern Canada and the Arctic region

Call: A rapid *week-a-teek-a-tee-tee-tee-tee*; abbreviated during feeding

Hot spots: Florida's beaches and marshes see many ruddy turnstones through the winter, so you are likely to find them just about anywhere you look. In the Keys, turnstones may visit your beachside table to steal crumbs and beg for handouts—enjoy the close-up look at these birds, but don't feed them.

RED KNOT
Calidris canutus

Larger than more-common sandpipers, the red knot's bright breeding color and short bill distinguish it from similar birds.

Field marks: Breeding adult has deep reddish-brown head, breast, and underside; short, black bill; gray and reddish scaled back and wings, white wing stripe visible in flight; dark legs. Nonbreeding bird is gray above and below, with white flanks barred in gray.

Size: L: 10"–11", WS: 20"–23"

Similar species: Dunlin is white and brown with black belly in breeding plumage, brownish with white underside in nonbreeding season, and has a longer, downward-curved bill. Dowitchers are taller, more heavily spotted or barred, and have a much longer bill.

Season: Winter

Habitat: Ocean beaches, tidal mudflats, muddy shores of lakes and rivers

Food source: Insects, aquatic invertebrates, small crustaceans

Nest: On the open tundra; Canadian Arctic and Alaska

Call: An elongated scream-like whistle, rising and falling

Hot spots: J. N. Ding Darling National Wildlife Refuge, Sanibel, 26.4540529 / -82.1155071; Outback Key, Tierra Verde, 27.6481906 / -82.7497702; Jetty Park, Port Canaveral, 28.4064535 / -80.5924523; Grayce Kenemer Barck North Beach Community Park, New Smyrna Beach, 29.0462527 / -80.9003905; Little Talbot Island, Jacksonville, 30.4240678 / -81.4124787

RUFF
Calidris pugnax

This rarity from Eurasia makes solo winter appearances in Florida—and it's something to see in breeding plumage.

Field marks: Breeding adult has red or white head, orange bill with black tip; wide, luxurious "ruff" collar of black, brown, or white feathers; rufous or white wings, white underside streaked in black; yellow legs. Nonbreeding bird is drab gray overall with white undertail coverts, white stripe at base of bill.

Size: L: 10"–12", WS: 19"–22"

Similar species: No other migratory or resident birds in Florida resemble this one in breeding plumage. In nonbreeding plumage, dowitchers have much longer, black bills; upland sandpiper is much slimmer and lighter brown.

Season: Winter, fall migration

Habitat: Mud along lakeshores, ponds, and riverbanks; also, flooded meadows

Food source: Insects, plants, some invertebrates and larvae

Nest: On the ground; Eurasia and northern Alaska

Call: A four-note *ruff, ruff, ruff, ruff,* not unlike a dog's bark; a *tu-tu-tu* as an alarm call .

Hot spots: A ruff sighting is a major event in Florida. The following hot spots have hosted a ruff for more than a day in the past several years: Sweetwater Wetlands Park, Gainesville, 29.6151026 / -82.3254061; Circle B Bar Reserve, Lakeland, 27.9959173 / -81.8652327; Brookridge sewage treatment facility on Grove Road, 28.5511767 / -82.4845053

DOMINIC SHERONY

STILT SANDPIPER
Calidris himantopus

This large sandpiper has a more streamlined silhouette than others in its size range.

Field marks: Breeding adult has dark head with rusty cheek and white eyebrow, long bill that curves downward, densely streaked chest and back, barred underside, dark tail with barred rump, yellow-green legs. Nonbreeding bird is pale gray throughout, with white underside.

Size: L: 8"–8.5", WS: 16"–18"

Similar species: Dowitchers are larger and have much longer bills, orange throat and breast in breeding plumage. Nonbreeding dowitchers are darker gray overall. Pectoral sandpiper is browner in all plumages and has a shorter bill.

Season: Spring and fall migration

Habitat: Meadows near beaches, higher ground with low trees

Food source: Small invertebrates, snails, some seeds

Nest: On the ground; northern Canada and Alaska tundra

Call: Repeated *quirp* chip note at intervals; ascending *whuup, whuup* in flight

Hot spots: Brookridge sewage treatment facility on Grove Road, 28.5511767 / -82.4845053; Sawgrass Road open field, Parrish, 27.581082 / -82.460788; Ten Thousand Islands National Wildlife Refuge, Marsh Trail, Marco Island, 25.973478 / -81.5542603; Stormwater Treatment Area 1E, auto entrance, Wellington, 26.6809958 / -80.3004992; T. M. Goodwin Waterfowl Management Area, Palm Bay, 27.8452341 / -80.7252359

SANDERLING
Calidris alba

Easy to identify as they run back and forth on beaches just above the waves, these birds often move in large flocks.

Field marks: Breeding adult has reddish head and neck, short black bill, white underside, scaled black and brown wings, black legs; white wing stripe visible in flight. Nonbreeding bird is pale gray above, white below, with black bill and legs.

Size: L: 8", WS: 15"–17"

Similar species: Least and semipalmated sandpipers are smaller and lack the reddish breeding plumage. Least sandpiper has greenish legs in all seasons.

Season: Winter

Habitat: Ocean beaches, tidal mudflats

Food source: Invertebrates, occasional insects

Nest: In a depression in the ground; on tundra in the Arctic region

Call: Whistling chatter or high-pitched *wip-wip-wip-wip*

Hot spots: No beach is complete without its flock of sanderlings, whether they form a single family unit or number in the hundreds. If you visit any of the Atlantic Ocean or Gulf of Mexico beaches in the proper season, you will see these birds running up the beach as they avoid the incoming surf, and then dashing down it in remarkable unison to partake of whatever the tide brought in. Their distinctive plumage and regimented behavior helps differentiate them from the least and semipalmated sandpipers.

DUNLIN
Calidris alpina

The downward-curving bill and black belly patch make this bird fairly easy to pick out of a group.

Field marks: Breeding adult has gray head, white breast with gray streaks, downward-curving bill, rufous back, scaly rufous and black wings, black patch on white belly, gray tail with white outer feathers, black legs. Nonbreeding bird has light brown head, grayish-brown back and wings, white underside.

Size: L: 7.5"–8.5", WS: 15"–17"

Similar species: Least and semipalmated sandpipers are smaller, have no rufous coloring, and lack the belly patch. Purple sandpiper is uniformly gray in winter and has yellow legs.

Season: Winter on the coasts; spring and fall migration throughout the region

Habitat: Ocean beaches, tidal mudflats, wetlands, lakeshores, riverbanks

Food source: Insects, aquatic invertebrates, snails, small crustaceans

Nest: On a dry, raised spot in open tundra; Arctic Canada and northern and coastal Alaska

Call: An elongated, scream-like *churr-eeeeee-errr*, rising in the middle

Hot spots: Dunlin flocks make landfall in Florida in late fall, and some flocks spend the winter along the shores of the Atlantic Ocean and the Gulf of Mexico. During their migration, it would be easier to tell you where they do not appear than to list all the places where they do. Check your local beach or your favorite mudflat from November to March before venturing further to find this bird.

LEAST SANDPIPER
Calidris minutilla

Florida's smallest sandpiper provides a simple way to tell it apart from others in its class: its yellowish legs.

Field marks: Breeding adult has brown head, chest, back, and wings, with black scales over the brown on wings; small bill that droops down at the end, white underside, yellow-green legs. Nonbreeding bird is gray instead of brown, but with a brownish head.

Size: L: 6", WS: 12"–13"

Similar species: Semipalmated sandpiper is slightly larger, has a straight bill and black legs. Western sandpiper is more rufous on head and back and has a longer bill and black legs.

Season: Late fall to early spring

Habitat: Ocean and lake beaches, tidal mudflats, moist open fields, stormwater treatment areas

Food source: Small invertebrates, insects, some plant seeds

Nest: In a hollow on the ground; northern Canada

Call: A high trill, interspersed with a *cheep* or *chirreep*

Hot spots: Least sandpipers are widespread and numerous, traveling in small flocks during spring and fall migration and remaining in larger flocks to canvas beaches and other fertile ground for food. You will encounter them on any beach or mudflat from October through early May, often in mixed flocks of sanderlings, semipalmated sandpipers, dunlins, and other small shorebirds.

WHITE-RUMPED SANDPIPER
Calidris fuscicollis

If the white rump is not visible, look for wings that extend past the tail, plus flanks streaked in dark brown.

Field marks: Breeding adult has brown cap and cheek, streaked head, wider streaks on breast and flanks, gray and brown scaly back and wing pattern, white undertail coverts, white rump, black legs; wing tips extend past the end of the tail. Nonbreeding bird is gray overall, with a pronounced white eyebrow.

Size: L: 7"–8", WS: 15"–17"

Similar species: Baird's sandpiper is slimmer and paler and has no white rump. Pectoral sandpiper is larger, has yellow-green legs, and its heavily streaked breast extends to its underside.

Season: Spring and fall migration

Habitat: Wet farm fields, mudflats, marshes, beaches

Food source: Insects, aquatic invertebrates, tiny crustaceans and mollusks, leeches, some seeds and plants

Nest: On the ground; Canadian Arctic region

Call: Very high-pitched *tcheep*, repeated at intervals

Hot spots: Fort De Soto Park, St. Petersburg, 27.6327266 / -82.718157; Lake Apopka Wildlife Drive, Apopka, 28.6691082 / -81.5574338; Merritt Island National Wildlife Refuge, Titusville, 28.6411839 / -80.7774067; Big Talbot Island State Park, Spoonbill Pond, Jacksonville, 30.5101704 / -81.4585671; Everglades National Park, Hole in the Donut Restorations, 25.3767388 / -80.6340014

BUFF-BREASTED SANDPIPER
Calidris subruficollis

Rare and highly desirable for Florida birders, this sleek sandpiper shows up in plowed fields in August and September, often in a mixed shorebird flock.

Field marks: Breeding adult has buff face, breast, and underside to the undertail coverts; brown cap, short bill, brown wings and back, yellow legs. Nonbreeding bird is similar but has a somewhat duller brown mantle.

Size: L: 8"–8.5", WS: 16"–18"

Similar species: Baird's and white-rumped sandpipers are similar in size but lack the buffy breast.

Season: Fall migration

Habitat: Farm fields, grasslands

Food source: Insect larvae, pupae, and adults; spiders, invertebrates

Nest: On the ground; northernmost Alaska

Call: A soft *whit-wa-WEET-wit, wut, wut*

Hot spots: Lake Apopka North Shore sod fields, Zellwood, 28.7204295 / -81.6290102; Avon Park Cutoff Road sod fields, Fort Meade, 27.6902924 / -81.6627073; West Kendall Agricultural Area, Miami, 25.650781 / -80.464181

PECTORAL SANDPIPER
Calidris melanotos

A dark, streaked breast gives this sandpiper its anatomical name.

Field marks: Breeding adult has brown head, slim white eyebrow, brownish breast heavily streaked with black, scaly brown and black wings, white belly, yellow legs. Nonbreeding bird is slightly less brown, but otherwise very similar to breeding plumage.

Size: L: 8"–9", WS: 16"–18"

Similar species: White-rumped sandpiper is smaller, has streaked flanks and a white rump visible in flight, black legs, and wings that extend past the tail. Baird's sandpiper has less streaking, a paler throat and chest, black legs, and wings that extend past the tail.

Season: Spring and fall migration

Habitat: Ponds, marshes, wetlands

Food source: Invertebrates from water and land

Nest: On the ground, disguised by leaves; Arctic Canada and northern Alaska

Call: A continuous, rising *oot-oot-oot-oot-oot*, gaining in speed in the middle and slowing toward the end

Hot spots: St. Marks National Wildlife Refuge, St. Marks, 30.1515653 / -84.1473314; Brookridge sewage treatment facility on Grove Road, 28.5511767 / -82.4845053; Fort De Soto Park, St. Petersburg, 27.6327266 / -82.718157; Palmer Lake, Fruitville, 27.3135761 / -82.3976111; Browns Farm Road, Sixmile Bend, 26.6321916 / -80.5711555

SEMIPALMATED SANDPIPER
Calidris pusilla

These tiny sandpipers travel in large flocks, often covering sections of beach during spring and fall migration.

Field marks: Breeding adult has gray-brown head, chest, back, and wings; short bill, white underside, black legs. Nonbreeding bird is similar but grayer.

Size: L: 6"–7", WS: 12"–14"

Similar species: Least sandpiper is slightly smaller and has yellow-green legs. Western sandpiper is more rufous in breeding plumage, and its bill droops downward.

Season: Spring and fall migration

Habitat: Ocean and lake shorelines, tidal and freshwater mudflats

Food source: Insects, spiders, aquatic invertebrates, tiny shellfish

Nest: In a depression in the ground; northern Canada and Alaska

Call: A measured *chirrup, chirrup*; a rattling, extended alarm call

Hot spots: Most beaches, mudflats, and sod fields bring in semipalmated sandpipers during spring and fall migration, so chances are you will find a few of them wherever you go to look for more unusual shorebirds. The following hot spots are proven favorites for larger flocks: Siesta Key Beach Access 7, 27.2703128 / -82.5628682; J. N. Ding Darling National Wildlife Refuge, Sanibel, 26.4540529 / -82.1155071; Marco Island, Tiger Tail Beach, 25.948098 / -81.74456; Dump Marsh, Cutler Bay, 25.5350068 / -80.3431249; Browns Farm Road, Sixmile Bend, 26.6321916 / -80.5711555

WESTERN SANDPIPER
Calidris mauri

Overwintering along the coast and migrating inland in spring and fall, the western sandpiper can be difficult to distinguish from semipalmated in nonbreeding plumage.

Field marks: Breeding adult has rufous crown and cheek; long, drooping bill; white breast and flanks spotted with black, white underside, black and rufous wings, black legs, white feathers on either side of tail. Nonbreeding bird is gray above and white below, with a white breast and throat.

Size: L: 6"–7", WS: 12"–14"

Similar species: Semipalmated sandpiper has a shorter, straight bill and a more heavily streaked throat in winter plumage. Least sandpiper is smaller and has yellow-green legs.

Season: Winter along the coast, spring and fall migration throughout the state

Habitat: Ocean and lake beaches, tidal mudflats, ponds and pools

Food source: Small aquatic invertebrates

Nest: On the ground; western Alaska tundra

Call: A raspy, rising series: *bee-dee-dee-dee-dee-dee-TWEE-elee-ah*

Hot spots: Just about any winter flock of "peeps" on Atlantic or Gulf beaches will include at least a few western sandpipers. In spring and fall, resting flocks are likely to feature more westerns than semipalmated sandpipers. Take the time to sort out the westerns from the semipalmateds to be sure you have both species.

DOMINIC SHERONY

LONG-BILLED DOWITCHER
Limnodromus scolopaceus

It's nearly impossible to tell this bird apart from its short-billed cousin except in breeding season, when the long-billed has heavily barred flanks.

Field marks: Breeding adult has dark orange head with white eyebrow stripe, long bill; rufous neck, breast, and belly; scaly brown, black, and white pattern on wings and back; flanks barred with black streaks; yellow legs. Nonbreeding bird is gray overall with white eyebrow, white underside.

Size: L: 11"–12", WS: 18"–20"

Similar species: Short-billed dowitcher has spotted breast and flanks and an imperceptibly shorter bill. Red knot is smaller and has a short bill.

Season: Winter

Habitat: Marshes, mudflats, wetlands

Food source: Worms, small crustaceans, snails, insect larvae, moss, seeds

Nest: On open tundra; northernmost Alaska

Call: A rattling call followed by a musical *peeta-peeta-wee-too*

Hot spots: Myakka River State Park, Myakka City, 27.2405033 / -82.3148167; T. M. Goodwin Waterfowl Management Area, Palm Bay, 27.8452341 / -80.7252359; Oil Well Road, Ave Maria, 26.2949452 / -81.4159482; Everglades National Park, Hole in the Donut Restorations, 25.3767388 / -80.6340014; Merritt Island National Wildlife Refuge, Titusville, 28.6411839 / -80.7774067

DOMINIC SHERONY

SHORT-BILLED DOWITCHER
Limnodromus griseus

Almost identical to the long-billed dowitcher, this one has spots on its breast and flanks instead of bars. Its call is strikingly different as well.

Field marks: Breeding adult has rufous head with white eye ring, black line through eye, long bill, orange breast and sides with black spots; scaly brown, black, and white pattern on wings and back; yellow legs. Nonbreeding bird is gray overall with white eyebrow, white underside.

Size: L: 11"–12", WS: 19"–22"

Similar species: Long-billed dowitcher has a more musical call and has bars instead of spots on its breast and flanks. Red knot is smaller and has a short bill.

Season: Spring and fall migration inland; winter on the coasts

Habitat: Marshes, mudflats, wetlands

Food source: Fly larvae and pupae, crab eggs, insects, some plants and seeds

Nest: On open tundra; southern Alaska

Call: A raspy *tcha-gri-gri, tcha-gri-gri,* spiraling down at the end

Hot spots: St. Marks National Wildlife Refuge (lighthouse area), Port Leon, 30.0751008 / -84.180; Cedar Key, 29.1354114 / -83.0340372; J. N. Ding Darling National Wildlife Refuge, Sanibel, 26.4540529 / -82.1155071; Browns Farm Road, Sixmile Bend, 26.6321916 / -80.5711555; Huguenot Memorial City Park, Jacksonville, 30.4112444 / -81.4206594

SPOTTED SANDPIPER

Actitis macularius

The spotted sandpiper's continuous dipping and nodding earns it the nickname "teeter-tail."

Field marks: Brown face with darker brown cap, white line above eye, black line through eye, orange bill; white breast heavily spotted in brown, white underside with lighter spotting, brown back and wings, short white wing stripe visible in flight. Nonbreeding plumage lacks the spots, and the bill is dull beige.

Size: L: 7.5", WS: 13"–15"

Similar species: Solitary sandpiper is larger and darker, has white spots on its back and wings, and has a gray bill.

Season: Winter

Habitat: Waterways, including ponds and moving streams

Food source: Insects, spiders, invertebrates, small crustaceans and mollusks

Nest: In a dip or hollow in the ground

Call: High-pitched *weet, weet, weet*

Hot spots: Florida is full of rivers, lakes, ponds, and marshes, so there are many, many places to find the spotted sandpiper. The selected sites have been consistent over the past three years, but check your local pond or wetland before traveling out of your way: Newnan's Lake, Palm Point Park, Gainesville, 29.6364 / -82.2382; Merritt Island National Wildlife Refuge, Titusville, 28.6411839 / -80.7774067; Dr. Von D. Mizell–Eula Johnson State Park, Hollywood, 26.0711624 / -80.1124978; Harns Marsh, Buckingham, 26.6496729 / -81.6869336; Mobbly Beach Park, Oldsmar, 28.0118846 / -82.6648053

SOLITARY SANDPIPER
Tringa solitaria

Watch for a lone sandpiper with a white eye ring working the mud along a pond or stream.

Field marks: Gray-streaked head and neck, white eye ring, straight bill, dark back with small white dots, white underside, dark rump, dark center of the tail, white outer tail feathers with black stripes, greenish legs. Nonbreeding plumage is grayer overall.

Size: L: 8"–9", WS: 17"–20"

Similar species: Spotted sandpiper is browner and shorter, with an orange bill and darkly spotted breast. Lesser yellowlegs is taller and slenderer, with a longer bill and yellow legs.

Season: Spring and fall migration

Habitat: Muddy areas along the edges of ponds and streams

Food source: Insects, spiders, small crustaceans, worms

Nest: In trees, in abandoned nests of other birds; Canada's lower provinces

Call: A very high *peet-weet;* also a continuous alarm call: *pit, pit, pit*

Hot spots: These locations have seen this bird for several springs in succession, making them important migration stopovers: Lake Apopka Wildlife Drive, Apopka, 28.6691082 / -81.5574338; Merritt Island National Wildlife Refuge, Titusville, 28.6411839 / -80.7774067; Browns Farm Road, Sixmile Bend, 26.6321916 / -80.5711555; Eagle Lakes Community Park, Naples, 26.0773686 / -81.7141414; Ollies Pond, Port Charlotte, 26.9848059 / -82.1511698

GREATER YELLOWLEGS
Tringa melanoleuca

Near-constant foraging behavior can make it tough to tell the two yellowlegs species apart (see photo inset for size comparison). Look for dark barring on the flanks and underside to pick out the greater yellowlegs.

Field marks: Black, gray, and white mottling overall; black streaks on head and neck, slightly upturned bill; white underside with black barring, yellow legs, white rump. In nonbreeding plumage, back and wings are browner.

Size: L: 14", WS: 23"–28"

Similar species: Lesser yellowlegs is shorter, has a straight bill, and has whiter flanks with no barring.

Season: Winter

Habitat: Beaches, mudflats in salt- and freshwater marshes, open fields, pools, lakeshores

Food source: Small invertebrates, fish, frogs, seeds

Nest: In the open on a mudflat; northern Canada

Call: Lyrical, continuous *pew-yoo, pew-yoo, pew-yoo*; also a three-note *tew-tew-tew* in flight

Hot spots: Yellowlegs of both varieties are among the most common shorebirds in Florida. Your favorite shorebird location is sure to have at least a few individuals, if not large flocks, so it's safe to plan your birding excursion around less-common birds, knowing that you will find yellowlegs as well.

LESSER YELLOWLEGS
Tringa flavipes

The lesser yellowlegs' straight bill, clear underside, and shorter stature sets it apart from its greater counterpart.

Field marks: Gray and white–streaked head and neck; mottled black and white breast, back, and wings; white underside, white rump, yellow legs. Mottling and streaking is muted in nonbreeding plumage.

Size: L: 10"–11", WS: 20"–24"

Similar species: Greater yellowlegs is up to 4 inches taller, has an upturned bill, and is barred with black on its underside in breeding season.

Season: Winter

Habitat: Beaches, fresh- and saltwater marshes, mudflats, open fields

Food source: Insects, invertebrates, seeds, tiny fish

Nest: On a pile of vegetation near water; northern Canada and west to Alaska

Call: *Tu-du* song singly and in pairs; also high-pitched, continuous notes as an alarm

Hot spots: Yellowlegs of both varieties are among the most common shorebirds in Florida. Your favorite shorebird location is sure to have at least a few individuals, if not large flocks, so it's safe to plan your birding excursion around less-common birds, knowing that you will find yellowlegs as well.

WILLET
Tringa semipalmata

The willet's white wing stripe makes it easy to spot as it arrives and lands on a beach or mudflat.

Field marks: Gray head, nape, wings, and back; long, straight gray bill with black tip; buffy breast with darker brown mottling, white underside with brownish barring, gray legs; wide white stripe on wings visible in flight. Nonbreeding adult is grayer overall with no barring.

Size: L: 15"–16", WS: 25"–30"

Similar species: Greater yellowlegs is darker, smaller, and has yellow legs.

Season: Year-round on the Atlantic and Gulf coasts; spring and fall migration inland

Habitat: Coastline beaches and lagoons, tidal mudflats, sandy shorelines on larger lakes

Food source: Small crustaceans, insects, invertebrates, tiny fish

Nest: On a clump of grass or on open ground

Call: A continuous *willa-will-willa, willa-will-willa*

Hot spots: Just about every beach, mudflat, and marsh has its share of the willet population. Plan to see it while you are searching for scarcer shorebirds along the Atlantic or Gulf coast.

SHUTTERSTOCK #101732059

AMERICAN WOODCOCK
Scolopax minor

One of a kind among sandpipers, this rounded, long-billed bird lives in forests and is best known for its unusual breeding display in mating season.

Field marks: Striking black, white, and buff head and nape; long, pink bill; wide gray collar, pale buff breast and underside, brown wings with black and white scaled pattern, buff undertail coverts, brown tail, pinkish legs.

Size: L: 11", WS: 18"

Similar species: Wilson's snipe is a similar size and shape, but it lacks the buff color and has a heavily barred breast and underside and a black and white–striped back.

Season: Winter

Habitat: Young woodlands with low trees and vegetation

Food source: Worms, insect larvae

Nest: On the ground in a field with high grasses

Call: Generally silent except during mating season, when the male utters a nasal *peent* at dusk before beginning his courtship ritual dance.

Hot spots: American woodcock is remarkably hard to find, as it is a shy bird that does not normally call outside of breeding season. Here are some places where lucky birders have flushed a woodcock more than once in the past several years: St. Marks National Wildlife Refuge, St. Marks, 30.1515653 / -84.1473314; Gainesville-Hawthorne Trail North, Gainesville, 29.6287187 / -82.3112231; Lake Apopka North Shore (trailhead only), Astatula, 28.6740878 / -81.7059258; Hal Scott Regional Preserve and Park, Wedgefield, 28.486186 / -81.1079327

WILSON'S SNIPE
Gallinago delicata

The snipe's distinctive patterning and rounded body make it a standout among mixed shorebird flocks.

Field marks: Black and buff–striped head, long gray bill, brown and buff–striped back, spotted brown breast, heavily barred flanks, white belly, orange tail, yellow legs.

Size: L: 10"–11", WS: 18"–20"

Similar species: American woodcock is larger and has a buff breast, flanks, and underside, with no barring.

Season: Winter

Habitat: Open, flooded fields; marshes, swamps, and other wetlands

Food source: Insect larvae, small crustaceans, tiny mollusks

Nest: In a hollow on the ground in a grassy field

Call: Repeated *kut-kut-kut* or rhythmic *tuck-a-tuck-a-tuck-a-tuck-a*

Hot spots: St. Marks National Wildlife Refuge, St. Marks, 30.1515653 / -84.1473314; Sweetwater Wetlands Park, Gainesville, 29.6151026 / -82.3254061; Welaka National Fish Hatchery and Aquarium, Welaka, 29.4419521 / -81.6499186; Lake Apopka Wildlife Drive, Apopka, 28.6691082 / -81.5574338; Frog Pond Wildlife Management Area, Lucky Hammock, Homestead, 25.396439 / -80.566581

PHALAROPE

WILSON'S PHALAROPE
Phalaropus tricolor

While other phalaropes turn up on islands in the ocean, Wilson's prefers coastal wetlands, grasslands, and mudflats.

Field marks: Breeding male has light orange hood, gray mantle, thin black bill, white face, white breast and underside, black legs. Breeding female is more strikingly marked with dark black stripe from base of bill through eye to shoulder, light orange throat, brown back, brown and gray wings. Nonbreeding adults lack the orange parts or black lines.

Size: L: 8.5"–9.25", WS: 15"–17"

Similar species: Red-necked and red phalaropes are rarely seen on the mainland except on coastal ponds.

Season: Spring and fall migration

Habitat: Grassy lakeshores, wetlands, fields with standing water

Food source: Mosquito and crane fly larvae, brine shrimp, some plant seeds

Nest: In a scrape on the ground; American West grasslands

Call: Measured *riff, riff, riff,* like a small dog; accelerating when agitated, adding a rattling trill in between

Hot spots: This bird's visits to Florida are infrequent and last only a day or two. Here are some places where they have put in more than one appearance over the last several years: St. Marks National Wildlife Refuge, St. Marks, 30.1515653 / -84.1473314; Palmer Lake, Fruitville, 27.3135761 / -82.3976111; Fort De Soto Park, St. Petersburg, 27.6327266 / -82.718157; Siesta Key public beach, 27.2703128 / -82.562868; agricultural fields, SW 217th Avenue and SW 384th Street, Florida City, 25.407384 / -80.5472946

FLAMINGO

AMERICAN FLAMINGO
Phoenicopterus ruber

Once a Florida avian highight, most flamingos are now escapees from zoos and bird collections at tropical attractions. Possibly wild birds from the Bahamas have appeared very recently, however, in south Florida and on the Panhandle during migration.

Field marks: Bright pink overall with long S neck, white bill with pink and black tip, hooked downward; long pink legs and feet. Black flight feathers visible in flight. Juveniles are paler pink or white overall, with more obvious black flight feathers at rest. Chicks are light gray.

Size: L: 45"–48", WS: 60"

Similar species: Roseate spoonbill is smaller, has a white head and neck, and has a long gray bill with a spoon-shaped tip.

Season: Spring and fall migration

Habitat: Coastal saltwater lagoons and mudflats

Food source: Tiny organisms in water and mud, including algae, shrimp, seeds, and mollusks. They get their pink color from the carotenoid in some of their food sources.

Nest: In colonies in the Caribbean and in South America

Call: A harsh, scratchy, continuous chortle

Hot spots: Sightings of truly wild, "countable" flamingos are extremely rare, but these spots have had more than one visit in the past several years: Siesta Key Beach, 27.2703128 / -82.562868; Palmer Lake, Fruitville, 27.3135761 / -82.3976111; agricultural fields, SW 217th Avenue and 384th Street, Florida City, 25.407384 / -80.5472946; Browns Farm Road and Sixmile Bend Ponds, Sixmile Bend, 26.6321916 / -80.5711555; Merritt Island National Wildlife Refuge, Titusville, 28.6411839 / -80.7774067

QUAIL

NORTHERN BOBWHITE
Colinus virginianus

More likely to be heard than seen, the bobwhite is the only member of the quail family in Florida.

Field marks: Male is small and rotund, with a distinctive white face patterned in rufous and black, reddish breast and shoulders, white underside with bold rufous lines and streaks, brown and buff wing pattern, short tail. Female has a buff face and a more muted facial pattern.

Size: L: 9"–10", WS: 13"

Similar species: Common ground dove also has some ruddy coloring, but lacks the bright facial pattern.

Season: Year-round

Habitat: Forests, farms, marshes; under feeders near these habitats

Food source: Seeds of many kinds

Nest: On the ground among tall grasses and other vegetation

Call: The onomatopoeic *bob-WHITE, bob-WHITE*

Hot spots: Elinor Klapp-Phipps Park, Tallahassee, 30.535666 / -84.28821; St. Marks National Wildlife Refuge, St. Marks, 30.1515653 / -84.1473314; Olustee Battlefield Historic State Park, Olustee, 30.2190252 / -82.3833847; Paynes Prairie Preserve State Park, Gainesville, 29.6068756 / -82.3031116; Clearwater Lake Recreation Area Trailhead, Paisley, 28.97664 / -81.5502

PEAFOWL

INDIAN PEAFOWL
Pavo cristatus

This exotic bird from India escaped from private collections to establish small populations in south Florida.

Field marks: Male has bright blue head with gray-white bands above and below the eye, fanlike crest, blue neck and breast, blue-green mottled underside, brown wings with tight white horizontal stripes; long, luxurious tail feathers displayed during breeding season; long gray legs and feet. Female has a darker green to brown head and neck, fanlike crest, white underside and dark back, and a much shorter, non-showy tail.

Size: L: Male up to 90", female 40"; WS: male 60"–63", female 49"–51"

Similar species: Ring-necked pheasant has a red face and yellow bill, a white neck ring, and a ruddy golden body, and is found only in game farms in Florida.

Season: Year-round in south and central Florida; occasionally found in summer farther north

Habitat: Forests are its natural home, but the Florida birds live in and around parks in human neighborhoods.

Food source: Seeds, insects, small reptiles, small mammals, fruit

Nest: A scrape on the ground, lined with leaves

Call: A loud, high-pitched *miaow, miaow*, scooping upward

Hot spots: The Miami-Dade metropolitan area is the easiest place to find peafowl. Black Point Park and Marina, Cutler Bay, 25.5400214 / -80.3274608; Charles Deering Estate, Palmetto Bay, 25.6258176 / -80.3055954; Crandon Park, Key Biscayne, 25.7089712 / -80.1536322; Brewer Park, Miller Drive Roost, South Miami, 25.7178837 / -80.2961969; Fairchild Tropical Botanic Garden, Coral Gables, 25.6764 / -80.2713

TURKEY

WILD TURKEY
Meleagris gallopavo

The nation's largest ground bird usually appears in flocks in grassy meadows.

Field marks: Large, heavy, iridescent body and thin, fleshy neck; rufous tail, orange legs. Male acquires long red wattles and a bright blue face and neck during breeding season, when he is often seen with his tail spread out in a fan shape.

Size: L: 44"–46", WS: 60"–64"; female much smaller: L: 37", WS: 50"

Similar species: Turkey vulture is smaller, has an all-red head and a much shorter tail. Black vulture is also smaller and has a short, squared-off tail.

Season: Year-round

Habitat: Oak and pine forests adjacent to open grassland

Food source: Plants, nuts, seeds, fruit, small invertebrates

Nest: On the ground at the base of a tree, or hidden in masses of tall grasses and weeds

Call: A comical *gobble-gobble-gobble*, like a chuckle. Females have a *cluck-cluck* alarm call.

Hot spots: Farm fields, suburban backyards, roadsides from the rural hills to the interstate, and even city neighborhoods now have their own wild turkeys, so no hotspot is required to see them. The spectacular success of the turkey's reintroduction in the late 1960s and early 1970s is in evidence all around us— and some would say that it has long since gotten out of hand. If you'd like to see some, take a drive down a country road and scan the fields for a healthy flock.

VULTURES

TURKEY VULTURE
Cathartes aura

Soaring in kettles over virtually any landscape, this very large bird is easily recognized by its flight pattern.

Field marks: Large, black body; red featherless head, gray flight feathers for the entire length of each wing, rectangular tail. This vulture glides with wings held in a distinctive dihedral V.

Size: L: 26"–30", WS: 67"–72"

Similar species: Black vulture has gray head, black wings with gray-white "fingers" at the outer ends. Immature bald eagle has black-feathered head and all-black or mottled wings, which it holds flat.

Season: Year-round

Habitat: Soaring over open areas, including farmland, forests, ocean dunes, and plains

Food source: Carrion

Nest: In a crevice or dead tree

Call: Usually silent

Hot spots: Turkey vultures soar over open lands, suburban areas, and even at the edges of cities in every part of Florida, often in kettles of thirty or more birds. You should have no trouble seeing them gliding over interstate highways as they search for the roadkill that drivers graciously provide for their daily repast.

BLACK VULTURE
Coragyps atratus

This large, dark raptor is usually spotted in the company of turkey vultures.

Field marks: Large, uniformly black body; gray, featherless head; whitish feather "fingers" at the outer tips of wings, squared-off tail.

Size: L: 24"–27", WS: 55"–60"

Similar species: Turkey vulture is larger and has a red featherless head and gray flight feathers.

Season: Year-round

Habitat: Usually found soaring over wide-open landscapes, including farmland, plains, marshland, and forests

Food source: Carrion, though this vulture sometimes kills its own prey.

Nest: In a hollow tree, cave, or stump, in woodlands or even inside buildings

Call: Generally silent

Hot spots: Black vultures are as prevalent as turkey vultures in Florida. Check your local landfill, and watch the skies over the interstate highways for both black and turkey vultures waiting for some yummy roadkill.

HARRIER AND ACCIPITERS

NORTHERN HARRIER
Circus hudsonius

A slim, sleek hawk with long wings, the harrier is usually spotted as it glides over open fields.

Field marks: Male is gray above and white below, with a spotted breast, black wing tips, a black trailing edge on its wings, and a gray and white–striped tail. Its most distinctive field mark is a white patch at the rump, easily visible in flight. Female and juvenile are brown above and buff below with brown streaks, also with the obvious white rump.

Size: L: 18"–22", WS: 41"–46"

Similar species: Cooper's hawk is smaller, with a rusty breast and longer tail. Snail kite also has a white rump, but the male is smaller, sleeker, and more uniformly gray, and both male and female kites have a bright yellow bill and red legs.

Season: Winter

Habitat: Open fields and meadows, as well as marshes and open dunes

Food source: Rodents, small birds, frogs, reptiles, insects

Nest: On the ground, often in colonies; throughout Canada and the subarctic region

Call: A sharp *vee-yah, vee-yah* in flight

Hot spots: Every wildlife refuge and open area has at least one harrier hunting for rodents over its fields throughout the winter. Stormwater treatment facilities are among the best places to find this bird as it soars along the edges of pools or perches on a fence post. Look up as you scan the landscape for birds on the ground, and watch for the harrier's white rump.

159

© SHUTTERSTOCK.COM/LAYNE V. NAYLOR

© SHUTTERSTOCK.COM/BRIAN E. KUSHNER

SHARP-SHINNED HAWK
Accipiter striatus

Small, heavily barred, and long-tailed, this little accipiter darts and glides under tree canopies to hunt in forests.

Field marks: Gray above with a rusty, barred breast and belly; long white tail with black bars, white undertail coverts, yellow bill and legs. Underside of wings is rufous-barred near the shoulders, gray-barred throughout the flight feathers.

Size: L: 10"–14", WS: 21"–26"

Similar species: Cooper's hawk is larger and has a pale nape below its gray-black crown. Merlin has a buff underside with dark brown streaks.

Season: Winter

Habitat: Forest edges, sometimes along the edges of yards with bird feeders

Food source: Small birds, supplemented with some lizards and small mammals

Nest: On a low tree branch; New England's northern forests

Call: Rapid *kik-kik-kik-kik-kik*

Hot spots: St. Marks National Wildlife Refuge, St. Marks, 30.1515653 / -84.1473314; Paynes Prairie Preserve State Park, Gainesville, 29.6068756 / -82.3031116; Lake Apopka Wildlife Drive, Apopka, 28.6691082 / -81.5574338; Mead Botanical Gardens, Winter Park, 28.5836 / -81.3586; Evergreen Cemetery, Fort Lauderdale, 26.1061594 / -80.1318741

COOPER'S HAWK
Accipiter cooperii

If there's a hawk hunting the birds that come to your feeders, chances are good it's a Cooper's hawk.

Field marks: Larger than a sharp-shinned hawk but very similar in appearance: gray above, white underside with heavy rufous barring, long white tail with black bars. The female is larger than the male and a paler gray. White nape between head and breast helps with identification in flight or perched in a tree or on a fence post.

Size: L: 15"–20", WS: 28"–34"

Similar species: Sharp-shinned-hawk is smaller and lacks the white nape.

Season: Winter in the Panhandle, on the Gulf coast and in south Florida; year-round in northern and central Florida

Habitat: Woodlands and forests

Food source: Birds, small mammals

Nest: High in a tree, usually above 20 feet

Call: Squeaky, continuous *kek-kek-kek-kek*; single *keh-hek* calls between male and female

Hot spots: Theodore Roosevelt Area, Timucuan Ecological and Historic Preserve, Jacksonville, 30.3697 / -81.482; Sem-Chi Rice Mill, Wellington, 26.6668727 / -80.4574621; Lake Gwyn Park, Wahneta, 27.954033 / -81.7189479; Eagle Lake Park, Clearwater, 27.934209 / -82.7651167; Boyd Hill Nature Park and Lake Maggiore, St. Petersburg, 27.7322367 / -82.6521206

BUTEOS AND EAGLE

RED-SHOULDERED HAWK
Buteo lineatus

Look on the edges of wooded areas near water for this year-round resident.

Field marks: Reddish-brown head, red patches at shoulders, white chest heavily barred with orange, chunky body, square black tail with narrow white bands. In flight, pale underneath with rusty orange chest and shoulders, wings lightly barred in black with light area at the wing tips. Juvenile may be streaked in brown instead of orange.

Size: L: 17"–24", WS: 35"–45"

Similar species: Red-tailed hawk is larger and has a red tail. Broad-winged hawk is smaller and nearly all white underneath.

Season: Year-round

Habitat: Forests and wooded areas near lakes, ponds, and ocean

Food source: Reptiles, amphibians, small mammals and birds, some insects

Nest: In a tree

Call: Repeated *kee-yah, kee-yah, kee-yah*; more rapidly when agitated

Hot spots: This ubiquitous hawk is one of the easiest raptors in Florida to spot, and it's likely to linger in place while you get a good look. You can find them in any wooded area near water, and they are often seen in trees along highways, and perched above less-traveled roads through forested land. All of Florida's national wildlife refuges and national parks have their own populations of red-shouldered hawks, so you should have no trouble locating at least one.

BROAD-WINGED HAWK
Buteo platypterus

Smallest of the local *Buteo* hawks, this hawk breeds in the Panhandle and overwinters in south Florida and the Keys.

Field marks: Brown head and body, evenly sized white and black bands on tail. Underside of wings appears all white in flight, with a black trailing edge. Adult's chest is white with heavy orange banding.

Size: L: 14"–19", WS: 35"–39"

Similar species: Red-tailed hawk is larger, has a red tail, and has a white breast with a brown-streaked bellyband. Red-shouldered hawk is larger and chunkier, with a shorter, squarer tail.

Season: Summer in the Panhandle, winter in south Florida; spring and fall migration throughout the state

Habitat: Forests with open edges; adjoining wetlands, meadows, roadways

Food source: Birds, small mammals, reptiles, amphibians, insects

Nest: In the crotch of a tree, usually a deciduous variety

Call: Single note: a very high, piercing *ti-weee*

Hot spots: Wakulla Springs State Park, Wakulla Springs, 30.2335 / -84.3037; San Felasco Hammock Preserve State Park, Yellow Trail, Gainesville, 29.7180976 / -82.4636471; Sawgrass Lake Park, St. Petersburg, 27.8398 / -82.6705; Everglades National Park, Flamingo, 25.1416 / -80.9255; Long Key State Park, Layton, 24.814968 / -80.82018

RED-TAILED HAWK
Buteo jamaicensis

The nation's most common hawk is often seen near roadways, soaring over fields, or sitting at the tops of trees.

Field marks: Brown head and body with bright reddish-orange tail, usually visible in flight or at rest; white underside with brown streaks around the middle, forming a distinctive bellyband. Juvenile may be paler underneath and lack the red tail.

Size: L: 19"–25", WS: 46"–55"

Similar species: Broad-winged hawk is much smaller and has a black and white tail. Red-shouldered hawk has orange-banded chest, black tail with white stripes.

Season: Year-round

Habitat: Open fields, meadows, and marshes that have tall trees or other high perches

Food source: Primarily small mammals, but with a preference for red-winged blackbirds

Nest: In large trees

Call: A loud, hoarse *kee-e-e-r-r-rh*, the quintessential hawk call used in countless movies and television shows (and often attributed to the bald eagle)

Hot spots: Red-tailed hawks are the most common and widespread hawks in Florida—and across the United States. You will see them standing atop utility poles and lampposts along interstate highways, watching fields from perches at the tops of trees, and being mobbed by starlings or crows when the hawks venture too close to a nest. Look for the white chest and underside with a jagged gray-to-brown bellyband, as well as the bright rufous tail.

DOMINIC SHERONY

© SHUTTERSTOCK.COM/AGAMI PHOTO AGENCY

SHORT-TAILED HAWK
Buteo brachyurus

An uncommon tropical hawk in Florida, this striking buteo prefers woodlands next to wide-open prairie or farmland.

Field marks: Solid, dark brown head and body with light bill and spray of white feathers around it; in flight, underside of wings is lighter with dark outer feathers and a whitish tail with thin dark stripes. Dark juveniles (see inset) are white-spotted in front from lower breast to undertail. A fraction of adults have a dark hood and back, rufous stripe at the neck, and all-white throat, breast, and underside.

Size: L: 16"–18", WS: 35"–39"

Similar species: Juvenile broad-winged hawk is smaller. Turkey vulture is nearly twice the size and has a featherless red head. Black vulture is also much larger and has a featherless gray head.

Season: Summer in mid-state; year-round in south Florida and the Keys

Habitat: Woodland edges near large expanses of open land, especially in mangrove or cypress swamps

Food source: Small birds, some small reptiles, rodents, insects

Nest: In trees, usually above 25 feet

Call: Long, high-pitched, descending *kreeee*, usually only near nest

Hot spots: Lettuce Lake County Park, Tampa, 28.0725 / -82.3754; Boyd Hill Nature Park and Lake Maggiore, St. Petersburg, 27.7322367 / -82.6521206; Harns Marsh, Buckingham, 26.6496729 / -81.6869336; Brewer Park, Miller Drive Roost, South Miami, 25.7178837 / -80.2961969; Research Road, Everglades National Park, 25.3712306 / -80.6889582

BALD EAGLE
Haliaeetus leucocephalus

This unmistakable raptor is the national bird of the United States.

Field marks: Adult has white head, yellow bill, all-brown body, white tail. Juvenile may be all brown or mottled brown and white.

Size: L: 30"–43", WS: 75"–95"

Similar species: Turkey vulture and black vulture are often mistaken for eagles, but they have featherless heads. The bald eagle soars while holding its wings flat, while the turkey vulture makes a wide V shape with its wings in flight. Osprey has a completely white underside, a white cap with a black band through its eye, and a dark tail.

Season: Year-round

Habitat: Areas with open water, including rivers, lakes, ponds, and ocean

Food source: Fish, road-killed carrion (especially deer)

Nest: Near the top of a large tree that can support a big nest made of twigs

Call: A very high series of notes and squeaks, ending in a rapid *wee-ee-ee-ee-ee-o*

Hot spots: Any habitat near a sizable body of water may provide a home for bald eagles, which have made an exponential comeback since the use of the pesticide DDT was banned in 1972. Today it's fairly easy to see adult and immature eagles throughout Florida, with several individuals often roosting in the same tree. Any wildlife refuge with abundant water, pond, managed wilderness area, or coastline is likely to have its own pair of eagles soaring above it, with mottled immature birds close by.

OSPREY AND FALCONS

OSPREY
Pandion haliaetus

This fish-eating raptor is easily spotted near any major waterway.

Field marks: White head and face with black band from eye to shoulder, dark body and tail, white underside with streaky black breastband. Juvenile has buff-colored upper breast.

Size: L: 21"–24", WS: 56"–72"

Similar species: Bald eagle, often seen in the same habitat, is larger and has an all-white head and white tail.

Season: Year-round

Habitat: Areas with open water that supports a healthy fish population; high perches

Food source: Fish

Nest: At the top of a tree, or on a platform or crosspiece at the top of a utility pole or lamppost

Call: Very high *pip-pip-pip-pip*

Hot spots: After scanning the sheer quantity of ospreys seen on a daily basis in Florida, I offer these tips for spotting one: Go to the seashore, a lake that supports fish in your own community, or the nearest river or marsh. Look for a utility pole or other high platform covered in a large nest made of twigs. Check this out with binoculars to see if there's a bird sitting in the nest; if not, chances are good there's an osprey within a few hundred yards. These very common "fish hawks" are never far from water and are very attentive to their nests.

CRESTED CARACARA
Caracara cheriway

A bird of open desert, this falcon shows up along roadsides throughout south Florida in its search for a roadkill meal.

Field marks: Dark brown cap extended to the nape, orange facial skin extending to bill, gray bill tip, white neck and throat, white breast mottled with brown, brown back and wings with white outer feathers, white undertail coverts, white tail with brown trailing edge, yellow legs and feet.

Size: L: 22"–24", WS 49"–50"

Similar species: Black vulture is much larger and is all black with white outer wing "fingers."

Season: Year-round in a concentrated area

Habitat: Open land including farm fields, prairie, and pastures; often seen perching on a fence post

Food source: Carrion, as well as fish, reptiles, birds, rodents, and amphibians

Nest: In the tallest tree or shrub they can find

Call: Generally silent; sometimes make a rattling sound of warning

Hot spots: Caracaras are fairly easy to see while you're driving through open land along any state road in south Florida. The drive to Immokalee from any direction, for example, can yield multiple sightings of this large, easily identifiable bird, as will a trip along Alligator Alley (now Everglades Parkway). Watch the roadside as you travel through this flat, expansive countryside.

MERLIN
Falco columbarius

An aggressive hunter, this adaptable falcon may prey upon the small birds at your feeder.

Field marks: Dark, streaked head with white stripe through the eye and grayish vertical stripes; dark back, mottled gray; white and rusty chest and underside; long, dark tail with light gray stripes. Wings are short and tapered.

Size: L: 10"–13", WS: 23"–25"

Similar species: American kestrel is much redder overall. Peregrine falcon is much larger, with pronounced black vertical stripes on its face.

Season: Winter

Habitat: Coniferous forest, often near an adjoining housing tract or farm where small birds are plentiful

Food source: Small birds and occasional small mammals, reptiles (including snakes), dragonflies

Nest: A tree cavity, high ledge, or abandoned bird nest

Call: A single, high-pitched *heee*; repeated rapidly when used as an alarm call

Hot spots: Bailey Tract, J. N. Ding Darling National Wildlife Refuge, Sanibel, 26.4276 / -82.0819; Audubon Corkscrew Swamp Sanctuary, Corkscrew, 26.375442 / -81.6040206; Harney Pond Canal Recreation Area, Lakeport, 26.995414 / -81.0675573; Tall Cypress Natural Area, Coral Springs, 26.2768695 / -80.214057; Frog Pond Wildlife Management Area, Lucky Hammock, Homestead, 25.396439 / -80.566581

AMERICAN KESTREL
Falco sparverius

Our smallest falcon stands out for its reddish wings and body, as well as its uncanny ability to hover while hunting.

Field marks: Gray cap, white face with gray vertical stripes, bright rust back and tail. Male has gray wings, a buff-colored breast with black streaks, and a buff patch on the back of the head. Female has rusty streaks on chest and lacks the buff patches.

Size: L: 9"–11", WS: 20"–24"

Similar species: Merlin is larger and has no rusty areas. Peregrine falcon is much larger and darker.

Season: Year-round in most of Florida; winter in south Florida and the Keys

Habitat: Farmland, open fields and meadows, as well as city parks and housing developments

Food source: Grasshoppers and other large insects, small mammals, birds, frogs and other amphibians

Nest: In a tree cavity

Call: High-pitched, gargled *klee-klee-klee-klee-klee*

Hot spots: Any farmer's field, marshland, airfield, open area in a neighborhood, or very large backyard may attract a kestrel to consider it as a hunting ground. These robin-size hawks are fairly easy to identify because of their bright plumage and their ability to hover—and they perch on the tops of utility poles and on wires, fence posts, and fences along roadsides. Drive down your favorite rural road when fields have been plowed before or after the growing season, and you are likely to find a kestrel hunting grasshoppers in the freshly turned earth.

PEREGRINE FALCON
Falco peregrinus

After being nearly wiped out by the pesticide DDT, this large falcon has returned to its accustomed habitat across the country.

Field marks: Black and white head with vertical black stripe through the eye, dark gray back and wings, white breast with heavy, dark barring from mid-breast to undertail coverts; long gray tail with darker gray barring. Juvenile is very similar, but browner.

Size: L: 16"–20", WS: 41"–45"

Similar species: Merlin and American kestrel are both smaller, and both have rusty barring on their breasts. Kestrel is more reddish overall.

Season: Winter

Habitat: Open spaces, including mountains and rocky coastlines with cliffs. Peregrines are renowned for their ability to nest and breed on top of tall buildings in major cities.

Food source: Birds, especially rock pigeons and doves; small reptiles

Nest: Up high, near the top of a cliff or on the ledge of a city skyscraper

Call: A rapid, repeated, cackled *ka-ka-ka-ka-ka*, sometimes for several minutes

Hot spots: Myakka River State Park, Myakka City, 27.2405033 / -82.3148167; Ten Thousand Islands National Wildlife Refuge Observation Tower, Marco Island, 25.973478 / -81.5542603; West Kendall Agricultural Area, Miami, 25.650781 / -80.464181; Stormwater Treatment Area 5/6, Clewiston, 26.4330582 / -80.9416786; "Viera" Ritch Grissom Memorial Wetlands, Melbourne, 28.228577 / -80.7604659

KITES

WHITE-TAILED KITE
Elanus leucurus

Watch the skies over south Florida's open fields for this sleek, white rodent hunter with black shoulders.

Field marks: White face, amber eye rimmed in black; white throat, breast, and underside; light gray wings with black shoulders, long white tail extending past dark wing tips when standing. Flies with wings held in dihedral position. Juvenile has buff-colored breast for first few weeks.

Size: L: 14"–16", WS: 39"–40"

Similar species: Swallow-tailed kite has black and white wings and long, black, forked tail. Mississippi kite is uniformly gray with a dark tail.

Season: Year-round

Habitat: Open grassland and savanna

Food source: Rodents, small reptiles, snakes, some insects

Nest: In tall trees at forest edges, or in a lone tree in an open area

Call: A crackling grunt, like metal rubbing a rough surface

Hot spots: Miami Canal, Lake Harbor, 26.6736972 / -80.8193108; Browns Farm Road, Sixmile Bend, 26.6321916 / -80.5711555; West Kendall Agricultural Area, Miami, 25.650781 / -80.464181; Frog Pond Wildlife Management Area, Lucky Hammock, Homestead, 25.396439 / -80.566581; Research Road, Everglades National Park, 25.3712306 / -80.6889582

SWALLOW-TAILED KITE
Elanoides forficatus

This striking raptor's deeply forked tail and unique wing pattern make it easy to identify in flight.

Field marks: White head, throat, breast, and underside; black back and wings, black tail with deep fork, white underwings with black flight feathers. Juvenile may have a buff wash over its face and breast.

Size: L: 21"–23", WS: 50"–52"

Similar species: White-tailed kite has gray wings with black shoulders, and a white fan tail.

Season: Breeding (summer)

Habitat: Marshes and swamps with trees; forests

Food source: Flying insects, frogs, lizards, snakes, some nesting birds

Nest: At the top of a tall tree

Call: Loud, high-pitched *kee-kee-kee-kee-kee-kaw*, *ki-kaw*, dropping to a lower pitch at the first *kaw*

Hot spots: Swallow-tailed kites can be found all over the state, with more frequent and numerous sightings farther south. Here are some particularly dependable spots: Lake Apopka North Shore sod fields, Zellwood, 28.7204295 / -81.6290102; Celery Fields, Fruitville, 27.3282173 / -82.4340248; Anhinga Trail, Everglades National Park, 25.3820583 / -80.6069362; Everglades National Park, Flamingo, 25.1416 / -80.9255; Eagle Lakes Community Park, Naples, 26.0773686 / -81.7141414

SNAIL KITE
Rostrhamus sociabilis

A Florida specialty, this dark kite has a white patch at the base of the tail.

Field marks: Male is dark gray overall with a hooked yellow-orange bill and red legs, long wings that extend past the tail when standing, and a bright white patch at the tail base. Female is dark brown with a brown and white–streaked breast and underside, and a black and white facial pattern.

Size: L: 16"–18", WS: 40"–43"

Similar species: Mississippi kite is lighter gray overall. Northern harrier has a white breast and underside with broken brown stripes and a shorter bill; the male's wings are white with black tips and a black trailing edge.

Season: Year-round

Habitat: Freshwater marshes and wetlands that contain snails

Food source: Apple snails; occasionally small turtles, crustaceans, or fish

Nest: In a tree in or near shallow water

Call: A chattery, continuous *kik-kik-kik-kik*, rising and falling in pitch

Hot spots: Joe Overstreet Road and Landing, Kenansville, 27.9426789 / -81.2050366; Francis S. Taylor Wildlife Management Area, Everglades Parkway rest area, Alligator Alley, 26.1469438 / -80.6291342; West Regional WTF Wetlands, Vero Beach, 27.6131434 / -80.5052376; Sweetwater Wetlands Park, Gainesville, 29.6151026 / -82.3254061; Paynes Prairie Preserve State Park, Gainesville, 29.6068756 / -82.3031116

© SHUTTERSTOCK.COM/BRENT BARNES

MISSISSIPPI KITE
Ictinia mississippiensis

This light gray kite's long, slender wings make it easy to mistake for a falcon.

Field marks: Adult is light gray overall with dark eye patch, gray wings with white secondary feathers, darker fan tail. Juvenile has a brown and white breast and underside, brown underwings at the shoulders, and faint stripes in tail.

Size: L: 14"–15", WS: 31"–32"

Similar species: Snail kite is darker overall with a white patch at the base of the tail. Peregrine falcon has a boldly patterned face and a black and white, horizontally striped breast and underside.

Season: Breeding in northern Florida; spring and fall migration in the Keys and south Florida

Habitat: Forests with mature trees

Food source: Large insects, reptiles, amphibians, small mammals; sometimes bats

Nest: In trees in lowland forests

Call: A wispy *PEW-phew*, dropping in pitch at the end

Hot spots: McCord Park, Tallahassee, 30.4730144 / -84.2623043 (and other wetlands with woods in the Tallahassee area); Torreya State Park, Bristol, 30.5656 / -84.9468; Depot Park, Gainesville, 29.6426364 / -82.3231369; Paynes Prairie Preserve State Park, Gainesville, 29.6068756 / -82.3031116; Little Marsh Island, Shell Bay, Jacksonville, 30.3963423 / -81.4990819

OWLS

DOMINIC SHERONY

BARN OWL
Tyto alba

Like a gray ghost in the night, this nocturnal bird is very difficult for birders to see clearly and well.

Field marks: Male has heart-shaped white face, black eyes, light pink bill; pale tan head, nape, back, and wings; white breast and underside, mottled gray and light brown wings with pure white underside visible in flight, dark legs. Female has a tawny breast.

Size: L: 16"–20", WS: 42"–44"

Similar species: Barred owl has vertical barring on its chest and horizontal barring around its neck and over its wings.

Season: Year-round

Habitat: Structures or wooded areas near open grasslands

Food source: Primarily rodents; also rabbits and bats

Nest: In a barn, church steeple, or other building; in a hollow tree, in a crevice on a rocky cliff, or on a ledge

Call: A chilling screech that sounds uncannily like an ill-fated Alfred Hitchcock heroine; also a high-pitched *kik-kik-kik* by the male approaching the nest

Hot spots: Paynes Prairie Preserve State Park, Gainesville, 29.6068756 / -82.3031116; Kissimmee Prairie Preserve State Park, Basinger, 27.5746341 / -81.0228825; Browns Farm Road, Sixmile Bend, 26.6321916 / -80.5711555; Miami Executive Airport, west side dike, Miami, 25.640304 / -80.447631; Frog Pond Wildlife Management Area, Lucky Hammock, Homestead, 25.396439 / -80.566581

GREAT-HORNED OWL
Bubo virginianus

A year-round resident throughout Florida, this large owl often perches in the open as evening approaches.

Field marks: Orange face with brown forehead and yellow eyes, large "horn" tufts, rufous and buff chest and underside with strong brown barring, brown back and wings with some rufous tint, buff underside of wings, brown tail.

Size: L: 20"–25", WS: 36"–44"

Similar species: Barred owl is smaller, with dark eyes and no ear tufts. Barn owl has a white face and no ear tufts, and a ruddy brown back and wings.

Season: Year-round

Habitat: Woodlands, swamps, farmland with wooded areas

Food source: Larger mammals and birds other than owls (ducks, quail, geese), rabbits, groundhogs, skunks, as well as squirrels and rats

Nest: In a large nest abandoned by another bird

Call: A four- or five-note series: *hoo-HOO, hoo, hoo*; also a shriek not unlike a red-tailed hawk

Hot spots: Just about every wooded area in the state has its own great horned owl, if not a pair. Check the park nearest you before venturing cross-country to find one—try an evening just before twilight or the hour or so before the sun rises, and listen for one calling. Rangers in parks often know where these owls are nesting, and if they have nearly fledged young that may be visible in the nest.

DOMINIC SHERONY

BARRED OWL
Strix varia

The barred owl's familiar "Who cooks for you?" call helps birders narrow down its location in the forest after dark.

Field marks: Gray facial disc, black eyes, gray barring around neck and throat, buff breast with heavy brown streaking, brown and white–mottled back and wings, buff and brown barred tail.

Size: L: 18"–23", WS: 42"–50"

Similar species: Short-eared owl, an occasional Florida visitor, is smaller and tawnier overall.

Season: Year-round

Habitat: Forests and woodlands near water

Food source: Rodents and other small mammals, fish, reptiles, amphibians, grasshoppers and other insects

Nest: In a tree cavity or in a nest built by a hawk or squirrel

Call: *Hoo, hoo, huh-hoo, hoo, hoo, huh-hoo-ah,* often defined as "Who cooks for you, who cooks for you all?" with a long descending note at the end

Hot spots: Sweetwater Wetlands Park, Gainesville, 29.6151026 / -82.3254061; Paynes Prairie Preserve State Park, Gainesville, 29.6068756 / -82.3031116; Guana Tolomato Matanzas National Estuarine Research Reserve, St. Augustine, 30.0074 / -81.3325; Kissimmee Prairie Preserve State Park, Basinger, 27.5746341 / -81.0228825; Fakahatchee Strand Preserve State Park, Janes Scenic Drive, Big Cypress, 25.9793 / -81.4109

COMINIC SHERONY

EASTERN SCREECH-OWL
Megascops asio

This year-round resident calls with an eerie, elongated trill that strikes fear in many species, including unsuspecting humans.

Field marks: Two morphs are possible: rufous/brown and gray. Facial disc is brown or gray with a white X from eyebrows to chin; yellow eyes, small ear tufts. Wings are brown or gray with white lines from shoulder. Breast is heavily barred with gray or brown streaks.

Size: L: 7"–9", WS: 18"–22"

Similar species: Barred owl is larger and lacks the ear tufts.

Season: Year-round

Habitat: Mixed deciduous and coniferous forest, parks, woods near streams or marshes, open fields

Food source: Small mammals and rodents

Nest: In a tree cavity, either natural or excavated by woodpeckers

Call: A long, soprano, descending trill, lasting 3 seconds or more; a trill on one note with no descent, also 3 or 4 seconds long

Hot spots: Elinor Klapp-Phipps Park, Tallahassee, 30.535666 / -84.28821; Paynes Prairie Preserve State Park, Gainesville, 29.6068756 / -82.3031116; Merritt Island National Wildlife Refuge, Titusville, 28.6411839 / -80.7774067; Kiwanis Park, Port Charlotte, 26.9845561 / -82.1324158; Brewer Park, Miller Drive Roost, South Miami, 25.7178837 / -80.2961969

BURROWING OWL
Athene cunicularia

These tiny owls live in colonies, in holes in the ground in flat, open plains.

Field marks: Mottled brown head, chest, and body; yellow eyes and bill, long legs, short tail. Males and females are similar.

Size: L: 8"–9", WS: 21"

Similar species: This is the only Florida owl that lives on the ground.

Season: Year-round

Habitat: Open grassland, airports, ball fields, and other flat, clear areas

Food source: Insects, small rodents, small reptiles, and amphibians

Nest: Burrows dug by other animals, including tortoises, armadillos, skunks, or ground squirrels, often on a small mound in an otherwise open area

Call: A high-pitched, two-note *cu-COO*

Hot spots: Orlando Melbourne International Airport, Melbourne, 28.1020068 / -80.6415436; Trilby Road, Dade City, 28.4568871 / -82.2273687; Kissimmee Prairie Preserve State Park, Peavine Trail, Okeechobee, 27.5495055 / -81.0227323; Pelican Boulevard Baseball Fields, Cape Coral, 26.5747491 / -81.9834566; Markham Park, Sunrise, 26.1279694 / -80.3596902

DOVES AND PIGEONS

© SHUTTERSTOCK.COM/DANNY YE

WHITE-CROWNED PIGEON
Patagioenas leucocephala

This bird of the Caribbean islands has expanded its range to include the southern tip of Florida.

Field marks: Bright white cap on an otherwise dark gray, dove-shaped bird with iridescent neck feathers.

Size: L: 13"–14", WS: 23"

Similar species: Rock pigeon is larger and heavier with more varied plumage. Mourning dove is uniformly beige.

Season: Year-round

Habitat: Forests with fruit trees

Food source: Fruits and berries of many different trees

Nest: In trees, often near water

Call: Elongated *woof, woof, woof, kaWOO*, or a vibrating *currrRRR-urr*

Hot spots: Dagny Johnson Key Largo Hammock Botanical State Park, Key Largo, 25.280242 / -80.2973986; Southern Glades Wildlife and Environmental Area—The Annex, Homestead, 25.384123 / -80.5657911; Everglades National Park, Flamingo, 25.1416 / -80.9255; A. D. Barnes Park, Miami, 25.7340827 / -80.3108552; Dr. Von D. Mizell–Eula Johnson State Park, Hollywood, 26.0711624 / -80.1124978

EURASIAN COLLARED DOVE
Streptopelia decaocto

Larger and lighter than a mourning dove, this widespread species is everywhere that people congregate.

Field marks: Light gray-tan overall with a thin black line around nape of neck; dark primary feathers on wings, gray undertail coverts, red eye, pink legs and feet. White outer tail feathers are visible in flight.

Size: L: 13", WS: 21"–23"

Similar species: Mourning dove is slightly smaller, darker tan, and has black spots on its wings. White-winged dove has a bright white line along the outer edge of its wings, most visible when standing.

Season: Year-round

Habitat: Human-populated areas including cities, suburbs, and farms, especially where bird feeders are found

Food source: Seeds, some berries and insects

Nest: On buildings or in trees, at least 10 feet off the ground

Call: Repeated *coo-COO coo*, as well as a distinctly different, elongated *waw* when alarmed, not unlike a blue jay

Hot spots: You won't need a specific place to look for this dove. If you don't have a yard with a bird feeder, watch electrical wires or light poles along roadsides and at shopping centers, or scan mowed lawns throughout the state.

© SHUTTERSTOCK.COM/GO_UBEV DMITRII

COMMON GROUND DOVE
Columbina passerina

Bright rufous underwings make this little dove fairly easy to spot.

Field marks: Scaly-feathered black and white crown and nape; ruddy face, breast, underside, and wings; red bill with black tip, light brown back, black spots in lines on wings, short wings, brownish tail.

Size: L: 6"–6.5", WS: 10"–11"

Similar species: No other small dove is found in Florida. Mourning dove is slimmer, twice the size, and has no rufous features. Eurasian collared dove is slightly larger than the mourning dove and is lighter gray.

Season: Year-round

Habitat: Open ground, often with very little vegetation, especially under bird feeders

Food source: Seeds from weeds and grass, as well as bird feeders

Nest: On the ground, or low in a shrub or other sturdy vegetation

Call: *Cooo, cooo, cooo*, in a series, each rising at the end

Hot spots: This dove may show up just about anywhere in Florida, but here are some surefire places to see them: St. Marks National Wildlife Refuge, St. Marks, 30.1515653 / -84.1473314; Paynes Prairie Preserve State Park, Gainesville, 29.6068756 / -82.3031116; Cedar Key State Museum, Cedar Key, 29.1506996 / -83.0480307; Watermelon Pond Wildlife and Environmental Area, Newberry, 29.5803805 / -82.6070997; Fort De Soto Park, St. Petersburg, 27.6327266 / -82.718157

WHITE-WINGED DOVE
Zenaida asiatica

The white edge along the wing makes this dove fairly easy to differentiate from the much more prevalent mourning dove.

Field marks: Gray-brown overall, orange eye with blue ring, black patch along jawline, white wing patch that forms a line along the bottom edge of the wing while at rest, becoming visible on upper wing during flight; black flight feathers, square tail with white trailing edge, red legs and feet.

Size: L: 11"–12", WS: 19"–20"

Similar species: Mourning dove has black spots on its wings and no white areas. Eurasian collared dove has a black line extending around the nape and is paler overall.

Season: Winter on the northern coasts; year-round throughout central and southern Florida

Habitat: Cities, towns, suburbs, and anywhere else where there are people

Food source: Seeds, both from plants and from feeders

Nest: In the crotch or on a sturdy branch of a large shade tree

Call: *Coo-coo-coo-COO-woo;* very like the "Who cooks for you?" of a barred owl

Hot spots: This ubiquitous bird can be found in virtually any parking area, picnic ground, beach, or backyard south of Orlando; they are particularly numerous at any restaurant with outdoor dining. They are also staples on trails in all of south Florida's wildlife refuges, parks, and wildlife management areas.

MOURNING DOVE
Zenaida macroura

A resident of suburban yards, parks, and shopping centers, this gentle creature can be seen and heard virtually anywhere in Florida.

Field marks: Light grayish brown overall with a black spot on the cheek and black spots on the wings; short, thin bill; long tail expands in flight to show white tips with a black edge; whitish undertail coverts.

Size: L: 12", WS: 17"–19"

Similar species: Rock pigeon is larger and heavier, and is either light gray and black or a combination of colors due to interbreeding with other dove species. Eurasian collared dove is lighter in color and has a black line around its nape. White-winged dove lacks the black spots, and has a solid white line visible just below its wings. White-crowned pigeon is uniformly dark gray with a white cap.

Season: Year-round

Habitat: Mowed lawns and platform or ground feeders in suburban areas, parks with trees and shrubs, and other areas frequented by people

Food source: Seeds, leaves, and plant matter found on the ground

Nest: In a tree, shrub, or on the ground

Call: A slow, mournful *ohh-WOO, hoo, hoo;* also a pronounced whistling made by the wings during flight

Hot spots: Mourning doves are among the most common birds in Florida and are easy to locate. Watch utility wires in your area for single birds, pairs, and flocks, and keep an eye on platform feeders, tops of lampposts, and other places where they can stand comfortably.

185

ROCK PIGEON
Columba livia

An introduced species from Europe, this member of the dove family (formerly known as rock dove or feral pigeon) took full advantage of its new territory and is now found on every city street in the country.

Field marks: Original coloring is a purple head, iridescent blue neck and breast, light gray back and upper wings, darker gray primary flight feathers, black stripe across both wings, black trailing edge; white rump, gray tail with a black tip. Interbreeding with domestic species has produced a variety of alternate plumages in mottled shades of brown, black, gray, and white.

Size: L: 12.5"–14", WS: 26"–34"

Similar species: Mourning dove is smaller, more delicate, and is always grayish brown with black spots on wings.

Season: Year-round

Habitat: Areas inhabited by humans, including cities, suburbs, buildings and barnyards in rural areas; also on agricultural lands

Food source: Seeds, berries, and human discards scavenged from streets, yards, and parks

Nest: On human-made ledges—windowsills, bridge girders, eaves, gutters, etc.

Call: Elongated, descending *coo* with a throaty rumble

Hot spots: Rock pigeons are everywhere humans are. Check city streets, gravel driveways, parking lots, rooftops of houses and barns, landfills, dumpsters, restaurants with outdoor dining, fairs and festivals, and other places where people may drop a morsel of food.

PARAKEETS, CUCKOOS, AND ANIS

MONK PARAKEET
Myiopsitta monachus

Probably descended from birds released by pet owners decades ago, established colonies of these gregarious birds from South America thrive all over central and south Florida.

Field marks: Bright green head with whitish face and orange bill, green back, green wings with bright blue primaries, grayish breast, gray-to-yellow belly, long diamond-shaped green tail.

Size: L: 11"–12", WS: 17"–19"

Similar species: A wide variety of similarly marked parrot and parakeet species have colonized south Florida, but the monk parakeet's pale gray forehead and breast set it apart from most of them.

Season: Year-round

Habitat: City parks and structures with lots of perches, especially power substations

Food source: Seeds, fruits, berries, nuts, flowers, insects

Nest: On top of a tall structure (a building or utility pole), or at the top of a very tall tree

Call: Rattling *chaa, chaa* calls with several syllables in succession; loud screeches

Hot spots: Pine Woods Park, Kendall, 25.647447 / -80.356726; Brian Piccolo Park, Hollywood, 26.03408 / -80.27048; YMCA Park, Key Largo, 25.092573 / -80.4383748; Pelican Boulevard baseball fields, Cape Coral, 26.5747491 / -81.9834566; Largo Central Park Nature Preserve, Largo, 27.9158428 / -82.7751357

NANDAY PARAKEET
Aratinga nenday

Formerly known as black-hooded parakeet, this South American native's black face and yellow eye ring are distinctive.

Field marks: Black crown and face, yellow eye ring around black eye, black bill; bright yellow-green neck, breast, and body; green wings with dark blue secondary feathers, paler green rump, long green tail with blue outer feathers.

Size: L: 12"–13" WS: 23"–24"

Similar species: Monk parakeet has a gray forehead and breast and a yellow underside; blue-crowned parakeet has a blue forehead and wide white eye ring. Many other exotic green birds live in small colonies throughout the same region.

Season: Year-round

Habitat: Open areas near trees, especially palm trees

Food source: Seeds, fruit, berries, palm nuts; will come to bird feeders

Nest: In a found hole in a tree

Call: A grating *kreeah, kreeah, kreeah*

Hot spots: Fort De Soto Park, St. Petersburg, 27.6327266 / -82.718157; Boynton Beach Inlet Park, Ocean Ridge, 26.5446541 / -80.0426102; Snook Islands Natural Area, Lake Worth, 26.6159905 / -80.0461936; Pine Woods Park, Kendall, 25.647447 / -80.356726; Manor Park, Fort Myers, 26.5997807 / -81.8783748

© SHUTTERSTOCK.COM/ERIC ISSELEE

WHITE-WINGED PARAKEET
Brotogeris versicolurus

The white and yellow wing patches differentiate this South American bird from monk parakeet.

Field marks: Green overall with bluish-gray face, white eye ring and white line to light-colored bill, white and yellow trailing edge of wing at rest, with obvious patches in flight.

Size: L: 8.5"–9", WS: 15"–16"

Similar species: Monk parakeet has a gray forehead and white breast and a yellow underside; blue-crowned parakeet has a blue forehead and wide white eye ring and is much larger. Many other exotic green birds live in small colonies throughout the same region.

Season: Year-round

Habitat: Open areas near trees, especially palm trees

Food source: Seeds, fruit, berries, palm nuts; will come to bird feeders

Nest: In a hole in a palm tree

Call: Rapid, chattering *kreeah, kreeah, kreeah*

Hot spots: Ocean Bank, 788-700 FL 953, Miami, 25.7792038 / -80.2642599; Evergreen Cemetery, Fort Lauderdale, 26.1061594 / -80.1318741; Kendall-Baptist Hospital Area, Miami, 25.68765 / -80.33864; Matheson Hammock Park, Coral Gables, 25.6806539 / -80.2726364

189

DOMINIC SHERONY

YELLOW-BILLED CUCKOO
Coccyzus americanus

Florida's more-common cuckoo prefers pastures, meadows with high grass, orchards, and other open areas with trees and shrubs.

Field marks: Brown cap, nape, and back; brown wings with bright reddish primaries; brown tail with white spots on outer tail feathers, large white spots visible on the underside of the tail; white throat, breast, and underside; yellow bill with black upper mandible; yellow eye ring.

Size: L: 11"–12", WS: 16"–18"

Similar species: Mangrove cuckoo is darker brown and has a pinkish wash over its underside.

Season: Spring migration; summer

Habitat: Grasslands with trees for roosting, especially willows

Food source: Caterpillars, cicadas, bird eggs, small reptiles, fruit

Nest: In a shrub or young tree

Call: Long, slow, descending rattle: *ki-ki-ki-ki-kow-kow-kow-kow*; a series of single *koo* sounds on one note

Hot spots: Kathryn Abbey Hanna Park, Jacksonville Beach, 30.3713664 / -81.4073128; Lake Apopka Wildlife Drive, Apopka, 28.6691082 / -81.5574338; Fort De Soto Park, St. Petersburg, 27.6327266 / -82.718157; Key Largo Hammocks State Botanical Site, Key Largo, 25.1758333 / -80.3694444; Dagny Johnson Key Largo Hammock Botanical State Park, Key Largo, 25.280242 / -80.2973986

© SHUTTERSTOCK.COM/AREND TRENT

MANGROVE CUCKOO
Coccyzus minor

Sitting motionless in a low tree as it waits for prey, the mangrove cuckoo makes itself very difficult to see.

Field marks: Dark gray-brown head, back, and wings; black band across the eye, two-tone black and yellow bill, white cheek and throat, pinkish wash on lower breast and underside; long tail with two rows of large white spots on the underside.

Size: L: 11"–12", WS: 17"

Similar species: Yellow-billed cuckoo is lighter colored overall and has a white breast and underside.

Season: Year-round

Habitat: Tropical forests, mangrove swamps

Food source: Caterpillars, insect larvae, frogs, spiders, small reptiles, bird eggs

Nest: On a branch in a small tree or shrub, often a mangrove

Call: Long, rapid series of harsh *kah-kah-kah-kah-kah-kah* sounds

Hot spots: Emerson Point Preserve, Palmetto, 27.5320111 / -82.6256604; J. N. Ding Darling National Wildlife Refuge, Sanibel, 26.4540529 / -82.1155071; John Pennekamp Coral Reef State Park, Key Largo, 25.1280556 / -80.41; Black Point Park and Marina, Cutler Bay, 25.5400214 / -80.3274608; Spanish River Park, Boca Raton, 26.3829 / -80.0692

SHUTTERSTOCK.COM/GUALBERTO BECERRA

SMOOTH-BILLED ANI
Crotophaga ani

Watch for the chunky black bill to tell this parrotlike bird from crows and grackles.

Field marks: All black, with disheveled feathers and a long tail; short, bulky bill like a parrot.

Size: L: 14"–15", WS: 18"–19"

Similar species: Groove-billed ani is slightly smaller but otherwise nearly identical, and is best distinguished by call. Fish crow is slimmer with a longer, thinner bill.

Season: Year-round

Habitat: Fields of low scrub, pastures, savannas

Food source: Insects, small reptiles, fruit, berries

Nest: In groups in a tree or bush

Call: *AH-nee, AH-nee*, high-pitched and repeated in quick succession

Hot spots: Lake Apopka North Shore, Astatula, 28.6740878 / -81.7059258; "Viera" Ritch Grissom Memorial Wetlands, Melbourne, 28.228577 / -80.7604659; Loxahatchee National Wildlife Refuge, Valencia Reserve, 26.4928139 / -80.2168894; Eagle Lakes Community Park, Naples, 26.0773686 / -81.7141414; J. N. Ding Darling National Wildlife Refuge, Bailey Tract, Sanibel, 26.4276 / -82.0819

© SHUTTERSTOCK.COM/ESTELLE R.

GROOVE-BILLED ANI
Crotophaga sulcirostris

Rare in Florida but seen annually for several years, this slimmer of the two anis has narrow grooves in its bill.

Field marks: All black, with disheveled feathers and a long tail; short, bulky bill like a parrot. Gray skin extends from the bill to the area around the eye. Grooves on bill may be visible with binoculars or a scope.

Size: L: 13"–14", WS: 17"–18"

Similar species: Smooth-billed ani is nearly identical, but a little larger and with less gray skin on the face, especially around the eye.

Season: All recent sightings have been in winter.

Habitat: Fields of low scrub, pastures, savannas

Food source: Insects, small reptiles, fruit, seeds

Nest: In groups in a tree or bush

Call: *Tuck-tuck-tuck-tuck*, slow and steady, with occasional whistles between *tucks*

Hot spots: Frog Pond Wildlife Management Area, Lucky Hammock, Homestead, 25.396439 / -80.566581; Winding Waters Natural Area, West Palm Beach, 26.773047 / -80.1249647; Miami Executive Airport, west side dike, Miami, 25.640304 / -80.447631

193

NIGHTJARS

DOMINIC SHERONY

EASTERN WHIP-POOR-WILL
Antrostomus vociferus

This rarely-seen nocturnal bird blends seamlessly with its surroundings. It is most easily identified by the song that gave it its name.

Field marks: Mottled brown and gray overall. Head with grayish cap and black stripe down the center, large black eye, white band at the throat, brown wings, gray or brown back with gray lines the width of the wing at each shoulder; gray and black tail with large white areas at the end on each side.

Size: L: 9"–10", WS: 17"–19"

Similar species: Common nighthawk has a bold white bar on each wing.

Season: Winter

Habitat: Open woodland

Food source: Flying insects it can catch in midair

Nest: On the edge of a woodland, on the ground among dead leaves

Call: High-pitched *whip-poor-WEE, whip-poor-WEE*, repeated several times in succession

Hot spots: Guana Tolomato Matanzas National Estuarine Research Reserve, St. Augustine, 30.0074 / -81.3325; Hal Scott Regional Preserve and Park, Wedgefield, 28.486186 / -81.1079327; Green Cay Wetlands & Nature Center, Boynton Beach, 26.4861584 / -80.1607561; Matheson Hammock Park, Coral Gables, 25.6806539 / -80.2726364; Oscar Scherer State Park, Nokomis, 27.1734149 / -82.466383

© SHUTTERSTOCK.COM/UNKNOWN

CHUCK-WILL'S-WIDOW
Antrostomus carolinensis

The largest of the nightjars, this nocturnal bird is named for its remarkably phonetic song.

Field marks: Flat head, gray crown with darker streaks, white line above the eye; rufous face, throat, and breast with white detail above the neck; mottled rufous and black back and wings (grayer in some birds), rufous and black–striped tail with buff outer tips.

Size: L: 12", WS: 25"–27"

Similar species: Eastern whip-poor-will is smaller and has white patches on the outer tail feathers. Nighthawks have a white bar on the wings at the "wrist."

Season: Breeding season north of Orlando; year-round in central and south Florida

Habitat: Pine and oak-hickory forests, as well as in thickets near open fields

Food source: Insects that they catch on the wing

Nest: In hedgerows or thickets, often near a roadside or open area

Call: *Chk-weeu-WIdow*, high and languid; also a low, throaty *oum* call, similar to a frog

Hot spots: Gulf Islands National Seashore, Fort Pickens, Pensacola Beach, 30.3231 / -87.2829; St. Marks National Wildlife Refuge, St. Marks, 30.1515653 / -84.1473314; Watermelon Pond Wildlife and Environmental Area, Newberry, 29.5803805 / -82.6070997; A. D. Barnes Park, Miami, 25.7340827 / -80.3108552; Everglades National Park, Long Pine Key Campground and Trail, Homestead, 25.3985091 / -80.6554395

LESSER NIGHTHAWK
Chordeiles acutipennis

A rare visitor to Florida, this small North American nighthawk has put in annual appearances for the past several winters.

Field marks: Male and female are mottled gray and brown above and below, with some buff color among the mottling on underside and underwings; whitish stripe toward the end of the wingtip; male has white bar close to the end of the tail, as well as a white collar. Tail is longer than common or Antillean nighthawk's tail.

Size: L: 9", WS: 22"–23"

Similar species: Common nighthawk's wing primaries reach beyond its tail, and the white bar on its wings is closer to the bend of the wing. Antillean nighthawk may have more contrast in its mottling pattern and may be more rufous. (Telling these species apart may require an expert's assistance.)

Season: Winter

Habitat: Open farm fields and areas with little vegetation, especially with a nearby lake

Food source: Insects they catch in flight

Nest: On the ground (not in Florida)

Call: Flight call is almost a giggled *whea-a-a-a-a*; on the ground, the call is a long, low trill easily mistaken for a frog

Hot spots: Lesser nighthawks have spent part or all of recent winters at these sites, though there is no guarantee they will choose them again: Lake Jesup Conservation Area, Marl Bed Flats, Sanford, 28.7377104 / -81.2400126; Canal 111E, Florida City, 25.4073113 / -80.5221838; Frog Pond Wildlife Management Area, Lucky Hammock, Homestead, 25.396439 / -80.566581

COMMON NIGHTHAWK
Chordeiles minor

Look for this darting hunter just after sunset, often catching bugs by the glow of industrial lighting systems at factories, stadiums, or shopping malls.

Field marks: Adult is mottled gray overall with tiny bill, slightly brown throat, white band across front of throat; brownish and gray back and wings, white feather at side below wing, broad white bar on each wing seen during flight; white stripe across tail just before terminal black stripe.

Size: L: 8"–10", WS: 22"–24"

Similar species: Whip-poor-will is similarly colored but lacks the wing stripe, and habitat does not generally overlap. Lesser nighthawk is rarely seen in Florida, and the white stripe on its wings is closer to the wing tip. Antillean nighthawk is slightly smaller, and its wings do not reach past the tail tip.

Season: Summer

Habitat: Very comfortable in human-populated areas, using buildings as roosting and nesting sites and lights to illuminate prey

Food source: Flying insects

Nest: In a hollow on the ground; on top of a flat-roofed building

Call: A nasal *peent*, not unlike a woodcock

Hot spots: Lake Apopka Wildlife Drive, Apopka, 28.6691082 / -81.5574338; Hal Scott Regional Preserve and Park, Wedgefield, 28.486186 / -81.1079327; Babcock-Webb Wildlife Management Area, Punta Gorda, 26.8582653 / -81.9401121; Frog Pond Wildlife Management Area, Lucky Hammock, Homestead, 25.396439 / -80.566581; Everglades National Park, Research Road, 25.3712306 / -80.6889582

ANTILLEAN NIGHTHAWK

Chordeiles gundlachii

Look for this nocturnal bird during your summer visit to the Keys.

Field marks: Mottled gray and brown overall, with thin white band at neck and at end of tail just before black tip. White band on wings between wing's bend and tip.

Size: L: 8.5"–9", WS: 21"

Similar species: Common nighthawk is slightly larger, with longer wings.

Season: Summer

Habitat: Flat, open areas like airports and ball fields

Food source: Insects it catches in flight

Nest: On bare ground, or on a flat roof

Call: A series of three rapid, stuttering syllables, like *ka-ty-tid*

Hot spots: Grassy Key, Marathon, 24.7580603 / -80.9612507; Marathon Airport, Marathon, 24.7248284 / -81.0523868; National Key Deer National Wildlife Refuge, Big Pine Key, 24.7299933 / -81.3913751; Little Hamaca City Park, Key West, 24.5571942 / -81.7673993

HUMMINGBIRD

RUBY-THROATED HUMMINGBIRD
Archilochus colubris

The eastern United States has only one reliable resident hummingbird, this sparkling jewel that readily comes to backyard feeders.

Field marks: Male has green cap and back, black bar through eye under cap, bright red throat, white breast, green sides, gray wings, gray and black tail with white wing tips. Female lacks the red throat.

Size: L: 3"–3.75", WS: 4.5"

Similar species: Rufous hummingbird has a bright orange throat and underside, orange at the base of the tail.

Season: Summer throughout most of the state; winter in south Florida and the Keys

Habitat: Backyards, parks, other areas with nectar-producing flowers; open woodlands

Food source: Nectar from flowers including petunias, fuchsia, and cardinal flower; some insects

Nest: Fastened to a tree branch with spiderweb silk

Call: Tiny, squeaky chip note repeated in rapid succession, sometimes in quick triplets

Hot spots: In the wild, just about any wooded area bordering a field of wildflowers may provide territory for hummingbirds. These birds develop a route through a neighborhood, park, or a wooded area with flowering plants, and they circle through that route over and over again throughout the day. If your feeder has clean, fresh nectar (one part sugar to four parts water, with no red food coloring), and some part of the feeder (not the nectar) is bright red, a hummingbird will find it eventually on its daily rounds. You can increase your chances of bringing hummingbirds to your yard by planting flowers like the ones listed above.

KINGFISHER

BELTED KINGFISHER
Megaceryle alcyon

Hunting over moving streams, rivers, ponds, and lakes, the easily recognized kingfisher can be fascinating to watch.

Field marks: Male has blue crest and face to just below the long bill, white collar, blue breast band over white breast, blue wings and back, white underside, blue tail with white bands. Female has a rust-colored band below the blue breastband, and some rust on flanks under the wings.

Size: L: 12"–14", WS: 20"–24"

Similar species: Pileated woodpecker is larger and has a bright red crest.

Season: Year-round in northern and central Florida; winter in south Florida

Habitat: Ponds, lakes, rivers, streams, saltwater waterways

Food source: Fish, mollusks, crustaceans, reptiles, amphibians, small mammals

Nest: The adults dig a tunnel in a riverbank and lay the eggs at the far end.

Call: Long, loud, rattling *ak-ak-ak-ak-ak*, often in flight

Hot spots: Just about every pond and lake in Florida has a kingfisher; if you don't have luck close to home, kingfishers are well known to favor the spots listed here: St. Marks National Wildlife Refuge, St. Marks, 30.1515653 / -84.1473314; Lake Apopka Wildlife Drive, Apopka, 28.6691082 / -81.5574338; Fort De Soto Park, St. Petersburg, 27.6327266 / -82.718157; Merritt Island National Wildlife Refuge, Titusville, 28.6411839 / -80.7774067; T. M. Goodwin Waterfowl Management Area, Palm Bay, 27.8452341 / -80.7252359

WOODPECKERS

RED-HEADED WOODPECKER
Melanerpes erythrocephalus

The only woodpecker with an all-red head, this charismatic resident populates Florida's forests.

Field marks: Bright red head, long gray bill, navy blue back and wings with large white patches on wings, white breast and underside, dark blue tail.

Size: L: 8.5"–9.5", WS: 16"–18"

Similar species: Pileated woodpecker has a large red crest and white face with dark blue pattern. Red-bellied woodpecker has a red stripe at the back of the head, a buff face, and black and white–barred wings.

Season: Year-round

Habitat: Open woodlands

Food source: Insects, invertebrates, nuts, seeds, berries

Nest: Cavity in a tree excavated by the woodpecker

Call: A low rattling trill, followed by a higher one; also a single-note *wurr*

Hot spots: Tall Timbers Research Station, Tallahassee, 30.6567786 / -84.2087889; Watermelon Pond Wildlife and Environmental Area, Newberry, 29.5803805 / -82.6070997; Longleaf Flatwoods Reserve, Hawthorne, 29.5654133 / -82.1889567; Ocala National Forest, Juniper Springs, Astor, 29.17814 / -81.71288; Rock Springs Run State Reserve, Sorrento, 28.7954932 / -81.450448

RED-BELLIED WOODPECKER
Melanerpes carolinus

A year-round resident, this midsize woodpecker with a bright red cap readily comes to suet and peanut feeders.

Field marks: Male has red cap extending from bill to shoulder; buff face, breast, and underside; black and white–barred back and wings, black trailing edge and wing primaries, white rump, black and white tail. Female's cap begins at the top of the head, leaving a buff forehead.

Size: L: 9"–10", WS: 16"–18"

Similar species: Yellow-bellied sapsucker has red cap, but its nape is white and it has a distinctive black and white facial pattern. Northern flicker has brown back with black barring, considerable spotting on buff breast, black bib, and gray cap with small red spot.

Season: Year-round

Habitat: Open woodlands, parks, backyards

Food source: Insects, seeds, fruit, suet, tree sap

Nest: In a tree cavity excavated by the pair or used in previous years by other woodpeckers

Call: Simple, mid-pitched *quirr* is most familiar; also chattering *kik-kik-kik-kik-kik.*

Hot spots: Red-bellied woodpeckers are everywhere in Florida. Any wooded area has at least a family of woodpeckers, and a morning walk along a forest trail may reveal half a dozen individuals or more. Active and expressive, they make themselves known with considerable movement up tree trunks and with their easily recognizable calls. If you feed birds with suet or peanuts in your yard, you are nearly certain to attract these birds.

DOMITIJIC SHERONY

YELLOW-BELLIED SAPSUCKER
Sphyrapicus varius

A winter resident, this is Florida's only sapsucker—so there's no confusion with the very similar red-naped sapsucker.

Field marks: Male has red forehead, bold black and white facial pattern, red throat with black border, black and white–barred back and wings, wide white stripe on wings, white rump, black and white–barred tail. Female has a white throat and some buff color on nape and breast.

Size: L: 8"–9", WS: 16"–17"

Similar species: Red-bellied woodpecker has a buff face and breast, and more red on the back of the head. Downy woodpecker is smaller and has a wide white area on its back. Hairy woodpecker is slightly larger and has a wide white stripe on its back.

Season: Winter

Habitat: Deciduous woods

Food source: Tree sap, berries, insects

Nest: In a tree cavity the pair excavates (not in Florida)

Call: High, nasal, single note: *pee-ow*, a rapid rattling *wikka-wikka-wikka* when confronted

Hot spots: Sapsuckers may be found in any leafy woods, but the areas noted here have multiple birds that remain throughout the winter: Tuscawilla Park, Ocala, 29.1916932 / -82.1325901; Orlando Wetlands Park, Orlando, 28.5753263 / -80.9966826; Highlands Hammock State Park, Sebring, 27.4707 / -81.5366; Babcock-Webb Wildlife Management Area, Punta Gorda, 26.8582653 / -81.9401121; Fran Reich Preserve SFWMD, Parkland, 26.3545316 / -80.2837256

DOWNY WOODPECKER

Dryobates pubescens

The smallest woodpecker in North America is also one of the most common, coming readily to feeders and nesting in neighborhoods with large trees.

Field marks: Male has black and white head with red spot on back of crown, small bill with white tuft at its base, black wings barred in white, large white patch on back, white breast and underside, dark tail. Female is identical but lacks the red spot.

Size: L: 6.75", WS: 11"–12"

Similar species: Hairy woodpecker is larger and has bill about twice the length.

Season: Year-round

Habitat: Deciduous forests; parks and backyards with leafy trees

Food source: Seeds, suet, nuts, insects

Nest: In a natural or excavated hole in a tree

Call: Elongated, descending *ti-ti-Tl-ti-ti-ti-ti-ti;* alternate is a high-pitched, one-note *tik.*

Hot spots: Downy woodpeckers are very common and easily spotted in any area with a healthy stand of trees. Look for them in your local parks, woodlands, or backyards with mature trees in your neighborhood, or attract them to your own backyard with a suet or peanut feeder.

HAIRY WOODPECKER
Dryobates villosus

Larger than a downy with a longer bill, hairy woodpeckers are otherwise nearly identical to the smaller bird. Vocal cues can help determine which is which.

Field marks: Male has black and white head with red spot on back of crown, long bill, black wings barred in white, large white patch on back, white breast and underside, dark tail. Female is identical but lacks the red spot.

Size: L: 9"–10", WS: 15"–17"

Similar species: Downy woodpecker is smaller, has a white tuft at the base of the bill, and has a shorter bill.

Season: Year-round

Habitat: Deciduous forests, parks, and neighborhoods with stands of mature trees

Food source: Gypsy moth caterpillars, spiders, insects, berries, seeds, nuts, suet

Nest: In a natural or excavated hole in a tree

Call: A single *pik*, followed by a long, high-pitched rattle; also *weeka, weeka, weeka*, like a squeaky wheel

Hot spots: Withlacoochee State Forest, Citrus Tract, Lecanto, 28.8016141 / -82.4179299; Withlacoochee State Forest, Croom Tract, Croom 28.5887423 / -82.2340393; Three Lakes Wildlife Management Area, Osceola County, 27.9312364 / -81.1522293; Babcock-Webb Wildlife Management Area, Punta Gorda, 26.8582653 / -81.9401121; Audubon Corkscrew Swamp Sanctuary, Corkscrew, 26.375442 / -81.6040206

RED-COCKADED WOODPECKER
Dryobates borealis

Once common, this southeastern specialty now confines itself to the few areas in Florida that have stands of healthy old-growth longleaf, loblolly, and slash pine.

Field marks: Black cap and bold black and white facial pattern with a bright white cheek, dark bill, black and white ladder pattern on back and wings, mottled black and white breast, white underside with faint streaks, black tail. Males have a nearly indistinguishable red line at the top of the white cheek.

Size: L: 8"–9", WS: 14"–14.5"

Similar species: Downy and hairy woodpeckers have a red dot on the back of the head (males), and a wide white stripe down the back. Yellow-bellied sapsucker has a red stripe on top of the head and a black stripe through the eye, dividing the white facial pattern.

Season: Year-round

Habitat: Old-growth pine forests with a clear understory from repeated fires

Food source: Insects that live under the bark on pine trees

Nest: In colonies in clusters of pine trees, in excavated holes in the trees

Call: A tumble of rapid, squeaky chatter when it arrives in its nesting area, as well as a high, one-syllable *chit*

Hot spots: Blackwater River State Forest, 3 Notch Road, Milton, 30.8392703 / -86.9411285; Apalachicola National Forest, Wright Lake and Road, Sumatra, 30.0001235 / -85.0019932; Tall Timbers Research Station, Tallahassee, 30.6567786 / -84.2087889; Withlacoochee State Forest, Citrus Tract, Lecanto, 28.8016141 / -82.4179299; Withlacoochee State Forest, Croom Tract, Croom 28.5887423 / -82.2340393

NORTHERN FLICKER
Colaptes auratus

Of the two races of northern flickers found across the country, the Florida variety is the yellow-shafted flicker. The yellow underwing offers proof of this.

Field marks: Male has gray head, light brown face, red spot on back of head, black malar stripe, black eye, long bill. Buff breast with many black spots, black bib at throat; back and wings are light brown and heavily barred with black; white rump is visible in flight. Tail is black with white barring. Female lacks red spot and black malar.

Size: L: 12"–14", WS: 19"–21"

Similar species: Yellow-bellied sapsucker has red throat and no brown areas.

Season: Year-round

Habitat: Open woodlands and edges, parks with mature trees, neighborhoods

Food source: Ants and other insects, fruit and berries, suet, nuts, sunflower seed from feeders

Nest: In a tree cavity or a hole in a utility pole; also in human-made birdhouses

Call: A rapid, repeated *flicker-flicker-flicker-flicker*, also a squeakier *wikka-wikka-wikka* call while interacting with other birds

Hot spots: Nearly every forest, park with mature trees, and neighborhood has a pair or colony of flickers within it. Flickers come to suet and nut feeders, especially platform feeders that allow them to stand horizontally and eat rather than perching or grabbing the mesh of a cage feeder. They are also seen frequently feeding on the ground after a rain, when ants are forced out of their nests.

PILEATED WOODPECKER
Dryocopus pileatus

When a pileated woodpecker arrives, it feels like an event. This large, colorful, charismatic bird entertains onlookers as it aggressively excavates a hole in a tree or dines at a suet feeder.

Field marks: Bright red crest, extending down the forehead in males; black and white face with black line through the eye, red malar stripe in males, white throat, black breast with white line extending from head, black underside, black wings with white secondaries, black tail.

Size: L: 16.5"–19.5", WS: 28"–30"

Similar species: No other woodpecker is as large or has similar color patterns.

Season: Year-round

Habitat: Forests of mature trees

Food source: Insect larvae, ants, fruit, nuts

Nest: In a large, excavated hole in a tree, usually about 10 to 15 feet up

Call: Loud *fluk-fluk-fluk-fluk-fluk*, much like a flicker but slower and lower-pitched

Hot spots: These big, striking birds frequent suet feeders in backyards and announce themselves in wooded areas throughout the state. Here are five places where you'll find the search particularly easy: Elinor Klapp-Phipps Park, Tallahassee, 30.535666 / -84.28821; Paynes Prairie Preserve, La Chua Trail, Gainesville, 29.6068756 / -82.3031116; Wekiwa Springs State Park, Apopka, 28.7337466 / -81.480324; Withlacoochee State Forest, Croom Tract, Croom 28.5887423 / -82.2340393; Sawgrass Lake Park, St. Petersburg, 27.8398 / -82.6705

FLYCATCHERS

EASTERN WOOD-PEWEE
Contopus virens

This common summer resident breeds in hardwood forests as far south as Gainesville, and passes through central and south Florida during migration. Listen for the call that gives the bird its name.

Field marks: Gray head with crest, thin eye ring, gray back, black wings with clearly visible white wing bars, grayish breast resembling a vest, yellowish underside, white undertail coverts, long dark tail.

Size: L: 6.25", WS: 10"

Similar species: Eastern phoebe is darker and stockier overall. Willow and alder flycatchers are smaller with brighter wing bars and whiter underside.

Season: Spring through fall in northern Florida; spring and fall migration in central and south Florida

Habitat: Hardwood forests, parks, suburban neighborhoods with mature trees

Food source: Flying insects

Nest: Built on the end of a tree branch

Call: A single *peeeoowee*, or repeated *peee-wee*, rising at the end

Hot spots: Elinor Klapp-Phipps Park, Tallahassee, 30.535666 / -84.28821; San Felasco Hammock Preserve State Park, Yellow Trail, Gainesville, 29.7180976 / -82.4636471; Mead Botanical Gardens, Winter Park, 28.5836 / -81.3586; Fort De Soto Park, St. Petersburg, 27.6327266 / -82.718157; Evergreen Cemetery, Fort Lauderdale, 26.1061594 / -80.1318741

DOMINIC SHERONY

ACADIAN FLYCATCHER
Empidonax virescens

Breeding in northern Florida and migrating through the rest of the state, this little flycatcher can be hard to distinguish from other *Empidonax* species.

Field marks: Olive-gray head and back; slim, pale yellow eye ring; two-tone black and yellow bill, dark wings with two white wing bars, white throat and breast, light yellow underside, long olive-gray tail.

Size: L: 5.75", WS: 8.75"–9"

Similar species: Willow and alder flycatchers are darker gray and brown and have a more distinct white eye ring.

Season: Summer north of Gainesville; spring and fall migration otherwise

Habitat: Forests with beech, hemlock, and maple trees, usually well into the forest rather than on the edges

Food source: Flying insects

Nest: On the end of a tree branch

Call: A soft *tee-chip*, or a simple *peet* chip note, repeated at intervals

Hot spots: Lake Talquin State Forest, Tallahassee, 30.4395582 / -84.4954097; St. Marks National Wildlife Refuge, St. Marks, 30.1515653 / -84.1473314; San Felasco Hammock Preserve State Park, Yellow Trail, Gainesville, 29.7180976 / -82.4636471; Poe Springs Park, High Springs, 29.8256037 / -82.6474857

WILLOW FLYCATCHER
Empidonax traillii

Do you see a willow flycatcher or an alder? The challenge is so great that the two birds were once considered a single species: Traill's flycatcher. Song and habitat are the best ways to tell these nearly identical birds apart.

Field marks: Dark brown-gray head and back, narrow white eye ring, two-tone black and yellow bill, white throat, grayish breast, whitish underside, dark wings with two bright white wing bars; long, straight tail.

Size: L: 5.75", WS: 8"–8.5"

Similar species: Alder flycatcher is virtually identical and is distinguishable in the field only by song. Least flycatcher is smaller, has a bolder eye ring, and lacks the yellowish underside.

Season: Fall migration

Habitat: Edges of wooded areas, including those along wetlands and pastures

Food source: Flying insects

Nest: In a shrub or young tree

Call: A dry *fitz-bew*, with a *whit* chip note

Hot spots: Sightings of this bird are few and far between in Florida, but these spots have been migratory stopovers in multiple years: Frog Pond Wildlife Management Area, Lucky Hammock, Homestead, 25.396439 / -80.566581; Bill Baggs Cape Florida State Park, Key Biscayne, 25.6733 / -80.1582; St. Marks National Wildlife Refuge, St. Marks, 30.1515653 / -84.1473314; Southern Glades Wildlife and Environmental Area—The Annex, Homestead, 25.384123 / -80.565; A. D. Barnes Park, Miami, 25.7340827 / -80.3108552

ALDER FLYCATCHER
Empidonax alnorum

Half of the Traill's flycatcher moniker, this bird is virtually indistinguishable from the willow flycatcher in the field. Check the habitat and listen for the song to make a positive identification.

Field marks: Dark brown-gray head and back, narrow white eye ring, two-tone black and yellow bill, white throat, grayish breast, whitish underside, dark wings with two bright white wing bars; long, straight tail.

Size: L: 5.75", WS: 8"–8.5"

Similar species: Willow flycatcher is essentially identical, but its song is distinctly different. Least flycatcher is smaller, has a bolder eye ring, and lacks the tinge of yellow on its underside.

Season: Summer

Habitat: Riparian areas with alder and birch trees, ponds, bogs, and other wetlands with woodland edges

Food source: Flying insects, berries, seeds

Nest: In a shrub or young tree, often very close to the ground

Call: Dry *fee-beer*, also a *wee-oo* whistle and simple *pip* call note

Hot spots: Crowder Road Landing, Lake Jackson, Tallahassee, 30.507019 / -84.313385; Paynes Prairie Preserve State Park, La Chua Trail, Gainesville, 29.6068756 / -82.3031116; Frog Pond Wildlife Management Area, Lucky Hammock, Homestead, 25.396439 / -80.566581; Bill Baggs Cape Florida State Park, Key Biscayne, 25.6733 / -80.1582; Southern Glades Wildlife and Environmental Area—The Annex, Homestead, 25.384123 / -80.565

LEAST FLYCATCHER
Empidonax minimus

The smallest of the local flycatchers sports a bold eye ring and chirps its rapid *che-bek* song to identify itself.

Field marks: Olive-gray head and back, bold white eye ring, two-tone black and yellow bill, whitish throat, grayish breast, white underside, two bright white wing bars, long tail.

Size: L: 5.25", WS: 7.75"–8.5"

Similar species: Willow and alder flycatchers are larger and have a narrow eye ring and yellower underparts.

Season: Winter in south Florida; migration farther north

Habitat: Leafy trees in parks, along roadsides, in neighborhoods

Food source: Flying insects, berries, seeds

Nest: On a branch in a bush or tree, sometimes close to the ground but often near the treetop

Call: Crisp *che-bek*, repeated in rapid succession; also a *tit, tit, tit, tit* chip note

Hot spots: Frog Pond Wildlife Management Area, Lucky Hammock, Homestead, 25.396439 / -80.566581; Bill Baggs Cape Florida State Park, Key Biscayne, 25.6733 / -80.1582; Lake Apopka North Shore, Astatula, 28.6740878 / -81.7059258; Paynes Prairie Preserve State Park, Gainesville, 29.6068756 / -82.3031116; Gulf Islands National Seashore, Fort Pickens, Pensacola Beach, 30.3231 / -87.2829

EASTERN PHOEBE
Sayornis phoebe

Like a flycatcher but larger, phoebes make themselves known with their tail-flicking behavior and distinctive song.

Field marks: Dark gray head, black bill, lighter gray nape and back, gray-smudged breast, pale yellowish underside, gray wings with no wing bars; long, straight tail.

Size: L: 7", WS: 10.5"–11.5"

Similar species: Eastern wood-pewee is smaller and lighter colored. All other local flycatchers have some kind of eye ring and wing bars.

Season: Summer

Habitat: Woodlands near open grasslands, pastures, or farms; suburban neighborhoods

Food source: Flying insects, berries, small fish caught from the water's surface

Nest: Glued with mud to the side of a building, or in a tree on top of an old nest

Call: A high, hoarse *PHEE-bee*, or quieter *tu-oo*

Hot spots: Eastern phoebe is among the most common birds that spend the winter in Florida. Any walk in the woods from November through March will yield at least one phoebe sighting; a focused birding day may turn up several.

VERMILION FLYCATCHER
Pyrocephalus rubinus

The Gulf coast of Florida is the only eastern wintering ground for this brilliantly colored western flycatcher.

Field marks: Male has a bright crimson head, throat, breast, and underside with a black band through the eye and a thin black bill; black back, wings, and tail. Female has a gray crown and cheek with a white face and thin black eye band, white breast streaked with gray, pink vent and undertail coverts, gray back and wings, black tail. Juvenile looks like female, but with no pink.

Size: L: 6", WS: 10"

Similar species: Scarlet tanager is larger and all red with black wings. Summer tanager has no black areas. Northern cardinal is larger and all red with a black area around the bill.

Season: Winter

Habitat: Open grassland with streams, near deciduous trees

Food source: Flying insects

Nest: In trees near streams (not in Florida)

Call: A series of tiny notes, speeding up and ending in a brisk trill: *pi-pi-pi-piiiitashee*

Hot spots: St. Marks National Wildlife Refuge, St. Marks, 30.1515653 / -84.1473314; Lake Apopka North Shore, Astatula, 28.6740878 / -81.7059258; Kissimmee Prairie Preserve State Park, Peavine Trail, Okeechobee, 27.5495055 / -81.0227323; Fort De Soto Park, St. Petersburg, 27.6327266 / -82.718157; Paynes Prairie Preserve State Park, Gainesville, 29.6068756 / -82.3031116

© SHUTTERSTOCK.COM/LAURIE E. WILSON

ASH-THROATED FLYCATCHER
Myiarchus cinerascens

Indisputably a western bird, individual ash-throated flycatchers have wintered in Florida regularly for the past several years.

Field marks: Brownish-gray head and back, gray bill, grayish throat and breast, very pale yellow wash on underside, light brown wings with pale beige-to-white wing bars, rufous primaries and tail.

Size: L: 8.5", WS: 12"

Similar species: Great-crested flycatcher is nearly identical but slightly larger and more brightly yellow and rufous.

Season: Winter

Habitat: Wide-open areas like dry scrublands and winter grasslands in Florida (deserts in the West)

Food source: Insects, spiders, some fruit and berries

Nest: In holes that occur naturally in trees, or left behind by other birds and animals (not in Florida)

Call: Sharp, high-pitched, trilling *ka-cheer*; also a single *pritt*

Hot spots: Bald Point State Park, Bald Point, 29.9377826 / -84.3381304; San Felasco Hammock Preserve State Park, Yellow Trail, Gainesville, 29.7180976 / -82.4636471; Lake Apopka Wildlife Drive, Apopka, 28.6691082 / -81.5574338; Dixie's Park, Merritt Island, 28.3836911 / -80.7148783; Weekiwachee Preserve (east of Shoal Line Boulevard), Spring Hill, 28.4630323 / -82.634697

GREAT CRESTED FLYCATCHER
Myiarchus crinitus

With its bright yellow underside and rusty orange tail, the largest local flycatcher provides plenty of hints to its identification.

Field marks: Gray-brown head with pronounced crest, paler throat, heavy black bill with pale pink base, olive back, dark wings with rufous primaries, white tips on flight feathers, gray breast, yellow underside, rufous tail.

Size: L: 8.5"–8.75", WS: 12"–14"

Similar species: Eastern phoebe is smaller and darker overall, with a dark gray tail. Ash-throated flycatcher is slightly smaller and paler overall, but very similarly marked.

Season: Summer throughout most of the state; winter south of US 41

Habitat: Woodlands with hardwood trees

Food source: Flying and crawling insects, caterpillars, butterflies, berries

Nest: In a natural or woodpecker-excavated cavity of a tree; in a human-made bird box

Call: One-syllable *wheeep*, often several in succession; also raspy *brrp, brrp, brrp*, repeated continuously

Hot spots: Every forest has its great-crested in season, so plan to look for this bird while you are out searching for breeding warblers and vireos in spring and early summer. A winter visit to any wildlife refuge or botanical garden in the Keys will almost certainly yield at least one great-crested sighting as well.

TROPICAL KINGBIRD
Tyrannus melancholicus

With its bright yellow belly and long bill, this western species looks decidedly different from the eastern and gray kingbirds found more commonly in south Florida.

Field marks: Gray head and back, dark mask; long, heavy bill; white chin, grayish breast, bright yellow underside, gray-brown wings and tail.

Size: L: 9"–9.5", WS: 14"–15"

Similar species: Western kingbird has a shorter bill and a whiter throat and breast. Eastern kingbird has a darker mantle, no yellow areas, and a white tail tip. Gray kingbird has no yellow plumage.

Season: Winter

Habitat: Woodlands near open areas

Food source: Flying insects, some small reptiles, spiders, fruit

Nest: High in a tree (not in Florida)

Call: A high, piercing series of twitters, sometimes in staccato bursts

Hot spots: St. Armand's Circle, Sarasota, 27.3199321 / -82.5768524; Stormwater Treatment Area 5/6, Clewiston, 26.4330582 / -80.9416786; Sem-Chi Rice Mill, Wellington, 26.6668727 / -80.4574621; Francis S. Taylor Wildlife Management Area, Everglades Parkway rest area, Alligator Alley, 26.1469438 / -80.6291342; Frog Pond Wildlife Management Area, Lucky Hammock, Homestead, 25.396439 / -80.566581

WESTERN KINGBIRD
Tyrannus verticalis

This western bird of open lands has expanded its wintering ground to south Florida.

Field marks: Gray head and back, small bill, grayish-white throat and breast, yellow underside, greenish-gray back, gray wings and tail with white tail edges in fresh adult plumage.

Size: L: 8.5"–9", WS: 15"–16"

Similar species: Tropical kingbird is slightly larger and has a large, heavy bill.

Season: Winter

Habitat: Open grassland near woodlands, often seen perched on a fence post or rail

Food source: Insects, some fruit

Nest: In deciduous trees (not in Florida)

Call: Tiny *pit-pit-pit*, followed by a rapid burst: *de-WEE-di-ti-ti*

Hot spots: Cox Road kingbird roost, Bartow, 27.8791651 / -81.7614834; Southern Glades Wildlife and Environmental Area—The Annex, Homestead, 25.384123 / -80.565; L31W Canal, Homestead, 25.3978115 / -80.5725288; Audubon Corkscrew Swamp Sanctuary, Corkscrew, 26.375442 / -81.6040206; Celery Fields, Fruitville, 27.3282173 / -82.4340248

EASTERN KINGBIRD
Tyrannus tyrannus

A black, gray, and white bird of open grasslands, this kingbird is easily identified by the white tip of its tail.

Field marks: Black head, gray back, white throat, grayish breast, white underside, dark gray wings, long black tail with white tip.

Size: L: 8.5", WS: 14"–15"

Similar species: Eastern phoebe is smaller, darker, has a yellowish wash on its underparts, and has no white tip on its tail. Gray kingbird is lighter gray and lacks the white tail tip.

Season: Summer

Habitat: Open grasslands, meadows, and farmland, where it often perches on fences and posts

Food source: Insects, berries, fruit

Nest: On a tree branch, or inside a barn or other structure

Call: Very high-pitched *dit-dit-dit-dit-dit-dit-derWEE, derWEE*; also a single *chee* note

Hot spots: Eastern kingbirds make themselves easy to see by perching on fences and fence posts, wires, the tops of buildings, and on top of shrubs, bobbing their white-tipped tails and singing almost continuously, especially in spring. Any drive through a rural area or a visit to a sanctuary or wildlife refuge with open fields will yield at least one sighting, probably a number of them.

© SHUTTERSTOCK.COM/TONOS

GRAY KINGBIRD
Tyrannus dominicensis

This Caribbean kingbird is very common along the edges of coastal swamps throughout the breeding season.

Field marks: Gray head, back, and tail; dark mask, darker gray wings with faint wing bars; white throat, breast, and underside; long, heavy bill.

Size: L: 9"–9.5", WS: 14"–15"

Similar species: Eastern kingbird is darker overall with a smaller bill and a white tail tip. Tropical and western kingbirds have a yellow underside.

Season: Summer

Habitat: Coastal wetlands, especially the edges of mangrove swamps; also frequently seen along the roadside

Food source: Insects, occasionally berries

Nest: In the branches of mangrove trees

Call: Song is a high, musical *peedle-TI-churee*; call is two quick, rising notes followed by a trill.

Hot spots: Crandon Park, Key Biscayne, 25.7089712 / -80.1536322; Everglades National Park, Long Pine Key Campground and Trail, 25.3985091 / -80.6554395; Point Ybel Lighthouse Beach Park, Sanibel, 26.4520609 / -82.0151281; Cedar Key State Museum, Cedar Key, 29.1506996 / -83.0480307; Bald Point State Park, Bald Point, 29.9377826 / -84.3381304

© SHUTTERSTOCK.COM/BRIAN LASENBY

SCISSOR-TAILED FLYCATCHER

Tyrannus forficatus

Unique among North American flycatchers for its luxuriously long tail, this southwestern bird often winters in south Florida.

Field marks: Pale gray overall with brown wings, pinkish flanks and undertail; very long, forked black tail (longer than its body) with white edges. Pink underwing patches are visible when flying.

Size: L: 14"–15", WS: 14"–15"

Similar species: No other Florida species has this coloring or lengthy tail.

Season: Winter

Habitat: Open grassland with occasional trees and brush

Food source: Insects, some fruit during winter

Nest: In a lone tree or shrub (not in Florida)

Call: Squeaky chatter, sometimes continuous and sometimes in phrases

Hot spots: Southern Glades Wildlife and Environmental Area—The Annex, Homestead, 25.384123 / -80.565; Frog Pond Wildlife Management Area, Homestead, 25.396439 / -80.566581; Everglades National Park, Flamingo, 25.1416 / -80.9255; Felda Church Road, Lehigh Acres, 26.5575107 / -81.4655674; Cox Road kingbird roost, Bartow, 27.8791651 / -81.7614834

SHRIKE

LOGGERHEAD SHRIKE
Lanius ludovicianus

Common in Florida, this little bird of prey perches on fence posts and wires for easy viewing.

Field marks: Gray cap, wide black mask from ear to ear, white throat, grayish-white breast and underside, gray shoulders and back, black wings with conspicuous white spot, long black tail. Black bill has an obvious hook.

Size: L: 8.5"–9.5", WS: 12"

Similar species: Northern mockingbird has a small black bill and no mask. Northern shrike is not generally found in Florida.

Season: Year-round

Habitat: Open areas with some trees and shrubs; usually found in or near farmlands and orchards

Food source: Insects, reptiles, amphibians, rodents, some birds

Nest: In trees or shrubs with thorns, or in large piles of brush or weeds

Call: Several variations: a harsh, buzzy *pffft*, a squeaky two-syllable *pi-TEET*, or a note filled with harmonics, followed by a high-pitched squeak

Hot spots: Every agricultural area and wildlife refuge has its population of shrikes, making this one of the most common birds of prey in Florida. Watch the electrical wires for it when you visit the most popular birding areas in the state for other species. You should have little trouble getting a good look at this bird.

VIREOS

RED-EYED VIREO
Vireo olivaceus

The most common and widespread member of the vireo family is the only one in the area with a red eye.

Field marks: Gray cap with black border, white eyebrow, red eye with dark gray line through it, white throat and breast, light olive green back, pale yellow undertail coverts, olive tail.

Size: L: 6", WS: 10"

Similar species: Philadelphia vireo has a black eye and bright yellow throat. Blue-headed vireo has distinct white "spectacles" around its black eyes. Black-whiskered vireo has a dark "whisker" stripe on its throat and a black eye. Yellow-green vireo has yellow cheeks and flanks, no black borders on its face, and a black eye.

Season: Spring migration in south Florida and the Keys; summer throughout the rest of the state

Habitat: Deciduous woodlands

Food source: Insects, gypsy moth caterpillars

Nest: On a tree branch, very close to the ground or as much as 60 feet up

Call: Repeated three-note phrases with a brief pause after each: *Here I am . . . where are you?*

Hot spots: Any woodland area with leafy trees is sure to contain at least one pair of red-eyed vireos. Suburban neighborhoods with mature trees often make hospitable environments for these virtually ubiquitous breeding birds.

YELLOW-THROATED VIREO
Vireo flavifrons

A little larger than other local vireos, this bird's bright yellow breast and wide, equally yellow eye ring makes it distinctive in spring woodlands filled with passerines.

Field marks: Yellow-green head, yellow spectacles, small gray bill, bright yellow throat and chest, extending to underside; white belly and rear, gray back, dark wings with two white wing bars, gray tail.

Size: L: 5"–6", WS: 9"–10"

Similar species: Yellow-throated warbler has distinctive black and white facial pattern. White-eyed vireo has yellow spectacles, but it has a white throat and gray underparts.

Season: Summer north of Tampa; spring and fall migration along the southern coasts

Habitat: Forests with mature oak and/or pine trees, often along rivers or streams

Food source: Caterpillars, insects, spiders, some berries

Nest: At the end of a tree limb, close to the ground or very high up

Call: Two syllables with a pause in between: *three-eight, three-o-eight*; or a slightly different *tree-o, treedie-o*, dropping at the end

Hot spots: Lettuce Lake County Park, Tampa, 28.0725 / -82.3754; Wekiwa Springs State Park, Apopka, 28.7337466 / -81.480324; San Felasco Hammock Preserve State Park, Yellow Trail, Gainesville, 29.7180976 / -82.4636471; Clearwater Lake Recreation Area Trailhead, Paisley, 28.97664 / -81.5502; Sweetwater Wetlands Park, Gainesville, 29.6151026 / -82.3254061

BLUE-HEADED VIREO
Vireo solitarius

Once known as solitary vireo, this bird can be mistaken for the similar Tennessee warbler, but its bespectacled face is the giveaway to its true identity.

Field marks: Bluish-gray head, bright white eye ring "spectacles," greenish-gray back, white throat and underside, yellowish flanks, dark wings with two distinct wing bars, greenish tail.

Size: L: 5.25"–5.5", WS: 8.5"–9.5"

Similar species: Tennessee warbler has a gray head and more yellow-green upper parts, no wing bars, and lacks the white spectacles. White-eyed vireo has yellow spectacles and a gray head.

Season: Winter

Habitat: Mixed deciduous and coniferous forests

Food source: Insects, berries

Nest: In a bush or tree, usually between 4 and 30 feet up

Call: A variety of squeaky syllables, either singly or in run-on groups: *twee-yoo, twee-mee, tweedle-yoo-twee-mee, tweedle-me-twee-yoo-twee-me*

Hot spots: Blue-headed vireo is a fairly common winter bird in Florida woodlands, at nature centers, and at wildlife refuges, and a trail walk through a county park often yields two or more. Before you travel to find one, take a walk in the woods in your own neighborhood and listen for its call.

WHITE-EYED VIREO
Vireo griseus

Look for the bright yellow spectacles and white iris to make a positive identification of this small vireo.

Field marks: Gray head, yellow eye ring and lores, small black bill, white throat, yellow flanks, grayish underside, olive back and wings, two bright white wing bars.

Size: L: 5", WS: 7.5"–8"

Similar species: Blue-headed vireo has white spectacles and a blue head. Yellow-throated vireo also has yellow spectacles, but it has a bright yellow throat.

Season: Year-round

Habitat: Ponds, dense woodlands, thickets

Food source: Insects, spiders, small reptiles, berries

Nest: In thickets, no more than 8 feet up

Call: Buzzy, wheezy *wink-doodly-do-a-vee*; variations of this

Hot spots: One of the dominant vireos throughout Florida, white-eyed vireo makes itself easy to find. Listen for its call on trails in any wooded area, and keep an eye out for it as it mingles with chickadees and kinglets. Mixed flocks of overwintering songbirds almost always include at least one of these birds.

© SHUTTERSTOCK.COM/JULIO SALGADO

BLACK-WHISKERED VIREO
Vireo altiloquus

This Florida specialty breeds in the Keys, making scattered spring appearances along the southern Atlantic and Gulf coasts.

Field marks: Gray crown, white line above the eye, gray line through the eye, large bill, dark gray "whisker" lines on throat, olive-brown back and wings, light yellow flanks, mostly white underside, olive tail.

Size: L: 6"–6.5", WS: 10"

Similar species: Red-eyed vireo has a black border along the white eyebrow and on both sides of the black stripe through its red eye; its back and wings are greener. Yellow-green vireo, a rarity in Florida, has no border along its eye stripe and has brighter yellow flanks and yellow underwing and undertail coverts.

Season: Breeding (summer) in the Keys and Everglades; spring along the coasts

Habitat: Mangrove swamps and hardwood hammocks at sea level

Food source: Insects, fruit

Nest: In the fork of a tree branch

Call: Several notes that slur downward at the end, with pauses between phrases; also a single-note *phweee* call

Hot spots: Long Key State Park, Layton, 24.814968 / -80.82018; No Name Key, Big Pine Key, 24.697714 / -81.3310146; Big Torch Key, Summerland Key, 24.7132512 / -81.4351607; National Key Deer National Wildlife Refuge, Big Pine Key, 24.7299933 / -81.3913751; Florida Keys Wildlife and Environmental Area, Sammy Creek Landing, Upper Sugarloaf Key, 24.6034609 / -81.5706199

JAYS

BLUE JAY
Cyanocitta cristata

Brightly colored, loud, and aggressive, the blue jay dominates bird feeders, neighborhoods, wooded parks, and forests throughout the eastern United States.

Field marks: Blue crest, black and white face, black bill, black ring across chest, white throat and underside, grayish breast, blue back and wings with one bright white wing bar, white tips on secondary flight feathers, long blue tail with white outer tips.

Size: L: 11", WS: 16"

Similar species: Eastern bluebird is smaller and has an all-blue mantle and ruddy breast. Florida scrub-jay has no crest or black facial markings, and its flanks and belly have faint gray-brown streaks.

Season: Year-round

Habitat: Wooded areas in neighborhoods and parks, forest edges, backyards

Food source: Seeds, nuts, fruit, berries, insects, very small rodents and reptiles, eggs from birds' nests

Nest: In trees, often close to the trunk; most likely in conifers

Call: A harsh *jaaaay*, singly or repeated four or five times; also mimic calls (mewing catbird, red-tailed hawk, and others), and a descending warble often compared to a rusty hinge

Hot spots: A popular and often numerous backyard bird, blue jays can be found in any yard with a feeder stocked with sunflower seeds or peanut pick-outs, as well as in neighborhood parks or random stands of mature trees.

FLORIDA SCRUB-JAY
Aphelocoma coerulescens

This very localized bird is the only bird species not found outside Florida. It's easy to see them at Merritt Island National Wildlife Refuge.

Field marks: Blue head, white forehead, fine white stripes on chin and throat, strong black bill, gray back, white breast and underside with faint tan or gray streaks, blue wings and tail. Juveniles have a gray head.

Size: L: 11"–12", WS: 13"–14"

Similar species: Blue jay has bold black and white facial pattern and tall blue crest. Eastern bluebird is smaller and has a ruddy breast.

Season: Year-round

Habitat: Low oak scrublands, mostly along the Atlantic and Gulf coasts

Food source: Insects, small snakes, mice, lizards, acorns, berries

Nest: In a sand live oak tree, close to the ground

Call: A harsh, rapid *weep, weep, weep*, or a single raspy *wsssht*

Hot spots: Pine Flatwoods Trail, Merritt Island National Wildlife Refuge, Mims, 28.7696529 / -80.7869339; Canaveral National Seashore Pay Station Area, Titusville, 28.6450209 / -80.682596; Lyonia Preserve, Deltona, 28.9238 / -81.2266; Ocala National Forest, Yearling Trail, Yellow Bluff, 29.2451613 / -81.6485506; Oscar Scherer State Park, Nokomis, 27.1734149 / -82.466383

CROWS

AMERICAN CROW
Corvus brachyrhynchos

Easily spotted in neighborhoods and parking lots, on buildings and beaches, and in large flocks in parks, crows are among the most common birds in America.

Field marks: All black with a long, solid black bill; wide wings, a short tail that fans in flight. Crows flap their wings continuously in flight.

Size: L: 17.5", WS: 35"–40"

Similar species: Fish crow is virtually identical but has a higher, more nasal call.

Season: Year-round

Habitat: Farm fields, woods, ocean coastline, areas inhabited by humans

Food source: Carrion, scraps scavenged from human discards, fruit, seeds, small animals and birds, bird eggs, insects

Nest: High in a tree, often more than 90 feet up

Call: The familiar *caw, caw*; also a rhythmic *caw-haw, cah-caw-haw* and a staccato series of clicks

Hot spots: Look in any parking area, on any beach, or in city parks to find this ubiquitous bird, as well as in your own backyard if you feed birds with a platform or ground feeder.

FISH CROW
Corvus ossifragus

Slightly smaller but nearly identical to the American crow, this year-round resident usually identifies itself with its more nasal call.

Field marks: All black with a black bill, wings almost as long as the tail, tail fan-shaped in flight.

Size: L: 15"–17", WS: 32"–38"

Similar species: American crow is virtually identical but larger, with a harsher call.

Season: Year-round

Habitat: Any body of water in the state

Food source: Aquatic invertebrates, bird eggs, berries, seeds, carrion

Nest: At the top of a tree or in a tall shrub

Call: Like an American crow with a sinus condition: a thin, nasal *caw-hah*, singly or in pairs; also a single, nasal *cook*

Hot spots: Fish crows are nearly as populous as American crows in Florida, though it can be tricky to pick one out if you don't hear it call. Visit any seashore, gulf shore, lake, river, or canal and watch for a flock of large black birds, or individuals standing on fences or posts. Wait to hear them call to be sure you've found the fish crows.

SWALLOWS AND SWIFT

PURPLE MARTIN
Progne subis

This colony nester often lives in human-made martin houses, near a convenient water feature or open beach.

Field marks: Male is deep purple-blue overall, with a small black bill and wings as long as its slightly forked tail. Female has deep blue cap, back, wings, and tail; gray forehead and collar, gray-smudged breast and underside.

Size: L: 7.5"–8.5", WS: 16"–18"

Similar species: All swallow species are smaller. Tree swallow has bright white underparts. Cliff swallow has an orange face and grayish underparts with a rufous wash.

Season: Summer

Habitat: Woodlands, neighborhoods, and open fields near a prominent water feature (ocean, bay, lake, river)

Food source: Flying insects

Nest: In colonies in a human-made martin house; in a series of tree cavities in a woodland area

Call: A series of whistles and gurgles, differing between male and female birds; also a simple *seet, seet, seet*

Hot spots: Many coastal and lake neighborhoods have martin houses that can be viewed from residential streets, making them the easiest places to see purple martins—but these are private property, so I can't list them here. The following public areas also host martin colonies: "Viera" Ritch Grissom Memorial Wetlands, Melbourne, 28.228577 / -80.7604659; Peaceful Waters Sanctuary, Wellington, 26.631443 / -80.2332294; Watermelon Pond Wildlife and Environmental Area, Newberry, 29.5803805 / -82.6070997; Point Ybel Lighthouse Beach Park, Sanibel, 26.4520609 / -82.0151281; Pinecraft Park, Southgate, 27.3189746 / -82.5037765

NORTHERN ROUGH-WINGED SWALLOW
Stelgidopteryx serripennis

Most swallows socialize in colonies, but this one prefers to nest and forage alone or in pairs.

Field marks: Mud-brown head, back, wings, and tail; lighter brown throat and breast, white underside, square tail. Juvenile may have bright reddish wing bars.

Size: L: 5.5", WS: 12"–14"

Similar species: Bank swallow has a bright white throat, chest, and underside; barn swallow has a long, thin tail with a fork at the end. Female tree swallow is dark gray and has white throat, breast, and underside.

Season: Summer north of US 41; winter in south Florida and the Keys

Habitat: Rivers, streams, ponds, wetlands, canals, other waterways

Food source: Insects, either flying above water or on the surface

Nest: Under a bridge, in a cavity on a cliff, in a retaining wall on a man-made waterway, or in a hollow dug in sand

Call: Single, high-pitched *jeet*

Hot spots: Bald Point State Park, Bald Point, 29.9377826 / -84.3381304; Sweetwater Wetlands Park, Gainesville, 29.6151026 / -82.3254061; Newnan's Lake, Palm Point Park, Gainesville, 29.6364 / -82.2382; Fort De Soto Park, St. Petersburg, 27.6327266 / -82.718157; Fran Reich Preserve SFWMD, Parkland, 26.3545316 / -80.2837256

BANK SWALLOW
Riparia riparia

Small and long-tailed, this swallow prefers lakes, creeks, and river-banks with trees nearby.

Field marks: Brown head, back, wings, and tail; white face with brown mask and pale forehead, white throat, brown collar, white breast and underside; thin, forked tail.

Size: L: 4.75"–5.25", WS: 11"–13"

Similar species: Northern rough-winged swallow has a light brown throat, breast, and underside; no collar; a square tail. Female tree swallow is grayer and lacks the dark collar.

Season: Spring and fall migration

Habitat: Lakesides, creeks, riverbanks, larger bodies of water

Food source: Flying insects

Nest: In colonies, digging tunnels in riverbanks

Call: Long, scratchy, unmusical chatter; also a single, two-syllable note: *t-jip*

Hot spots: Lake Apopka Wildlife Drive, Apopka, 28.6691082 / -81.5574338; Fort De Soto Park, St. Petersburg, 27.6327266 / -82.718157; Stump Pass Beach State Park, Manasota Key, 26.9022934 / -82.346805; Browns Farm Road, Sixmile Bend, 26.6321916 / -80.5711555; Frog Pond Wildlife Management Area, Lucky Hammock, Homestead, 25.396439 / -80.566581

TREE SWALLOW
Tachycineta bicolor

The bright blue tree swallow often nests or roosts in boxes meant for eastern bluebirds.

Field marks: Male has bright blue head, back, and rump with white undertail coverts; bright white throat, breast, and underside; black wings and tail; tail is slightly forked. Female is gray above and white below.

Size: L: 5.75", WS: 12.5"–14.5"

Similar species: Cliff swallow has a rufous face, dark throat, and a grayish-white breast with rufous streaks. Barn swallow has a darker blue back, an orange face and lighter orange underside, and a deeply forked tail.

Season: Winter

Habitat: Open fields with stands of trees near marshes, swamps, lakeshores, rivers, or ponds

Food source: Flying and crawling insects, spiders

Nest: In boxes usually meant for bluebirds; also in tree cavities (not in Florida)

Call: High-pitched, buzzy, chattery *cheet-cheet-cheet* calls with variations in speed and pitch; also simple *treet* note in flight

Hot spots: When you visit any salt marsh, riverside, lakeshore, or other body of water in winter, tree swallows will be very much in evidence. Darting back and forth over the water to catch mosquitoes and other flying insects, they rarely stop to allow you a long look, but you will have the chance to admire their bright blue backs and wings as they glide past you.

CLIFF SWALLOW
Petrochelidon pyrrhonota

This colony nester builds closely packed, volcano-shaped mud cylinders and raises its young within a community.

Field marks: Dark blue cap, orange face, dark blue throat, small black bill, buff collar, grayish underside with some light rufous streaking, light rufous rump, dark wings and tail.

Size: L: 5.5", WS: 12"–13.5"

Similar species: Barn swallow has an orange face and throat, a lighter orange underside, and a deeply forked tail.

Season: Spring and fall migration

Habitat: Open farm fields, meadows, or lakes near buildings or cliffs

Food source: Flying and crawling insects

Nest: In colonies, building adjoining mud cylinders on the sides of cliffs or buildings

Call: A repeated, descending *peeer*, also a crackling series of calls like the sound of crumpling plastic wrap

Hot spots: Lake Apopka Wildlife Drive, Apopka, 28.6691082 / -81.5574338; Browns Farm Road, Sixmile Bend, 26.6321916 / -80.5711555; Point Ybel Lighthouse Beach Park, Sanibel, 26.4520609 / -82.0151281; Celery Fields, Fruitville, 27.3282173 / -82.4340248; FL 50 John's River bridge, Christmas, 28.5434989 / -80.9335837

BARN SWALLOW
Hirundo rustica

The bird that gives all swallowtails their name, this brightly colored migrant and summer resident often follows working farm machinery to catch insects unearthed by plows and harvesters.

Field marks: Male has dark blue cap, mask, back, wings, and tail; orange face and throat, lighter orange breast and underside; long, deeply forked tail. Female has a somewhat whiter underside.

Size: L: 6.75"–7.5", WS: 13"–15"

Similar species: Cliff swallow has a gray collar and underside, a duller orange face, and a dark blue throat.

Season: Spring and fall migration through central and south Florida; summer in northern Florida

Habitat: Farm fields with barns, neighborhoods, lakes, wetlands

Food source: Insects of open fields: grasshoppers, crickets, moths, and others

Nest: In colonies, in the corners of barns and garages or under bridges

Call: High-pitched, constant chatter in groups of three or four notes; also a *chee-deep* chip note

Hot spots: The most common swallow in the region, barn swallows can be found in season in any area of open land, especially if there is a structure—a bridge, pavilion, barn, or porch—under which they can build nests. A summer drive through agricultural lands or through your favorite wildlife management area in northern Florida or the Panhandle will almost certainly yield views of barn swallows hunting down insects. Watch the utility wires along these roadsides for rows of swallows (which may include bank or tree swallows in the proper seasons).

BRAD CARLSON

CAVE SWALLOW
Petrochelidon fulva

Just a few colonies of these birds live in south Florida; of the two races in the United States, Florida hosts the Caribbean one.

Field marks: Small, flat head with dark blue cap, dark patch over eye, rufous head, blue back, brown wings and tail, buff chest, white underside. Juveniles have more brown and are less vibrant.

Size: L: 5"–6", WS: 12"–13"

Similar species: Cliff swallow has a buff rump, and its rufous areas are darker. Barn swallow has a blue hood and a deeply forked tail.

Season: Summer in south Florida; a few individuals migrate along the coasts.

Habitat: As there are few if any caves in Florida, these birds nest under bridges.

Food source: Flying insects

Nest: Mud packed onto cement walls under bridges

Call: A repeated *sreet*—continuous, disorganized notes

Hot spots: Cutler Ridge roost, SW 216th Street and Florida's Turnpike, Miami, 25.56639 / -80.36215; Portofino Plaza swallow colony, Miami, 25.4747572 / -80.4456301; Sixmile Bend Ponds, Belle Glade, 26.6442271 / -80.5842876; Browns Farm Road, Sixmile Bend, 26.6321916 / -80.5711555; Kendall Indian Hammocks Park, Kendall, 25.6953 / -80.3734

CHIMNEY SWIFT
Chaetura pelagica

Birders refer to this swift as "a cigar with wings," noting its elongated oblong shape in flight.

Field marks: Gray and black overall, paler at the throat; rounded at the head and tail, sometimes with the tail fanned in flight. Wings extend well beyond the tail when in repose (clinging to the side of a building, for example).

Size: L: 5.25"–5.5", WS: 12"–14"

Similar species: Bank swallow is brown above and white below. Northern rough-winged swallow is brown overall with bright rufous wing bars. Tree swallow is distinctly blue above and white below; juvenile tree swallows also have a white face, breast, and underside.

Season: Spring and fall migration in south Florida and the Keys; breeding season throughout most of the state

Habitat: Buildings with tall chimneys: schools, churches, industrial structures; also open habitat for feeding on the wing

Food source: Insects, captured entirely in flight

Nest: In a nest made from twigs and the bird's saliva, stuck to the inside of a chimney or belfry

Call: A high, rapid, continuous chattering in flight

Hot spots: Chimney swifts are rarely seen perched or clinging to a wall; they are nearly always seen best when they congregate around a smokestack or chimney before they roost for the night. College campuses, the tops of parking garages, and small town squares are often the best places to see them shortly before dusk. During the day, these swifts can be seen catching insects over bodies of water or any area with a lot of bugs. Every wildlife refuge, park, and wetland in Florida has its own summer population.

TITMOUSE AND CHICKADEE

TUFTED TITMOUSE
Baeolophus bicolor

From forests to feeders, this friend of chickadees is a dependable sighting on any woodland outing.

Field marks: Gray crest, back of head, back, wings, and tail; white face with large black eye and black forehead; grayish-white throat, breast, and underside; light orange flanks, white undertail coverts.

Size: L: 6.5", WS: 9.75"–10.75"

Similar species: Blue-gray gnatcatcher is smaller and bluer, has no crest, and has a white eye ring and a black tail.

Season: Year-round

Habitat: Deciduous forests, neighborhoods with mature trees, parks, backyards

Food source: Insects, spiders, nuts, seeds, suet

Nest: In a tree cavity or birdhouse

Call: A musical *peter, peter, peter, peter,* also a rough, scolding *shrii, shrii, shrii* and a series of very high *ti, ti, ti* sounds

Hot spots: Tufted titmouse is one of the most common birds of the Florida woodlands and neighborhoods north of the Everglades, and virtually every backyard feeder filled with sunflower seeds receives daily visits from this bird. The titmouse often associates with Carolina chickadees, so if you're on a woodland walk and you haven't detected a titmouse, watch groups of chickadees to see which of their many allies they have with them.

241

CAROLINA CHICKADEE

Poecile carolinensis

Florida's only chickadee is just a little drabber than its black-capped cousin, but where their range overlaps farther north, they often hybridize—making it even harder to tell them apart.

Field marks: Black cap dipping below the eye, black throat, white face and breast, buffy underside; gray wings and tail.

Size: L: 4.5"–5", WS: 7"–8"

Similar species: Black-capped chickadee is nearly identical with a little whiter edging on its wings, and its range does not extend to Florida. White-breasted nuthatch is larger, with a black hood that does not extend to the eye, and a bluish back and wings with striking black and white detail. Blackpoll warbler has black and white streaks on its flanks, a white underside, and brown and white wings.

Season: Year-round through northern and central Florida

Habitat: Wooded areas, including forests, swamps, parks, and residential neighborhoods with trees

Food source: Insects, as well as seeds from bird feeders

Nest: In a hole they excavate or find in a tree

Call: A descending four-note whistle: *TOO-dee-di-di*; also a high-pitched twiddle followed by a raspy *dee-dee-dee-dee-dee-dee* series

Hot spots: Any birding outing in a wooded park or neighborhood north of Tampa should yield at least one chickadee, and probably many more. Sightings are more numerous in human-populated areas where feeders are plentiful and kept filled.

NUTHATCHES AND CREEPER

RED-BREASTED NUTHATCH
Sitta canadensis

This little winter visitor prefers the forests of northern and central Florida.

Field marks: Male has black cap and eye stripe, white eyebrow and throat, sharp black bill, red-orange underparts, gray-blue back and tail, white stripes on outer tail feathers. Female is slightly less brightly colored.

Size: L: 4.5", WS: 8"–8.5"

Similar species: White-breasted nuthatch is larger, lacks the eye stripe, and has a white breast. Brown-headed nuthatch has a brown cap, no eyebrow, a white-to-buff underside, and less white on the outer tail feathers.

Season: Winter

Habitat: Mixed forests of deciduous and coniferous trees, as well as backyards and feeders in neighborhoods

Food source: Nuts, seeds, insects, spiders, clusters of insect eggs

Nest: In a tree cavity (not in Florida)

Call: *Toot, toot, toot,* like a toy horn; also an extended trill

Hot spots: Northern Florida is the southern boundary of this bird's range, and sightings tend to be a single bird for a week or so. Here are some places where these nuthatches have spent more than one winter recently: Elinor Klapp-Phipps Park, Tallahassee, 30.535666 / -84.28821; Guana Tolomato Matanzas National Estuarine Research Reserve, St. Augustine, 30.0074 / -81.3325; Pine Meadows Conservation Area, Eustis, 28.88406 / -81.66308

WHITE-BREASTED NUTHATCH
Sitta carolinensis

Feeding upside down on a tree trunk, the larger local nuthatch frequents feeders as well as mature trees.

Field marks: Black cap, white face, black eye; long, upturned bill; gray back and wings, white breast and underparts, rufous tinted undertail coverts (white in female), gray tail.

Size: L: 5"–6", WS: 10"–11"

Similar species: Red-breasted nuthatch is smaller, has a black eye stripe, and has reddish underparts. Brown-headed nuthatch is smaller and has a brown cap.

Season: Year-round

Habitat: Mixed forests with oak trees, neighborhoods with mature trees, parks

Food source: Insects, seeds, nuts, suet

Nest: In a nest box, tree cavity, or hole abandoned by woodpeckers

Call: A honking *waah, waah, waah, waah*, all on one note; also a faster series of a single higher note

Hot spots: Elinor Klapp-Phipps Park, Tallahassee, 30.535666 / -84.28821; Tall Timbers Research Station, Tallahassee, 30.6567786 / -84.2087889; St. George Island State Park, Eastpoint, 29.7155 / -84.7535; Harriman Circle Park, Tallahassee, 30.4745686 / -84.2529586; Wakulla Springs State Park, Wakulla Springs, 30.2335 / -84.3037

BROWN-HEADED NUTHATCH
Sitta pusilla

If you hear one squeaky little nuthatch, chances are there are several close by.

Field marks: Brown cap extending through the eye, white cheek; long, dark bill; white spot on nape, buff breast and underside, gray shoulders and back, gray and brown wings, gray tail with some white on outer feathers.

Size: L: 4.5"–5", WS: 7.5"–8"

Similar species: White-breasted nuthatch is larger, has a black hood and bright white face, and blue-gray back and wings. Red-breasted nuthatch has a black crown, a bright white eyebrow, a black line through the eye, and a rosy underside.

Season: Year-round

Habitat: Forests of southern pine species: loblolly, longleaf, shortleaf, and slash

Food source: Insects, spiders, and other creatures that live under pine bark

Nest: In a dead tree, or in a hole made by another nuthatch or a woodpecker in a tree or utility pole

Call: A high, repeated squeak, much like a pet's chew toy

Hot spots: Bald Point State Park, Bald Point, 29.9377826 / -84.3381304; Longleaf Flatwoods Reserve, Hawthorne, 29.5654133 / -82.1889567; Wekiwa Springs State Park, Apopka, 28.7337466 / -81.480324; St. Sebastian River Preserve State Park, Micco, 27.839059 / -80.5438571; Everglades National Park, Long Pine Key Campground and Trail, 25.3985091 / -80.6554395

BROWN CREEPER
Certhia americana

Remarkably suited to blend seamlessly into the trees it climbs, this bird starts at the bottom of the tree and makes its way up as it hunts for food, then starts over at the bottom.

Field marks: Mottled brown head, back, and wings; distinctive buff band above primaries on each wing, downward-curving bill, white breast and belly, buff rear, solid brown rump and tail.

Size: L: 5.25", WS: 7"–8"

Similar species: No other local species looks or behaves like a brown creeper.

Season: Winter

Habitat: Mixed woodlands, with deciduous trees preferred

Food source: Insects, seeds, nuts, suet

Nest: Wedged behind the bark of a tree

Call: Very high-pitched *tsee-tsitsowa-SEE-tsee;* also *tsee-tila-see-see-see-see*

Hot spots: Brown creeper's range is very limited in Florida, with scattered sightings generally no farther south than Gainesville. These spots have reported single overwintering birds in the past few years; sightings at other parks have been single individuals for a day or two: St. Marks National Wildlife Refuge, St. Marks, 30.1515653 / -84.1473314; Elinor Klapp-Phipps Park, Tallahassee, 30.535666 / -84.28821; Hogtown Creek Greenway between Northwest 8th and 16th Avenues, Gainesville, 29.661262 / -82.3633862

WRENS

CAROLINA WREN
Thryothorus ludovicianus

Don't be deceived by the name—this expressive wren's range extends southward to the tip of Florida.

Field marks: Brown cap, bright white eyebrow edged in black, brown eye line, buff cheek, white throat; buff-orange chest, flanks, and underside; brown back, brown wings barred in black, white undertail coverts with black barring, short brown tail.

Size: L: 5.5", WS: 7.5"

Similar species: All other local wrens are smaller. Marsh wren has white eyebrow, but its crown is black.

Season: Year-round

Habitat: Edges of woodlands with lots of brushy shrubs

Food source: Insects, spiders

Nest: In a crack between rocks, or in a crevice or hole in a building

Call: Often transcribed as *teakettle, teakettle, teakettle*; sometimes very quick, but often slower

Hot spots: Carolina wrens are widespread and numerous in Florida, and they should be fairly easy to find because of their enthusiastic and highly recognizable song. Before you cross the state looking for one, check the brushy areas in your own neighborhood or the shrubs and thickets in your nearest park. These wrens are fond of residential areas and sometimes visit suet feeders in winter.

HOUSE WREN
Troglodytes aedon

Tiny birds with a lot to say, house wrens spend the winter in Florida. Check parks, woodlands, and brushy areas of your own backyard for this fierce little migrant.

Field marks: Light brown (or light gray) head and body with buff or pale gray throat and breast; faint white eyebrow and long, downward-curving yellow bill; brownish (or grayish) wings with darker horizontal barring. Warm brown undertail coverts and tail with black barring; tail is often held upright at a nearly 90-degree angle from the body.

Size: L: 4"–5", WS: 6"–7"

Similar species: Winter wren is smaller and more distinctly barred. Carolina wren is larger, more rufous, and has a bright white eyebrow extending from bill to nape.

Season: Winter

Habitat: Wooded areas in parks, neighborhoods, and along farm fields; also in forest thickets and shrubs

Food source: Insects found on trees and shrubs, caterpillars, spiders

Nest: In a sheltered opening in a shrub, a tree cavity, or a human-made nest box

Call: One of the most exuberant in the avian kingdom: a series of musical trills, whistles, and song phrases sung without breaks; repeated note for note at regular intervals

Hot spots: If you don't have house wrens in your residential area, here are some spots where birders see them regularly, and often in quantity: Mead Botanical Gardens, Winter Park, 28.5836 / -81.3586; Fort De Soto Park, St. Petersburg, 27.6327266 / -82.718157; Babcock-Webb Wildlife Management Area, Punta Gorda, 26.8582653 / -81.9401121; Lake Apopka North Shore, Astatula, 28.6740878 / -81.7059258; Elinor Klapp-Phipps Park, Tallahassee, 30.535666 / -84.28821

WINTER WREN
Troglodytes hiemalis

The region's smallest wren brings us a sparkling song from deep within thickets and forest understory.

Field marks: Brown cap with distinct buff eyebrow, light brown face, buff throat, thin straight bill, brown back and tail, short tail held nearly at a right angle to the body, dark brown flanks with heavy black barring, yellow legs.

Size: L: 4", WS: 5.5"–6"

Similar species: House wren is larger and lighter colored. Carolina wren is larger, has a downward-curving bill and a bright white eyebrow.

Season: Winter

Habitat: Brushy areas, thickets, woodland understory near streams

Food source: Insects and tiny invertebrates among leaf matter on the ground

Nest: In a shrub or thicket or among a fallen tree's roots (not in Florida)

Call: A high-pitched, lengthy phrase of twitters, whistles, and at least one long trill, repeated at intervals exactly the same way. While the house wren's song has a laughing, chattering quality, the winter wren's song is more similar to a piccolo.

Hot spots: Sightings of winter wren tend to be single birds lingering for a few days or up to a month. These spots have hosted a winter wren for longer than a few days: St. Marks National Wildlife Refuge, St. Marks, 30.1515653 / -84.1473314; Lake Jackson Mounds Archaeological State Park, Tallahassee, 30.501421 / -84.3134842; Ponce de Leon Springs State Park, Ponce De Leon, 30.7225061 / -85.9310246

DOMINIC SHERONY

SEDGE WREN
Cistothorus platensis

This shy wren spends the winter in Florida's open grasslands and marshes.

Field marks: Tawny head and body with white throat, darkly striped crown with buff eyebrow, back streaked in black, light brown wings with dark barring, tawny breast and flanks; short, vertical-angled tail barred in black.

Size: L: 4.5", WS: 5.5"–6"

Similar species: Marsh wren is bright rufous with a black cap and white eyebrow.

Season: Winter

Habitat: Open grasslands and marshes with tall reeds, sedges, and cattails

Food source: Insects, spiders

Nest: Woven from surrounding vegetation, low among tall grasses

Call: Two single *chit* notes, followed by a quick series of six or seven dry, staccato notes on the same pitch; also a single, dry *chit* note

Hot spots: While sedge wrens use the whole state through the winter months, sightings are far more plentiful north of Orlando. Bald Point State Park, Bald Point, 29.9377826 / -84.3381304; Barr Hammock Preserve, Levy Loop Trail, Micanopy, 29.5165735 / -82.3061907; Merritt Island National Wildlife Refuge, Black Point Wildlife Drive, Titusville, 28.6411839 / -80.7774067; Celery Fields, Fruitville, 27.3282173 / -82.4340248; Lake Apopka North Shore, Astatula, 28.6740878 / -81.7059258

MARSH WREN
Cistothorus palustris

Living up to their name, these tiny wrens fill low marshland with their chip notes and rattling song.

Field marks: Black cap, white eyebrow, brown cheek, long gray bill, whitish throat and breast, rufous back and wings, light rufous flanks and undertail coverts, darker wing primaries, rufous tail barred in black and held at a nearly 90-degree angle from body.

Size: L: 5", WS: 6"–7"

Similar species: Sedge wren is lighter colored overall. Carolina, winter, and house wrens all prefer woodland habitat.

Season: Year-round in the Panhandle, winter throughout the rest of the state

Habitat: Open freshwater marshes with tall vegetation, wetlands near the Atlantic and Gulf coasts

Food source: Insects, tiny invertebrates

Nest: Near the ground and built to be entered from the side, toward the base of tall grasses and reeds

Call: Buzzy but musical elongated trill, repeated at intervals; also one- or two-syllable *chut* note

Hot spots: St. Marks National Wildlife Refuge, St. Marks, 30.1515653 / -84.1473314; Paynes Prairie Preserve State Park, Gainesville, 29.6068756 / -82.3031116; Lake Apopka North Shore, Astatula, 28.6740878 / -81.7059258; Merritt Island National Wildlife Refuge, Black Point Wildlife Drive, Titusville, 28.6411839 / -80.7774067; Estero Bay Preserve State Park, Winkler Point, Fort Meyers, 26.4800134 / -81.898452

KINGLETS AND GNATCATCHER

GOLDEN-CROWNED KINGLET
Regulus satrapa

Watch for constant motion in woodlands with conifers to find this tiny bird, the smaller of the two local kinglets.

Field marks: Bright orange and yellow cap outlined in black, white eyebrow, black eye line, white throat, greenish-gray back and breast, grayish-white underparts, black and greenish wings with white bar across secondaries, greenish tail with dark gray end.

Size: L: 3.5"–4", WS: 6.5"–7"

Similar species: Ruby-crowned kinglet is slightly larger and lacks bold facial pattern; males have a raised red crest during breeding season. Golden-winged warbler is larger and grayer overall, with bright yellow patches on wings.

Season: Winter

Habitat: Mixed woodlands with conifers, boreal woodlands

Food source: Insects, tree sap, seeds

Nest: On a branch in a conifer, generally 30 feet up or more

Call: Very high-pitched *tsee* or *tsee-tsee-tsee*; also a song that begins with high *tsee-tsee* notes and ends in a tumbling warble

Hot spots: St. Marks National Wildlife Refuge, St. Marks, 30.1515653 / -84.1473314; Elinor Klapp-Phipps Park, Tallahassee, 30.535666 / -84.28821; Blackwater River State Forest, Milton, 30.8392703 / -86.9411285; Escambia Water Management District, Century, 30.9661102 / -87.2358227; Big Lagoon State Park, Perdido Key, 30.3138313 / -87.4133835

RUBY-CROWNED KINGLET
Regulus calendula

Always in motion, the larger of the two area kinglets makes it very difficult to get a good look at its ruby crown.

Field marks: Male has light olive green head and back, white eye ring, bright red crest (visible only in breeding season), olive-washed breast, lighter flanks, whitish undertail coverts, dark wings with one white wing bar, dark tail. Female is identical but lacks the ruby crown.

Size: L: 4.25", WS: 6.5"–7.5"

Similar species: Golden-crowned kinglet has a bright orange and yellow crown in all seasons. Tennessee warbler is larger and has a gray head and bright white underparts.

Season: Winter

Habitat: Woodlands and forests with both deciduous and coniferous trees

Food source: Insects, seeds, fruit

Nest: Hidden in a tree, suspended from a high branch

Call: Three to five *tsee-tsee-tsee* notes, followed by an exuberant series of musical chirps and trills

Hot spots: Ruby-crowned kinglets are plentiful throughout the winter months, and just about any grove of trees, thicket, nature center, or park will have its own population. While they once confined themselves to the northern parts of the state, they now appear in Flamingo at the southern tip of Everglades National Park and even in Key Largo's botanical gardens. They are early migrants, heading north by the end of March and vanishing from the Panhandle in the first few days of April.

BLUE-GRAY GNATCATCHER
Polioptila caerulea

The unbroken color, bright white eye ring, and long, black tail with white outer feathers will help you identify this frenetic bird.

Field marks: Bright blue-gray cap, nape, and back; black forehead (male only), gray cheek, whitish throat, grayish-white breast and underside, gray wings with white tertials, black tail with white outer feathers.

Size: L: 4.25"–4.5", WS: 6"–6.75"

Similar species: Warbling vireo has no cap or eye ring, has a pale white eyebrow, and is plain gray above and whitish below with yellowish flanks.

Season: Year-round; winter only in south Florida

Habitat: Deciduous woodlands

Food source: Gnats, as well as many other insects, butterflies, spiders, bees, and wasps

Nest: Fastened to a tree branch, with no specific height preference

Call: *Bees, bu-bu-bees, bees*, with a buzzy spiraling downward note on each *bees*; also a *speez, speez, speez* call, all on one note

Hot spots: Just about every area with trees attracts this gnatcatcher, so chances are good that you will come across at least one when you go looking for warblers and other passerines in spring, or for resident birds in winter. They often will come close to you in what seems like a deliberate play for attention, hopping from branch to branch as actively as a kinglet and singing their buzzy song.

THRUSHES

EASTERN BLUEBIRD
Sialia sialis

Bright blue above and bright orange below, this folk symbol of happiness battles all spring and summer to keep its nest box, eggs, and nestlings safe from house sparrows and other aggressive raiders.

Field marks: Male has bright blue head, back, wings, and tail; orange throat, breast, and flanks; white belly and undertail coverts, black primaries. Female has gray head and back, blue leading edge of wing and primaries; light orange throat, breast, and flanks; white belly and undertail, blue tail.

Size: L: 7"–7.75", WS: 12"–13"

Similar species: Cerulean warbler is smaller, has black streaks on its flanks and two white wing bars, and lacks the orange throat and breast. Black-throated blue warbler is smaller and has a black face, black stripe on flanks, and no orange. Blue jay is much larger, has a high crest and a white breast, and has no orange. Florida scrub-jay is much larger and has no orange areas.

Season: Year-round

Habitat: Open grasslands, farm fields, pastures, parks with grassy areas and trees

Food source: Insects and invertebrates; readily comes to mealworm feeders in backyards

Nest: In a tree cavity, nest box, disused woodpecker hole, or a hole in a utility pole

Call: A short series of syrupy notes and trills, sometimes interlaced with sharp, raspy *chic* notes

Hot spots: Many farm fields and other open areas attract bluebirds throughout the season, so check in your local area before traveling a long distance to find them. The following hot spots offer very dependable bluebird sightings: Paynes Prairie Preserve State Park, La Chua Trail, Gainesville, 29.6068756 / -82.3031116; Elinor Klapp-Phipps Park, Tallahassee, 30.535666 / -84.28821; Myakka River State Park, Myakka City, 27.2405033 / -82.3148167; Babcock-Webb Wildlife Management Area, Punta Gorda, 26.8582653 / -81.9401121; Three Lakes Wildlife Management Area, Osceola County, 27.9312364 / -81.1522293

AMERICAN ROBIN
Turdus migratorius

The unofficial harbinger of spring in most of North America, robins come in winter to every mowed lawn, park, neighborhood, wooded area, and roadside rest stop in Florida.

Field marks: Dark gray head, broken white eye ring, yellow bill, thin white lines on throat, bright orange breast and belly, white undertail coverts, gray back and wings, gray tail with white outermost tail feathers. Juveniles have a lighter breast and belly covered in gray spots.

Size: L: 10", WS: 14"–17"

Similar species: Eastern towhee has an all-black head, white breast, and rufous flanks. Female eastern bluebird is smaller, a lighter gray overall, and has blue wing feathers.

Season: Winter, with some scattered individuals in northern Florida year-round

Habitat: Open woodlands, neighborhoods, commercial and industrial areas with mowed lawns, gardens, farm fields, and grasslands with trees.

Food source: Worms, grubs, berries, fruit, some insects

Nest: In a tree or on a human-made platform under shelter (like the joist of a porch roof), often in full view

Call: Series of musical notes and triplets with brief pauses: *wheedie, wee, wheedio, wheedie, wee*; also a less-melodious five-note phrase: *chi-chi-chi-chi-chi*

Hot spots: Look out any window onto a lawn in winter, and robins will be performing their hop-and-listen behavior as they hunt for invertebrates just under the ground's surface. Every neighborhood and mowed, landscaped open space in Florida becomes a robin hot spot once the weather turns colder up north.

WOOD THRUSH
Hylocichla mustelina

The wood thrush's bright rufous cap, nape, and back differentiate it from other thrushes, but its song is the real identifier—one many birders consider the most beautiful in the forest.

Field marks: Bright rufous cap, nape, and back; black and white–striped cheek, white eye ring, black and pink bill, white throat streaked with black; white breast and belly with large, heavy black spots; white undertail coverts, brownish-orange wings and tail. The wood thrush stands taller and more upright than other thrushes.

Size: L: 7.75", WS: 13"–14"

Similar species: Veery has a lighter orange back and light brown spots on its breast, with a clear white underside. Swainson's thrush is light brown with a buff and brown–striped cheek and light yellow spectacles. Gray-cheeked thrush is light brown with a gray cheek and buff breast with a dense covering of dark spots. Hermit thrush has a light brown cap, nape, back, and wings and a bright red tail.

Season: Spring and fall migration

Habitat: Deciduous woods with a lush, thriving understory

Food source: Insects, fruit

Nest: In a tree or shrub, at least 6 feet off the ground

Call: A three-part song, often described inadequately as *ee-o-lay*, begins with a series of high piccolo notes, followed by a lower note and ending in a harmonically rich, buzzy trill; also a *wap-wap-wap* call note and a very rapid *bip-bip-bip-bip-bip* clucking call.

Hot spots: Elinor Klapp-Phipps Park, Tallahassee, 30.535666 / -84.28821; Paynes Prairie Preserve State Park, Bolen Bluff Trail, Gainesville, 29.5587838 / -82.3245401; Mead Botanical Gardens, Winter Park, 28.5836 / -81.3586; George C. McGough Nature Park, Largo, 27.8830494 / -82.8426218; Delnor-Wiggins Pass State Park, Naples, 26.2816555 / -81.8292456

VEERY
Catharus fuscescens

A bright little woodland bird with a remarkable song, veery is usually heard long before it's seen.

Field marks: Uniformly reddish-brown cap, nape, back, wings, and tail; whitish lores and throat, subtle white eye ring, yellow bill, buff breast with reddish-brown spots, white belly and undertail coverts.

Size: L: 7"–7.5", WS: 11"–12"

Similar species: Wood thrush is more brightly orange with heavy black spots on its breast and underside. Swainson's, gray-cheeked, and Bicknell's thrush are all light brown with more heavily spotted breasts. Hermit thrush is light brown with a red tail and a densely spotted breast.

Season: Spring and fall migration

Habitat: Deciduous woodlands with streams or wet areas

Food source: Berries, insects, spiders

Nest: On a sturdy branch in a tree or tall shrub

Call: Two-part series of spiraling trills with unusual harmonics, like several instruments playing in unison

Hot spots: Lantana Nature Preserve, Lantana, 26.5843827 / -80.0415768; Bill Baggs Cape Florida State Park, Key Biscayne, 25.6733 / -80.1582; Pinecraft Park, Southgate, 27.3189746 / -82.5037765; Fort De Soto Park, St. Petersburg, 27.6327266 / -82.718157; Paynes Prairie Preserve State Park, Bolen Bluff Trail, Gainesville, 29.5587838 / -82.3245401

SWAINSON'S THRUSH
Catharus ustulatus

Watch for the buffy areas on the face and neck to tell a Swainson's from a gray-cheeked thrush.

Field marks: Light brown cap, nape, back, wings, and tail; buff lores, cheek stripes, and throat; two-toned yellow and black bill; buff breast with a large cluster of dark brown spots, fading toward the belly; white belly, light brown flanks, white undertail coverts.

Size: L: 6"–7", WS: 11"–12"

Similar species: Wood thrush is more brightly orange with heavy black spots on its breast and underside. Veery has a lighter orange back and light brown spots on its breast, with a clear white underside. Gray-cheeked thrush has a gray cheek and a more heavily spotted breast. Hermit thrush is light brown with a red tail and a densely spotted breast.

Season: Spring and fall migration

Habitat: Coniferous forests, thickets around or near willow trees

Food source: Insects, invertebrates

Nest: On a branch in a conifer tree, usually between 12 and 20 feet high and near the trunk

Call: An ascending series of warbles and trills, ending with a wispy, upward-spiraling hiss; also a simple *weep* note, similar to an eastern towhee

Hot spots: Elinor Klapp-Phipps Park, Tallahassee, 30.535666 / -84.28821; Newnan's Lake State Forest, East Trail, Gainesville, 29.6611775 / -82.2544858; Guana Tolomato Matanzas National Estuarine Research Reserve, St. Augustine, 30.0074 / -81.3325; Mead Botanical Gardens, Winter Park, 28.5836 / -81.3586; Boyd Hill Nature Park and Lake Maggiore, St. Petersburg, 27.7322367 / -82.6521206

DOMINIC SHERONY

GRAY-CHEEKED THRUSH
Catharus minimus

This uncommon thrush stops briefly during its migration to northern Canada, making a sighting a fairly big event among local birders.

Field marks: Gray-brown cap, nape, back, and shoulders; gray cheek and pale gray patch in front of eye, yellow and black bill, buff breast with heavy coverage of brown spots, light brown spots on white belly, olive-brown flanks, white undertail coverts, darker brown tail.

Size: L: 7"–8", WS: 12"–13"

Similar species: Swainson's thrush is browner, has a buff-yellow pattern on its face, and has lighter spotting on its breast.

Season: Spring and fall migration

Habitat: Coniferous and deciduous forests

Food source: Insects, spiders, earthworms, fruit

Nest: Relatively close to the ground (no more than 10 feet up) on a tree or shrub branch

Call: A musical series of notes and sounds, somewhat thinner and more nasal than other thrushes and finishing with a descending, buzzy trill; also a simple *weer* call note

Hot spots: Fort De Soto Park, St. Petersburg, 27.6327266 / -82.718157; Pinecraft Park, Southgate, 27.3189746 / -82.5037765; Lantana Nature Preserve, Lantana, 26.5843827 / -80.0415768; Mead Botanical Gardens, Winter Park, 28.5836 / -81.3586; Paynes Prairie Preserve State Park, Bolen Bluff Trail, Gainesville, 29.5587838 / -82.3245401

HERMIT THRUSH
Catharus guttatus

This common woodland thrush flicks its bright red tail continuously as it rustles through leaves on the forest floor.

Field marks: Olive-brown cap, nape, back, and wings; white eye ring, pink and black bill, white throat and breast covered in black spots, white belly with light brown spots, light rusty flanks, white undertail coverts, red wing primaries, red tail.

Size: L: 6.75", WS: 11.5"

Similar species: Wood thrush has a bright orange-brown cap, nape, back, and tail. Veery has a lighter orange back and light brown spots on its breast, with a clear white underside. Swainson's thrush is light brown with a buff and brown–striped cheek and light yellow spectacles. Gray-cheeked thrush is light brown with a gray cheek and buff breast with a dense covering of dark spots.

Season: Winter

Habitat: Deciduous, coniferous, and mixed woodlands; open woods with a thick understory

Food source: Insects, invertebrates, fruit

Nest: On the ground or in a shrub, usually deep in the forest

Call: A single piccolo note, followed by a harmonically rich, descending trill; also a clucking *chut-chut-chut* and a simple *vee* call note

Hot spots: San Felasco Hammock Preserve State Park, Yellow Trail, Gainesville, 29.7180976 / -82.4636471; Wakulla Springs State Park, Wakulla Springs, 30.2335 / -84.3037; Paynes Prairie Preserve State Park, La Chua Trail, Gainesville, 29.6068756 / -82.3031116; Mead Botanical Gardens, Winter Park, 28.5836 / -81.3586; Pinecraft Park, Southgate, 27.3189746 / -82.5037765

MIMIC THRUSHES

GRAY CATBIRD
Dumetella carolinensis

The catbird's trademark *mew* call is not the only unique thing about it. It's also the only solidly bill-to-tail gray bird in North America.

Field marks: Uniformly gray with a black cap, black eye, rufous undertail coverts, and black tail.

Size: L: 8.5"–9", WS: 11"–12"

Similar species: Northern mockingbird is gray above and whitish below with large white patches on its wings.

Season: Winter, with a few individuals year-round in northern Florida

Habitat: Forest and marsh edges, wooded edges of farm fields and grasslands, neighborhoods with mature trees

Food source: Insects, spiders, fruit, seeds; sometimes comes to jelly feeders used by orioles

Nest: In the lower branches of a tree or in a shrub

Call: A chattery series of notes that may vary from one bird to the next, derived from the catbird's ability to mimic other birds; also a single *mew* note, very like a cat

Hot spots: Every city park, neighborhood, cemetery, nature center, sanctuary, forest, and farm has its resident catbird, and many of these areas have several. The only places you are not likely to encounter these birds is in areas of dense forests with few discernible edges.

NORTHERN MOCKINGBIRD
Mimus polyglottos

Nicely adapted to city parks, neighborhoods, cemeteries, and other human-inhabited areas, the mockingbird can incorporate everything from other birds' calls to car alarms in its own song.

Field marks: Gray cap, nape, and back; black eye line, yellow eye, white lores; white throat, breast, and belly; darker wings with two wing bars, large white wing patches, visible during flight; white undertail coverts; long, dark tail often held at an upward angle.

Size: L: 9"–10", WS: 12"–14"

Similar species: Gray catbird is uniformly gray all over. Northern shrike has a black mask, black wings, and a black tail. American pipit is smaller, has a light breast with black streaks, and is found on open ground like beaches and fallow fields.

Season: Year-round

Habitat: Parks, neighborhoods, farmland with hedgerows and wooded areas

Food source: Many kinds of insects, fruit, worms, some small reptiles

Nest: In shrubs or low in trees

Call: Varied phrases that may be different from one bird to the next. Each mimicked call is usually repeated in sets of five or six, and may incorporate the songs of killdeer, Carolina wren, Baltimore oriole, ovenbird, and a wide range of others. Some have learned to imitate car alarms, emergency vehicle sirens, and the beeping of construction vehicles backing up.

Hot spots: Northern mockingbird is a common bird in residential and commercial areas. While it generally does not come to feeders, it often frequents the wooded edges of backyards, as well as rail-to-trail conversions and other nature trails. In Florida, it favors apartment complexes and other areas with lots of human activity.

© SHUTTERSTOCK.COM/ELLIOTTE RUSTY HAROLD

BAHAMA MOCKINGBIRD
Mimus gundlachii

A rare but annual visitor to the Atlantic coast of south Florida, this bird looks distinctly different from the far more common northern mockingbird.

Field marks: Brownish-gray head, back, and wings; white throat, light gray breast, whitish underside with black streaks on flanks, light yellow undertail coverts (sometimes extending to underside), two faint white wing bars, gray tail with white tip on some tail feathers.

Size: L: 11"–12", WS: 14"–15"

Similar species: Northern mockingbird is grayer with bolder white wing bars, bright white patch on wings visible in flight, no streaking or yellow on underside or undertail.

Season: Late spring/summer

Habitat: Tropical shrubs flanking dry open areas

Food source: Insects and fruit

Nest: In a tree or shrub (not in Florida)

Call: A series of repeating chirps and whistles, rising and falling in pitch—not a mimic call, despite the bird's name

Hot spots: There are no dependable sites in Florida for this bird, but these have seen visits in the past three years: Gulfstream Shores, Key Largo, 25.1912724 / -80.3546906; Windy Key Fossil Reef Geological State Park, Islamorada, 24.9498572 / -80.5963683; Bill Baggs Cape Florida State Park, Key Biscayne, 25.6733 / -80.1582; Lantana Nature Preserve, Lantana, 26.5843827 / -80.0415768; Crandon Park, Key Biscayne, 25.7089712 / -80.1536322

THRASHER

BROWN THRASHER
Toxostoma rufum

The eastern United States' only thrasher is also a mimic, but its songs are always sung in couplets, so a careful listener can pick it out of a dawn chorus.

Field marks: Bright reddish-brown cap, nape, back, wings, and tail; gray cheek, pink and black bill curving slightly downward, white throat with black malar stripes, light breast and belly striped in black and reddish-brown, two black and white stripes on wings, buff undertail coverts, long tail.

Size: L: 11.5", WS: 13"–14"

Similar species: Wood thrush is equally reddish, but its breast is heavily spotted rather than streaked, and its bill is shorter.

Season: Summer

Habitat: Shrubby areas, including farm fields with hedgerows, forest edges, parks

Food source: Insects, fruit, grains, some small amphibians

Nest: Close to the ground in a shrub, often one with thorns

Call: A range of distinctly musical phrases, incorporating whistles, rasps, warbles, and other sounds, always sung with one or two repetitions before moving on to the next

Hot spots: Thrashers are numerous in northern and central Florida and a little less so the farther south you go. Here are some fairly surefire spots to find them: St. Marks National Wildlife Refuge, St. Marks, 30.1515653 / -84.1473314; Newnan's Lake State Forest, East Trail, Gainesville, 29.6611775 / -82.2544858; Freedom Point Ponds and CCRC Area, The Villages, 28.9490933 / -81.9616748; Lyonia Preserve, Deltona, 28.9238 / -81.2266; Boyd Hill Nature Park and Lake Maggiore, St. Petersburg, 27.7322367 / -82.6521206

STARLING, MYNA, AND PIPIT

EUROPEAN STARLING
Sturnus vulgaris

This introduced species arrived in North America in the 1800s and is now one of the most widespread and numerous birds on the continent.

Field marks: Starlings have three distinct plumages. Breeding adult has iridescent purple head, black eye, yellow bill, greenish back, greenish-black breast and belly, spotted flanks, black wings, and short black tail with feathers outlined in brown. Nonbreeding adult has black head with white edges on each feather; black back, breast, belly, and flanks covered with white spots; scaly brownish wings and tail. Juvenile is softly brownish gray with a light gray throat, slightly darker wings.

Size: L: 8.5", WS: 15.5"–16"

Similar species: Purple martin is more uniformly blue-black. Molting indigo bunting is smaller and lacks the spotting of a winter starling.

Season: Year-round

Habitat: Very comfortable in residential and commercial areas, and a frequent visitor to backyard feeders

Food source: Insects, invertebrates, spiders, fruit, berries, plants, seeds from feeders, human discards

Nest: In a tree cavity, on a girder under a bridge, in a hole in a building or tree, or in a nest box

Call: Most often a high-pitched, descending *zheeer, zheeer,* a long, chattering phrase of syllables gleaned from other birds' songs. Starlings also have a rasping, nonmusical, one-note *hashhh* call to signify danger.

Hot spots: Any gathering place for people has a population of starlings, whether it's in the middle of a city or along an open beach. Look for them around the edges of shopping malls, on city streets, at fairgrounds or outdoor festivals, in any farm field, along the paths of electrical lines, and in your own backyard if you feed birds regularly. Starlings often form colonies of tens of thousands of birds in winter to scavenge for food together, creating clouds of birds that move in unison to avoid predators. (Search "murmuration" on YouTube for some astonishing examples.)

COMMON MYNA
Acridotheres tristis

This South Asian native and much-favored cage bird has established a healthy feral population in south Florida.

Field marks: Black head and breast with yellow ring around the eye, bright yellow bill, brown body, white patch on primary wing feathers and underwing, black and brown tail with white tip, yellow legs.

Size: L: 9.5"–10", WS: 18"

Similar species: Common hill myna is all black with white wing patch, a yellow patch on its face from cheek to nape, and a bright orange bill.

Season: Year-round

Habitat: Cities and suburbs, including parks, shopping areas, and residential neighborhoods

Food source: Insects, invertebrates, spiders, fruit, berries, plants, seeds from feeders, human discards

Nest: In a hole in a wall or tree

Call: A collection of clicks, chips, and loud, piercing musical phrases

Hot spots: West Kendall Baptist Hospital area, The Hammocks, 25.6826869 / -80.4526034; Crandon Park, Key Biscayne, 25.7089712 / -80.1536322; Ocean Bank, 788-700 FL 953, Miami, 25.7792038 / -80.2642599; Mutineer Restaurant stormwater pond, Florida City, 25.44645 / -80.474733; Fairchild Tropical Botanic Garden, Coral Gables, 25.6764 / -80.2713

SHUTTERSTOCK #348429803

AMERICAN PIPIT
Anthus rubescens

The pipit's muted features serve as excellent camouflage for flocks while overwintering in open fields and beaches.

Field marks: Brownish-gray cap, nape, back, and wings; brown face with buff eye stripe, yellow and black bill, buff or white breast and belly with light gray streaks; wings darker brown with two buff wing bars, light brown flanks, darker tail with white outer feathers. In winter, all plumage fades to shades of gray.

Size: L: 6.5", WS: 10"–11"

Similar species: Field sparrow has a darker brown cap, back, and wings; a white eye ring, a small pink bill, and a darker tail. Clay-colored sparrow has a brown patch on its face with a wide white outline.

Season: Winter

Habitat: Fields with sparse vegetation, farm fields, occasionally on beaches

Food source: Insects, tiny mollusks, crustaceans, marine invertebrates, spiders

Nest: On the ground near a rock or small shrub

Call: Continuous *chee-chee-chee* notes, not unlike a cricket; also a single *pweet* note

Hot spots: Lake Jesup Conservation Area, Marl Bed Flats, Sanford, 28.7377104 / -81.2400126; River Lakes Conservation Area, Moccasin Island, Melbourne, 28.2299949 / -80.8110523; T. M. Goodwin Waterfowl Management Area, Palm Bay, 27.8452341 / -80.7252359; Babcock-Webb Wildlife Management Area, Punta Gorda, 26.8582653 / -81.9401121; Lake Apopka Wildlife Drive, Apopka, 28.6691082 / -81.5574338

BULBUL

© SHUTTERSTOCK.COM/TAO JIANG

RED-WHISKERED BULBUL
Pycnonotus jocosus

This South Asian bird has established several localized colonies in Miami neighborhoods.

Field marks: High black crest, brown head and back, red patch behind the eye, white cheek outlined in black, small bill, white breast with a dark crescent extending from shoulder, white underside, tan flanks, brown back and wings, long brown fan tail with white tip, red undertail coverts.

Size: L: 6.5"–7.5", WS 11"–11.5"

Similar species: Cedar waxwing is a soft golden brown with a black mask. Female cardinal is a warm brown with a bright orange bill, reddish wings, and a red tail.

Season: Year-round

Habitat: Tropical trees and shrubs in neighborhoods

Food source: Mostly berries

Nest: In a bush or small tree

Call: A quick burst of musical notes, five or six in rapid succession

Hot spots: Pine Woods Park, Kendall, 25.647447 / -80.356726; Kendallwood neighborhood, Miami, 25.6937451 / -80.3378892; Kings Creek Village, Glenvar Heights (Miami), 25.6939865 / -80.3280576; West Kendall Baptist Hospital area, The Hammocks, 25.6826869 / -80.4526034

WAXWING

CEDAR WAXWING
Bombycilla cedrorum

Elegant winter visitors, waxwings move among the treetops in flocks as they devour berries in winter and insects in all other seasons.

Field marks: Warm yellow-brown crest, neck, breast, and back; black mask outlined in white, white malar stripe against black throat, gray-brown upper wing, darker wing tips with red-tipped secondaries, lighter belly, white undertail coverts, black tail with yellow tip.

Size: L: 7"–7.25", WS: 11"–12"

Similar species: Bohemian waxwing is grayer overall, has white spots and yellow tips on its primaries, reddish undertail coverts, and a reddish forehead (and generally does not find its way to Florida).

Season: Year-round

Habitat: Woodlands, neighborhoods, arboretums, orchards and other areas with many fruit trees

Food source: Insects, caterpillars, berries, fruit, sap, some flowers

Nest: On a branch in a tree with plenty of leaf canopy

Call: A single, high-pitched *pseeet*, often repeated

Hot spots: Waxwings move in large flocks, so any area with many trees may play host to dozens of them at once. Here are some particularly popular spots for them: Chapmans Pond, Halle Plantation, 29.6183484 / -82.4164295; Huguenot Memorial City Park, Jacksonville, 30.4112444 / -81.4206594; Blue Spring State Park, Orange City, 28.942476 / -81.3418172; Fort De Soto Park, St. Petersburg, 27.6327266 / -82.718157; J. N. Ding Darling National Wildlife Refuge, Bailey Tract, Sanibel, 26.4276 / -82.0819

WARBLERS

NORTHERN PARULA
Setophaga americana

Look in moist forests with conifers for this small warbler, which prefers woodlands bordering freshwater marshes and streams.

Field marks: Male has gray head, white eye ring, black and yellow bill, yellow throat, rufous and black breastband with yellow below, white underside, greenish-brown back, gray wings with two white wing bars, gray tail. Female has slightly less yellow and may have no breastband.

Size: L: 4.25"–4.5", WS: 7"

Similar species: Nashville warbler has yellow throat and breast with no breastband, olive green back, and yellow underside (in males). Mourning warbler has gray head, black throat, and mostly yellow underside.

Season: Summer; winter in south Florida and the Keys

Habitat: Coniferous woods, especially bordering freshwater marshes, streams, and rivers

Food source: Insects, spiders, caterpillars, moths

Nest: Hidden among moss and lichens in trees

Call: An elongated, insect-like trill, terminating in a single staccato *chip*

Hot spots: Corkscrew Regional Ecosystem Watershed Bird Rookery Swamp Trails, Corkscrew, 26.3140166 / -81.6349089; Kendall Indian Hammocks Park, Kendall, 25.6953 / -80.3734; Turkey Creek Sanctuary, Palm Bay, 28.0156 / -80.5957; Wekiwa Springs State Park, Apopka, 28.7337466 / -81.480324; Withlacoochee State Forest, Citrus Tract, Lecanto, 28.8016141 / -82.4179299

ORANGE-CROWNED WARBLER
Leiothlypis celata

This warbler's orange crown patch is almost never seen in the wild, so don't let this elusive field mark sway your identification.

Field marks: Olive green above and dull yellow below, with a thin black eye line on the otherwise olive head. Breast and flanks are streaked with lighter yellow and olive, lighter yellow undertail coverts, olive tail.

Size: L: 4.75"–5", WS: 7"–8"

Similar species: Philadelphia vireo is gray above with a white eyebrow and much lighter undersides. Tennessee warbler has a gray head and white undersides.

Season: Winter

Habitat: Deciduous forest edges, thickets, and shrubs, with a preference for willows

Food source: Invertebrates, berries, flower nectar

Nest: Low in a shrub or thicket, or on the ground; breeding in southern Canada and north to Alaska

Call: A high, one-pitch trill, ending on a single *cheet* note

Hot spots: St. Marks National Wildlife Refuge (lighthouse area), Port Leon, 30.0751008 / -84.180; Huguenot Memorial City Park, Jacksonville, 30.4112444 / -81.4206594; Lake Woodruff National Wildlife Refuge, Leon Springs, 29.1092685 / -81.3752445; Mead Botanical Gardens, Winter Park, 28.5836 / -81.3586; Loxahatchee National Wildlife Refuge, Valencia Reserve, 26.4928139 / -80.2168894

TENNESSEE WARBLER
Leiothlypis peregrina

A late migrant moving through in April and May and again from late September through early November, Tennessee warbler announces itself with a loud, three-part song from the very tops of the trees.

Field marks: Male has gray head; olive back, wings, and tail; white eyebrow, throat, belly, and undertail coverts. Female has pale yellow head, is olive above, with two faint wing bars.

Size: L: 4.75", WS: 7.75"–8"

Similar species: Orange-crowned warbler has an olive head and yellow underparts. Nashville warbler has a bright white eye ring and bright yellow underparts. Mourning warbler has a black patch at the throat.

Season: Spring and fall migration

Habitat: Mixed woodlands, shrubs and thickets; prefers the tops of trees

Food source: Insects, spiders, seeds, berries

Nest: On the ground, hidden among moss or under shrubbery

Call: Three-part song: three *chips*, two *wops*, and an extended, rhythmic trill

Hot spots: Fort Zachary Taylor Historic State Park, Key West, 24.5463 / -81.8106; Plantation Preserve, Plantation, 26.1156777 / -80.2391624; Sawgrass Lake Park, St. Petersburg, 27.8398 / -82.6705; Sweetwater Wetlands Park, Gainesville, 29.6151026 / -82.3254061; St. Marks National Wildlife Refuge, St. Marks, 30.1515653 / -84.1473314

273

© SHUTTERSTOCK.COM/MTKHALED MAHMUD

CONNECTICUT WARBLER
Oporornis agilis

The bold white eye ring and longish bill help differentiate this warbler from other gray-headed species.

Field marks: Gray head and breast, unbroken white eye ring, longer bill than most warblers, greenish back and wings, pale yellow underside.

Size: L: 5.5"-6", WS: 9"

Similar species: Nashville warbler has a yellow throat and a brighter yellow underside. Mourning warbler has a thinner, broken eye ring, a darker face, and a black breast patch. Tennessee warbler has a white eyebrow, a gray line through the eye, and a white throat, breast, and underside.

Season: Spring migration

Habitat: Open forests in wet areas with a strong understory

Food source: Insects and spiders, feeding on the ground

Nest: On or close to the ground in thick vegetation (not in Florida)

Call: *wip-WIPpy, wip-WIPpy, wip-WIPpy;* also a small *wip* call note

Hot spots: This warbler stops annually along the Florida coast during spring migration, but rarely if ever in the same place. These spots have enjoyed visits for several days at a time: Rotary Park at Merritt Island, 28.3257929 / -80.6852353; Hugh Taylor Birch State Park, Fort Lauderdale, 26.1414 / -80.1048; Richardson Historic Park and Nature Preserve, Wilton Manors, 26.1517688 / -80.141809; Lantana Nature Preserve, Lantana, 26.5843827 / -80.0415768; Ocean Bay Riverside Park, Jensen Beach, 27.3381582 / -80.2365983

BLUE-WINGED WARBLER
Vermivora cyanoptera

This warbler and golden-winged warbler have strikingly different plumage, but they often hybridize together, creating variants known as Brewster's and Lawrence's warblers. Florida birders sight these hybrids infrequently but regularly.

Field marks: Dull yellow nape and back; bright yellow crown, face, throat, breast, and underside; black eye line, small dark bill, blue-gray wings with two bright wing bars, white undertail coverts, blue-gray tail.

Size: L: 4.75", WS: 7"–7.5"

Similar species: Prothonotary warbler has a bright yellow head and body with no markings, and gray wings with no wing bars. Wilson's warbler has a black cap, an all-yellow body, and olive wings with no wing bars. Yellow warbler has yellow wings with black-edged primaries and bright red streaks on its breast and underside.

Season: Spring and fall migration

Habitat: Open pastures and farmland with scrubby hedgerows, shrubs, and wooded edges

Food source: Insects, spiders

Nest: Just off the ground in low shrubs, hidden from outside view

Call: *Beeez-buzzz*, dropping in pitch from the first note to the second

Hot spots: Gulf Islands National Seashore, Fort Pickens, Pensacola Beach, 30.3231 / -87.2829; Maritime Hammock Preserve, Cocoa Beach, 28.3311287 / -80.6110239; Lantana Nature Preserve, Lantana, 26.5843827 / -80.0415768; Green Cay Wetlands & Nature Center, Boynton Beach, 26.4861584 / -80.1607561; Audubon Corkscrew Swamp Sanctuary, Corkscrew, 26.375442 / -81.6040206

GOLDEN-WINGED WARBLER
Vermivora chrysoptera

Suburban development and reductions in farmland have taken their toll on the golden-winged population, making them hard to find in the eastern United States.

Field marks: Yellow cap and forehead, black mask with a wide white stripe above and below it, black throat; gray back, sides, and wings; bright yellow wing patches, white undertail coverts, gray tail. Female lacks the black markings, and its yellow areas are duller than the male.

Size: L: 4.75"–5", WS: 7.5"–8"

Similar species: Magnolia warbler has white wing patches and a yellow breast and underside heavily streaked with black. Chestnut-sided warbler has a similar head pattern, but it has a wide chestnut stripe along its flanks and white wing bars instead of patches. Yellow-rumped warbler has a yellow cap and black mask, but its throat is white and its yellow patches are on its flanks and rump. Yellow-throated warbler has a yellow throat and white wing bars instead of patches.

Season: Spring and fall migration

Habitat: Farm fields and pastures with young, successional trees and shrubby edges

Food source: Insects, caterpillars

Nest: Deep in a shrub or young tree, close to the ground

Call: *Beeez, zee-zee-zee-zee*, with the *beeez* on a higher note; also a simple *tchip* note

Hot spots: Golden-winged warbler has become a rarity throughout much of its range. Only the following hot spots offer a strong likelihood of a sighting from one year to the next: George C. McGough Nature Park, Largo, 27.8830494 / -82.8426218; Fort De Soto Park, St. Petersburg, 27.6327266 / -82.718157; Point Ybel Lighthouse Beach Park, Sanibel, 26.4520609 / -82.0151281; Wakodahatchee Wetlands, Delray Beach, 26.4781984 / -80.144738; Mead Botanical Gardens, Winter Park, 28.5836 / -81.3586

NASHVILLE WARBLER
Leiothlypis ruficapilla

Bright and vocal, Nashville warblers move through during spring and fall migration, primarily following the coastlines in both directions.

Field marks: Male has gray head with bright white eye ring, small black bill; small reddish patch at top of head may be visible during breeding season; greenish back and wings, bright yellow breast and underside, yellow undertail coverts, short greenish tail. Female does not have the reddish patch and is paler yellow.

Size: L: 4.75", WS: 7.5"

Similar species: Mourning warbler has a gray head and black throat. Tennessee warbler has a gray head, olive green back, and white underside.

Season: Spring and fall migration, with some individuals remaining through the winter

Habitat: Mixed forests with shrubs, wooded areas along edges of wetlands

Food source: Insects

Nest: On the ground, hidden at the base of a shrub or behind grasses

Call: Two-part call: high-pitched *seedle, seedle, seedle, seedle, bit-bit-bit-bit-bit;* also a simple *chit* note

Hot spots: Sweetwater Wetlands Park, Gainesville, 29.6151026 / -82.3254061; Mead Botanical Gardens, Winter Park, 28.5836 / -81.3586; Maritime Hammock Preserve, Cocoa Beach, 28.3311287 / -80.6110239; Tall Cypress Natural Area, Coral Springs, 26.2768695 / -80.214057; Bill Baggs Cape Florida State Park, Key Biscayne, 25.6733 / -80.1582

YELLOW WARBLER
Setophaga petechia

America's most numerous and widespread warbler—with an estimated population of 39 million birds—is also one of its most delightful, with its cheery song and showy plumage.

Field marks: Male has bright yellow head, dull yellow back and tail, black eye and bill, yellow breast and underside with bright reddish streaks, light olive wings with black-outlined flight feathers. Female is very similar but lacks the red streaks.

Size: L: 5", WS: 7.75"–8"

Similar species: Prothonotary warbler has no red streaks, and its wings are blue-gray. American goldfinch is lemon yellow with a black cap and black wings.

Season: Spring migration; summer in the Everglades and Keys

Habitat: A combination of mixed woodlands and water features, including bogs, marshes, and swamps; also farmland, thickets, and residential areas

Food source: Insects, spiders, berries in a pinch

Nest: On a branch in a young tree

Call: A high-pitched warble, popularly parsed as *sweet-sweet-sweet-sweedle-sweet*; also a series of simple *tsp* notes when alarmed

Hot spots: St. Marks National Wildlife Refuge, St. Marks, 30.1515653 / -84.1473314; Point Ybel Lighthouse Beach Park, Sanibel, 26.4520609 / -82.0151281; Frog Pond Wildlife Management Area, Lucky Hammock, Homestead, 25.396439 / -80.566581; Green Cay Wetlands & Nature Center, Boynton Beach, 26.4861584 / -80.1607561; Lake Apopka Wildlife Drive, Apopka, 28.6691082 / -81.5574338

CHESTNUT-SIDED WARBLER
Setophaga pensylvanica

Check second-growth forests—the ones with fairly dense new growth after extensive logging or farming—for this common local breeder.

Field marks: Male has yellow cap, black eye line, white cheeks, black line from bill to throat, white nape with fine black streaks, black-streaked back and wings, white throat and underparts, bold chestnut streak on flanks, two white wing bars, black tail. Female is similar with a more muted facial pattern and short chestnut streak. Nonbreeding male in fall has a gray face with no black pattern, a bold white eye ring, and a yellow back.

Size: L: 5"–5.25", WS: 7.75"–8.25"

Similar species: Male bay-breasted warbler has a chestnut face and cap, which disappear in fall.

Season: Spring and fall migration

Habitat: Second-growth (young) woodlands, thickets, shrubby areas

Food source: Insects, some fruit

Nest: In a shrub or a low tree, built fairly close to the ground

Call: Commonly described as *pleased-pleased-pleased-pleased-ta-MEETcha*, with a more musical lilt than yellow warbler. Its alarm note is a tuneless *chp*.

Hot spots: Newnan's Lake, Palm Point Park, Gainesville, 29.6364 / -82.2382; Black Creek Park, Fleming Island, 30.0478 / -81.7101167; Mead Botanical Gardens, Winter Park, 28.5836 / -81.3586; Boyd Hill Nature Park and Lake Maggiore, St. Petersburg, 27.7322367 / -82.6521206; Fort De Soto Park, St. Petersburg, 27.6327266 / -82.718157

MAGNOLIA WARBLER
Setophaga magnolia

This northern warbler loves coniferous woods, particularly spruce, fir, and hemlock. Be careful not to confuse a magnolia with a yellow-rumped warbler—both species have a yellow rump.

Field marks: Male has gray cap, white eyebrow, wide black mask, black bill, yellow throat, yellow breast and underside with bold black streaks, white undertail coverts, black wings with white patches, yellow rump, black tail. Female is substantially similar but with white eyebrow and no black mask. Nonbreeding male has gray cap extending to cheek, white eye ring, muted colors with no white wing patches.

Size: L: 5", WS: 7.5"

Similar species: Cape May warbler has an orange facial patch (gray in female). Blackburnian warbler has finer black mask, bright orange throat, and buff wash on flanks with light streaking. Yellow-rumped warbler has a white throat and yellow flanks.

Season: Spring and fall migration

Habitat: Thickets, shrubs, and woodland edges; once settled into breeding, magnolia warblers prefer coniferous woods, especially northern woods with spruce and balsam fir.

Food source: Caterpillars, especially spruce budworm; berries

Nest: On a fairly low tree branch, usually not more than 10 feet up

Call: A sweetly warbled *weeto-weeto-weetie*; also a quickly repeated *chit*

Hot spots: St. Marks National Wildlife Refuge, St. Marks, 30.1515653 / -84.1473314; Newnan's Lake State Forest, East Trail, Gainesville, 29.6611775 / -82.2544858; Mead Botanical Gardens, Winter Park, 28.5836 / -81.3586; Saddle Creek Park, Lakeland, 28.0620436 / -81.8838501; Point Ybel Lighthouse Beach Park, Sanibel, 26.4520609 / -82.0151281

CAPE MAY WARBLER
Setophaga tigrina

The male's bright orange cheek quickly sets this bird apart from other warblers migrating north.

Field marks: Male has black cap, yellow face with orange cheek, black eye line, yellow breast and belly with black streaks, yellow nape, gray back, gray-brown wings with large white wing patch, gray-brown tail with white outer feathers, white undertail coverts. Female is grayer overall with gray cap and cheek, muted yellow face and breast, gray streaks on breast and flanks.

Size: L: 4.75"–5", WS: 7"–8"

Similar species: Blackburnian warbler has orange face with black mask and a bright orange throat. Black-throated green warbler lacks the cheek patch and has a black throat, white underside, and bold black streaks on flanks.

Season: Spring and fall migration

Habitat: Spruce forests for breeding; wooded areas of all kinds during migration

Food source: Insects, especially spruce budworms

Nest: On a high branch toward the top of a spruce tree

Call: Four very high-pitched, ascending notes, not unlike an insect

Hot spots: St. George Island State Park, Eastpoint, 29.7155 / -84.7535; Sweetwater Wetlands Park, Gainesville, 29.6151026 / -82.3254061; Paynes Prairie Preserve State Park, Bolen Bluff Trail, Gainesville, 29.5587838 / -82.3245401; Dunedin Hammock City Park, Dunedin, 28.0324 / -82.781; Lantana Nature Preserve, Lantana, 26.5843827 / -80.0415768

BLACK-THROATED BLUE WARBLER
Setophaga caerulescens

Bright blue with a black mask, this boldly patterned warbler offers a unique presentation—and the striking difference in the female's plumage makes it easy to miss in the excitement of spring migration.

Field marks: Male has bright blue cap, nape, back, wings, and tail; black face and throat, white underside with wide black stripe on flanks, white wing patch on primaries, white outer tail feathers with black tips. Female is plain gray-brown with thin white eyebrow, bluish wings, white spot on wings at the lower (outer) edge of primaries, white undertail coverts, muted blue tail.

Size: L: 5.25", WS: 7"–7.75"

Similar species: Cerulean warbler has blue face, two white wing bars, blue collar on white throat, white underside with blue streaks on flanks. Indigo bunting has a uniformly blue body and black wings.

Season: Spring and fall migration

Habitat: Mixed woodlands with a substantial understory

Food source: Insects and invertebrates; during migration, black-throated blues are frequently seen feeding on the ground.

Nest: In a bush or small tree, close to the ground

Call: A buzzy, insect-like series of four notes, steadily climbing: *zee-zee-zee-zeeEEE*. Chip note is a toneless *chuk, chuk.*

Hot spots: Fort De Soto Park, St. Petersburg, 27.6327266 / -82.718157; Delnor-Wiggins Pass State Park, Naples, 26.2816555 / -81.8292456; John Pennekamp Coral Reef State Park, Key Largo, 25.1280556 / -80.41; Bill Baggs Cape Florida State Park, Key Biscayne, 25.6733 / -80.1582; Plantation Preserve, Plantation, 26.1156777 / -80.2391624

CERULEAN WARBLER
Setophaga cerulea

Uncommon to rare, this blue warbler is considered a vulnerable and declining species because its favorite habitat—mature forest—is also in sharp decline.

Field marks: Male has blue head with brighter blue cap, black eye line, small bill, white throat; blue nape, back, wings, and tail; blue collar, white underside with bold blue streaks on flanks, white undertail coverts, two white wing bars. Female has sky blue to turquoise head and face with white eyebrow; same blue back, wings, and tail; white throat, white underside with gray streaks on flanks, two white wing bars.

Size: L: 4.75", WS: 7.75"

Similar species: Black-throated blue warbler is solid blue with a black face and throat, wide black streaks on flanks. Indigo bunting is uniformly blue from head to tail.

Season: Spring and fall migration

Habitat: Mature forests with very tall deciduous trees

Food source: Insects, caterpillars

Nest: On a tree branch at least 15 feet off the ground, often as high as 90 feet up

Call: A three-part song, ending on an ascending note: *cheer-cheer-cheer-cheer-chichichichichi-zweeet*; also a tiny, high, barely audible *cht* note

Hot spots: St. George Island State Park, youth camp area, Eastpoint, 29.7155 / -84.7535; St. Marks National Wildlife Refuge, St. Marks, 30.1515653 / -84.1473314; Evergreen Cemetery, Fort Lauderdale, 26.1061594 / -80.1318741; Point Ybel Lighthouse Beach Park, Sanibel, 26.4520609 / -82.0151281; Pinecraft Park, Southgate, 27.3189746 / -82.5037765

BLACKBURNIAN WARBLER
Setophaga fusca

A top contender for the title of Most Beautiful Warbler, the blackburnian's bright orange throat makes it unique among the East's warbler pantheon.

Field marks: Male has black cap, orange face with distinctive black pattern, bright orange throat and breast, yellow belly with thin black streaks, white undertail coverts, black wings with wide white wing patch, black tail. Female is similar but not as boldly marked, with subtler facial pattern, yellow-orange throat and breast, and two white wing bars instead of patch. Nonbreeding male is like female, but with lemon-yellow throat and white breast with black streaks.

Size: L: 5", WS: 8.5"

Similar species: No other local warbler species has a bright orange throat and breast.

Season: Spring migration

Habitat: Mixed woodlands with coniferous trees, including spruce and hemlock

Food source: Insects, caterpillars

Nest: Near the top of a mature conifer

Call: *Cherrie-chee-chee-chee-chee-TWEEdee*, on one pitch until the accent on the last syllable; also a very high-pitched, wheezy series of *sweetie, sweetie, sweetie* notes

Hot spots: St. George Island State Park, youth camp area, Eastpoint, 29.7155 / -84.7535; Elinor Klapp-Phipps Park, Tallahassee, 30.535666 / -84.28821; Fort De Soto Park, St. Petersburg, 27.6327266 / -82.718157; Point Ybel Lighthouse Beach Park, Sanibel, 26.4520609 / -82.0151281; Rotary Park Environmental Center, Cape Coral, 26.5467025 / -81.9806344

YELLOW-RUMPED WARBLER
Setophaga coronata

Florida sees the "myrtle" race of this abundant bird—and plenty of them, as the planet hosts more than 90 million of this species.

Field marks: Male has yellow cap, black mask with a white eyebrow and throat; gray back, wings, and tail; white breast and underside with heavy black streaks, yellow flanks, two white wing bars, white undertail coverts, yellow rump. Female is less boldly marked, with a gray cap and more muted mask.

Size: L: 5.5", WS: 9.25"

Similar species: Magnolia warbler has a yellow throat, breast, and underside. Black-throated green warbler has a yellow-green face, olive green back, and black throat.

Season: Winter

Habitat: Woodlands, thickets, shrubby areas, beach dunes, residential areas, parks, and others

Food source: Insects, berries

Nest: Usually high in a conifer, but possibly in lower vegetation in some areas (not in Florida)

Call: A rapid, two part song: *twee-twee-twee-twee-twee, tooey-tooey,* also an irregularly spaced series of very high *tsi, tsi* notes

Hot spots: This common warbler can turn up anywhere, from a national forest to your front yard. Easily confused with a number of other warbler species, yellow-rumpeds require a careful look even if you've already seen a dozen of them that day. Slight variations in plumage between the male, female, and immature are enough to confuse even the most experienced birders, but their "butter butt" nickname is a good reminder to check for yellow at the base of the tail.

BLACK-THROATED GREEN WARBLER
Setophaga virens

This warbler's buzzy call makes it fairly easy to find in its preferred coniferous forest habitat.

Field marks: Male has dull yellow cap, yellow face with olive eyebrow, black throat, white underside with yellow wash and wide black streaks, olive back, dark gray wings with two white wing bars, dark gray tail with white outer feathers, white undertail coverts. Female is similar except throat is white, with a black breast patch.

Size: L: 4.75"–5", WS: 7.75"–8"

Similar species: Hooded warbler has a black throat, but also has a black cap, olive back and wings, and clear yellow breast and underside. Cape May warbler has a yellow face with an orange cheek and a yellow throat striped with black. Golden-winged warbler has a white face with a black mask, a yellow cap, and a black throat, but its body and wings are gray, and its wings have bright yellow patches.

Season: Spring and fall migration; summer

Habitat: Coniferous woods, especially with pine and hemlock trees

Food source: Insects, berries, seeds

Nest: On a conifer branch, fairly high in the tree

Call: A buzzy *zooooo-zee, zoo-zoo zee,* sometimes at a faster pace: *zee-zee-zee-zee zoo-zeet*

Hot spots: Frog Pond Wildlife Management Area, Lucky Hammock, Homestead, 25.396439 / -80.566581; Matheson Hammock Park, Coral Gables, 25.6806539 / -80.2726364; Evergreen Cemetery, Fort Lauderdale, 26.1061594 / -80.1318741; Audubon Corkscrew Swamp Sanctuary, Corkscrew, 26.375442 / -81.6040206; Fort De Soto Park, St. Petersburg, 27.6327266 / -82.718157

PRAIRIE WARBLER
Setophaga discolor

Listen before you look for this little yellow bird. It often gives its location away with its distinctive, steadily rising song.

Field marks: Male has olive head with yellow face, black eye line, black line from bill to below the eye, yellow throat and breast, black shoulder line, black streaks on yellow flanks, olive underside to white undertail coverts, olive back with rufous streaks, olive wings with faint yellow wing bars, olive tail. Female has olive face with a white patch above and below the eye, fainter black streaks on its flanks.

Size: L: 4.75", WS: 7"–7.5"

Similar species: Pine warbler has an olive head with yellow spectacles, olive streaks on its flanks, and gray wings. Female Cape May warbler has a gray face, back, and wings. Yellow warbler has an unmarked yellow face and red streaks on its breast and flanks; female has a clear yellow breast and flanks.

Season: Winter in south Florida and the Keys; spring and fall migration throughout the rest of the state

Habitat: Open grasslands, including wetlands, pastures, farm fields, and scrubby woods

Food source: Insects

Nest: Near the ground in a small tree or shrub

Call: A rapid, emphatic *ziziziziziziZEEZEEZEEZEE*, rising steadily in pitch

Hot spots: Just about any open area may have its individual or pair of prairie warblers in the proper season. These birds migrate through areas that forest-loving warblers shun, so you may have a fairly easy time sorting out which small, yellow birds are prairie warblers throughout south-central Florida and along the coasts. Scrublands adjoining beaches, open pastures, and parks with low vegetation are all likely places to find this very vocal little bird.

PALM WARBLER
Setophaga palmarum

This red-capped winter resident is usually spotted in the company of pine warblers.

Field marks: Breeding adult has bright rufous cap, yellow eyebrow, grayish-brown face with black eye line, small black bill, yellow throat, tan back and wings, yellow breast and underside with red streaks, yellow undertail coverts, tan tail. Fall (nonbreeding) adult has brown head with yellow eyebrow, whitish throat, dull underside with yellow wash, yellow undertail coverts; brown back, wings, and tail.

Size: L: 5.5", WS: 8"

Similar species: Yellow warbler has clear yellow face and head and yellow-olive back. Cape May warbler has bright orange patch on face and black streaks on underside.

Season: Winter

Habitat: Open fields, wetland edges

Food source: Insects

Nest: On the ground under a tree, in a clump of weeds and grass

Call: An unmusical trill, much like a cicada song but short

Hot spots: Any winter visit to a mowed field or park will reveal at least one palm warbler, often several. This widespread resident grazes through mowed grassy areas, often in mixed flocks that include equally common pine warblers.

PINE WARBLER
Setophaga pinus

The pine warbler's yellow plumage stands out for winter birders as this bird mingles with palm warblers.

Field marks: Male has olive head and face with yellow spectacles, yellow dot above bill, yellow throat and breast, olive streaks on breast and flanks, white belly and undertail coverts, olive back, gray wings with two white wing bars, gray tail. Female lacks the streaking on breast, but has light streaks on flanks. *Fall plumage:* Gray head and back with white eye ring, pale neck patch, light gray underside with indistinct streaks on flanks, gray wings with white wing bars.

Size: L: 5.5", WS: 8.75"

Similar species: Female Cape May warbler has more distinct dark streaks on the breast and underside. Fall Cape May lacks the eye ring and has a greenish rump. Fall blackburnian warbler has yellow throat.

Season: Summer

Habitat: Mixed or coniferous forests with pine trees

Food source: Insects, seeds, fruit

Nest: At the end of a pine tree branch at least 20 feet up, hidden by needles

Call: A long, melodious trill, similar to a chipping sparrow but slower

Hot spots: Pine warblers are widespread and numerous throughout the winter, usually found feeding in mowed areas near wetlands in the company of palm warblers. Small mixed flocks of these two birds may visit backyards as well, though they generally do not come to feeders.

DOMINIC SHERONY

BAY-BREASTED WARBLER
Setophaga castanea

One of the largest warblers, the bay-breasted can be found in woods with spruce trees as it moves northward during spring migration.

Field marks: Male has rufous cap, black face, creamy white back of head, rufous throat, buff breast with irregular rufous stripe along flanks, buff undertail coverts, black wings with two white wing bars, black tail with white outer feathers. Female has small rufous cap; buff face, nape, and throat; rufous stripe on breast and along flanks, buff flanks and undertail coverts, black back and wings with two wing bars, black tail. *Fall plumage:* Male has greenish-yellow head and back, white throat, greenish breast, buff underside with rufous stripe on flanks, black wings with two wing bars, black tail. Nonbreeding female lacks the rufous flanks.

Size: L: 5.5", WS: 9"

Similar species: No other local warbler has the bright rufous throat and flanks.

Season: Fall migration, with a few individuals in spring

Habitat: Deciduous woodlands, spruce forests

Food source: Moths and other insects, caterpillars, canker worms

Nest: On a branch in a conifer, high above the ground

Call: High, wheezy *a-seetie-seetie-seetie-seetie-seet;* also a simple *chip*

Hot spots: Point Ybel Lighthouse Beach Park, Sanibel, 26.4520609 / -82.0151281; Fort De Soto Park, St. Petersburg, 27.6327266 / -82.718157; St. George Island State Park, youth camp area, Eastpoint, 29.7155 / -84.7535; Bill Baggs Cape Florida State Park, Key Biscayne, 25.6733 / -80.1582; Spanish River Park, Boca Raton, 26.3829 / -80.0692

BLACKPOLL WARBLER
Setophaga striata

The blackpoll warbler brings up the rear in spring migration, passing through Florida on its way to its Canadian breeding grounds.

Field marks: Male has black cap descending to the eye, white face, black malar stripe, black and gray bill, white throat, white underside with black streaks from throat to flanks, black back and wings with two thin white wing bars, white undertail coverts, black tail with white outer feathers. Female has gray cap, face, back, and wings with darker gray streaks; whitish throat, grayish underside with darker streaks, white undertail coverts, two white wing bars, dark tail. *Fall plumage:* Male has gray cap; yellowish face, throat, and breast; white flanks and undertail coverts, gray streaks from throat to flanks, dark gray back and wings with two white wing bars, dark gray tail. Nonbreeding female lacks throat stripe and is more subtly streaked.

Size: L: 5.5", WS: 9"

Similar species: Black-and-white warbler has black crown stripe and a wide white eyebrow, as well as heavy black streaking on the breast, flanks, and back.

Season: Spring migration

Habitat: Coniferous woods

Food source: A variety of insects and spiders

Nest: On a branch in a young conifer (not in Florida)

Call: A series of rapid, high-pitched notes: *zizizizizi*, sometimes in a shorter phrase; also a very high *zit* note

Hot spots: Maritime Hammock Preserve, Cocoa Beach, 28.3311287 / -80.6110239; Ocean Bay Riverside Park, Jensen Beach, 27.3381582 / -80.2365983; Delnor-Wiggins Pass State Park, Naples, 26.2816555 / -81.8292456; Point Ybel Lighthouse Beach Park, Sanibel, 26.4520609 / -82.0151281; Leffis Key, Bradenton Beach, 27.4522656 / -82.6890434

YELLOW-THROATED WARBLER
Setophaga dominica

This warbler's creeping behavior, black and white head pattern, and bright yellow throat are standout field marks.

Field marks: Gray cap, white eyebrow, black eye line, white lower half eye ring, black and white cheek, long bill, bright yellow throat, gray back and wings with two white wing bars, white underside with gray streaks, white undertail coverts, gray tail.

Size: L: 5.25"–5.5", WS: 8"–8.5"

Similar species: Magnolia warbler has a yellow underside. Yellow-rumped warbler (myrtle race) has a white throat and yellow flanks; Audubon race has a yellow throat, but is not normally seen in Florida.

Season: Year-round in northern and central Florida; winter only south of Sarasota (though more birds are being found in summer in south Florida)

Habitat: Mature mixed forests, both wet and dry, especially if they contain pine trees

Food source: Insects, spiders

Nest: Close to the ground in a clump of pine needles or moss

Call: A languid, musical *sweet-sweet-sweet-sweet-sweet-sweet-a-deet-a-deet;* also a dry, one-note *chip*

Hot spots: St. Marks National Wildlife Refuge, St. Marks, 30.1515653 / -84.1473314; Road to Nowhere, Jena, 29.5705764 / -83.3788609; Bayport Park, Spring Hill, 28.5342292 / -82.650066; Oscar Scherer State Park, Nokomis, 27.1734149 / -82.466383; Black Creek Park, Fleming Island, 30.0478 / -81.7101167

HOODED WARBLER
Setophaga citrina

The lemon-yellow face surrounded by a black, hijab-like hood makes this bird unique among local warblers.

Field marks: Male has yellow face, black hood and throat, black eye; yellow breast, belly, underside, and undertail coverts; solid olive back and wings, olive tail with white patches and black tip. Female may be identical, or may have a partial black hood and throat.

Size: L: 5.25", WS: 7"

Similar species: No other local warbler has a similar face, head, and throat pattern.

Season: Summer in northern Florida; spring and fall migration in central and south Florida

Habitat: Woods and forests with considerable understory; wetlands with woods

Food source: Insects

Nest: Near the ground in a shrub or small tree

Call: Clear, loud *tuwee, tuwee, tuwee, THREEo*

Hot spots: St. Marks National Wildlife Refuge, St. Marks, 30.1515653 / -84.1473314; George C. McGough Nature Park, Largo, 27.8830494 / -82.8426218; Evergreen Cemetery, Fort Lauderdale, 26.1061594 / -80.1318741; Point Ybel Lighthouse Beach Park, Sanibel, 26.4520609 / -82.0151281; Mead Botanical Gardens, Winter Park, 28.5836 / -81.3586

WORM-EATING WARBLER
Helmitheros vermivorum

This comparatively drab but distinctive warbler passes through Florida in small numbers during spring and fall migration. Despite its name, there's no evidence that this bird eats earthworms.

Field marks: Buff head with thin black crown stripe and eye line, black eye with thin white eye ring, large black and gray bill; clear buffy throat, breast, and underside; gray-brown wings and tail. Male, female, and nonbreeding plumages are the same.

Size: L: 5.25", WS: 8.5"

Similar species: Ovenbird has an orange crown stripe, a large white eye ring, and a white breast with heavy black bars. Northern and Louisiana waterthrushes have a dark brown crown stripe; dark brown back, wings, and tail; and white or buff breast with heavy brown streaking.

Season: Spring and fall migration

Habitat: Hillsides with thick foliage

Food source: Insects, slugs, caterpillars

Nest: On the ground, well-hidden in understory (not in Florida)

Call: One continuous trill, rising in the middle and falling again at the end

Hot spots: St. Marks National Wildlife Refuge, St. Marks, 30.1515653 / -84.1473314; Fort De Soto Park, St. Petersburg, 27.6327266 / -82.718157; Audubon Corkscrew Swamp Sanctuary, Corkscrew, 26.375442 / -81.6040206; Bill Baggs Cape Florida State Park, Key Biscayne, 25.6733 / -80.1582; Turkey Creek Sanctuary, Palm Bay, 28.0156 / -80.5957

PROTHONOTARY WARBLER
Protonotaria citrea

A flash of yellow during spring migration or summer may be all that Floridians see of this bright yellow visitor.

Field marks: Bright yellow head, throat, breast, belly, and flanks; black eye and sharp black bill, darker yellow back, blue-gray wings and tail, white undertail coverts. Male and female plumage is similar. *Fall plumage:* Darker yellow head, throat, and breast; light yellow wash on belly and flanks, olive back, blue-gray wings and tail, white undertail coverts.

Size: L: 5.5", WS: 8.75"

Similar species: Yellow warbler has a darker yellow back and wings and red streaks on its breast and flanks. Blue-winged warbler has a black eye stripe and gray wings with white wing bars.

Season: Spring migration, summer in north and central Florida

Habitat: Wooded wetlands, including forests with areas of standing water

Food source: Insects, some fruit, seeds

Nest: In a tree cavity or nest box

Call: Languid, musical series of the same note, usually in groups of eight: *sweet-sweet-sweet-sweet-sweet-sweet-sweet-sweet*; sometimes preceded by a higher chip note

Hot spots: Tate's Hell State Forest, Ralph G. Kendrick Boardwalk, Eastpoint, 29.8348482 / -84.7932824; St. Marks National Wildlife Refuge, St. Marks, 30.1515653 / -84.1473314; Paynes Prairie Preserve State Park, Bolen Bluff Trail, Gainesville, 29.5587838 / -82.3245401; Sweetwater Wetlands Park, Gainesville, 29.6151026 / -82.3254061; Leffis Key, Bradenton Beach, 27.4522656 / -82.6890434

BLACK-AND-WHITE WARBLER
Mniotilta varia

The black-and-white warbler climbs trees like a nuthatch and is comfortable upside down on a tree trunk—a unique quality among eastern warblers.

Field marks: Male has black and white–striped head with wide black eye stripe, patchy black throat, white underside with black stripes from breast to undertail, black and white–striped back and wings, two horizontal white wing bars, black tail. Female has black and white–striped head with thin eye stripe, pale cheek and throat, gray nape, white underside with gray stripes, buff flanks, black and white–striped back and wings with two horizontal wing bars. *Fall plumage:* Male plumage does not change in nonbreeding season. Female becomes more buff under the wings and on the flanks.

Size: L: 5.25", WS: 8.25"

Similar species: Blackpoll warbler has a solid black cap that extends down the head to the eye, and a solid gray back.

Season: Winter

Habitat: Deciduous forests, parks, residential areas

Food source: Caterpillars, spiders, insects, insect eggs found under bark

Nest: On the ground at the bottom of a tree or stump (not in Florida)

Call: A high, wheezy, squeaky song of ten or eleven notes: *ziti-ziti-ziti-ziti-ziti* or *weezee-weezee-weezee-weezee-weezee*; also a single *zeet* chip note

Hot spots: Check your favorite neighborhood park or woods for this very common warbler, which will be likely wherever you normally find chickadees, nuthatches, and yellow-rumped warblers. Just about every park with leafy trees will provide food and shelter to black-and-white warblers throughout the winter.

AMERICAN REDSTART
Setophaga ruticilla

Common and gregarious, this flashy bird and its attractive mate regularly confuse birders with their variety of songs.

Field marks: Male has black head, back, throat, wings, and tail; orange stripe from shoulder to flank, orange wing stripe, wide orange areas on tail before black tip. Female has gray head, throat, breast, and flanks; yellow shoulders, olive back and wings, yellow wing patches, wide yellow patches at base of tail. *Fall plumage:* Male has gray head, white eye ring, black streaks at neck, olive back and wings, yellow shoulders and wing stripe, yellow at base of dark gray tail. Female has gray head, throat, breast, flanks, and undertail coverts; white eye ring, yellow wash at sides, no wing bars, and yellow base of tail.

Size: L: 5.25", WS: 7.75"

Similar species: Baltimore oriole is larger and has a black head and wings and an orange body.

Season: Spring and fall migration

Habitat: Mixed woodlands

Food source: Insects, caterpillars, spiders, seeds, berries

Nest: On a tree branch at least 10 feet above the ground (generally not in Florida)

Call: Sometimes a wheezy *zeedle-zeedle-zeedle-zee;* sometimes *zhee-zhee-zhee-zhee-seet,* dropping in pitch at the end; sometimes a series of rattle notes ending in a slower *chibby, chibby, chibby, chim;* sometimes a slow *teet, teet, teet, teet,* followed by a trill. Other variations are likely as well.

Hot spots: Redstarts migrate in large flocks and can be found in any kind of woodland during migration. They begin to appear in Florida as early as August on their way south, and continue through the region until early November. In spring, begin watching for them in early April.

OVENBIRD
Seiurus aurocapilla

The best way to find this warbler is to follow its astonishingly loud *teacher-teacher-teacher* song. It gets its name from the oven-like shape of its nest.

Field marks: Orange crown stripe bordered by a black stripe on each side; light brown head, back, wings, and tail; large white eye ring, yellow bill, white throat with black vertical stripes, white underside with black streaks, light brown rear, white undertail coverts. Male, female, and nonbreeding plumages are all similar.

Size: L: 6", WS: 9.5"

Similar species: Wood thrush has a deep rufous head and back and is spotted rather than streaked on its underside. Swainson's thrush is larger, has a solid brown head and buff-yellow spectacles, and is lightly spotted on its breast instead of streaked. Other thrushes are similarly spotted, with solid-color heads. Worm-eating warbler is smaller, has no streaking on its lower body, and has very thin black stripes on its head.

Season: Spring and fall migration through the Panhandle; winter throughout the rest of the state

Habitat: Mature forests with open understory

Food source: Insects, worms, spiders, snails

Nest: On the ground, built like an oven to be entered from the side

Call: A loud, musical *teacher-teacher-teacher-teacher-teacher;* also a *whip, whip chip* note

Hot spots: With its loud, penetrating call and its propensity for rustling through dry leaves on the forest floor, the ovenbird makes no secret of its location. Find them in any wooded area during migration and throughout winter. Check low branches and the brushy understory of your favorite local woods, and use your ears as well as your eyes to locate them.

© SHUTTERSTOCK.COM/HAYLEY CREWS

YELLOW-BREASTED CHAT
Icteria virens

Infuriatingly difficult to see, this shy warbler is the largest in the wood-warbler family.

Field marks: Solid olive-brown head, nape, back, and wings; white spectacles pattern across eyes, above bill, and forming a malar "mustache," black bill, yellow breast, white underside, light peach wash on flanks, white undertail coverts, dark legs. Male and female are identical.

Size: L: 7"–8", WS: 9.5"–10"

Similar species: Common yellowthroat has a wide black mask. Kentucky warbler is smaller and has a bold black pattern around the eye and cheek.

Season: Summer along the Pandhandle's coast and in northern Florida, migration along the central state's coastlines, winter along the southern coast and in the Everglades and Keys

Habitat: Brushy areas and thickets, especially along forest edges and on the shores of ponds, streams, and swamps

Food source: Insects and spiders

Nest: In low vegetation, especially in blackberry or raspberry bushes

Call: Many different variations, including mewing, whistling, a harsh chuckle, and others, not unlike a mockingbird but slower and more measured. They may emit a defensive *chk* chip note while moving through brush near a nest or a winter roost.

Hot spots: Lakes Park, Fort Myers, 26.5271649 / -81.8765643; Orlando Wetlands Park, Orlando, 28.5753263 / -80.9966826; Paynes Prairie Preserve State Park, Bolen Bluff Trail, Gainesville, 29.5587838 / -82.3245401; Sweetwater Wetlands Park, Gainesville, 29.6151026 / -82.3254061; Frog Pond Wildlife Management Area, Lucky Hammock, Homestead, 25.396439 / -80.566581

NORTHERN WATERTHRUSH
Parkesia noveboracensis

Where woodlands shelter slow-moving streams or motionless pools, northern waterthrush makes its home. Watch for this thrush-like bird's narrow white eyebrow and buffy flanks.

Field marks: Brown cap, narrow white eyebrow, black eye-line, dark cheek, white or buff throat heavily streaked in black, underside consistently white or buff with heavy black streaks, white undertail coverts; uniformly dark brown back, wings, and tail. Male, female, and nonbreeding plumages are similar.

Size: L: 6", WS: 9.5"

Similar species: Louisiana waterthrush has a wider white eyebrow and less streaking on flanks and underside.

Season: Spring and fall migration

Habitat: Streams, rivers, or pools in the midst of fairly dense woodland areas

Food source: Insects, fish, snails, tiny crustaceans

Nest: In a riverbank, or on the woodland floor at the base of a tree

Call: A musical *cheewhit, whit, whit, whit, wee-wee-wee-wee-o*, dropping in pitch at the end; also a metallic *chit, chit, chit* note

Hot spots: Paynes Prairie Preserve State Park, Bolen Bluff Trail, Gainesville, 29.5587838 / -82.3245401; Mead Botanical Gardens, Winter Park, 28.5836 / -81.3586; Lantana Nature Preserve, Lantana, 26.5843827 / -80.0415768; Point Ybel Lighthouse Beach Park, Sanibel, 26.4520609 / -82.0151281; Long Key State Park, Layton, 24.814968 / -80.82018

DOMIN C SHERONY

DOM/NIC SHERONY

LOUISIANA WATERTHRUSH

Parkesia motacilla

Slimmer than a northern waterthrush and sporting a clear white throat, this close cousin prefers more swiftly moving waterways.

Field marks: Brown cap, wide white eyebrow, wide black eye line, brown cheek, clear white throat, brown malar stripe, white breast and underside with sparse brown streaks, white undertail coverts; uniformly brown back, wings, and tail.

Size: L: 6", WS: 10"

Similar species: Northern waterthrush has a chunkier profile, a narrower white eyebrow, a streaked throat, and heavy streaking on its breast and underside.

Season: Summer

Habitat: Brooks and rivers flowing down hillsides, wetlands formed by rivers, woodland streams

Food source: Insects, small frogs, invertebrates

Nest: Among tree roots, along a streambank in a sheltered spot with an overhanging ledge, or in a hollowed-out stump

Call: Five distinct notes: *seeit-seeit-seeit-suet-up*, sometimes followed by a catbird-like series of warbles and sounds; other variations also possible

Hot spots: Lake Apopka North Shore, Astatula, 28.6740878 / -81.7059258; San Felasco Hammock Preserve State Park, Yellow Trail, Gainesville, 29.7180976 / -82.4636471; Big Cypress National Preserve, Kirby Storter Roadside Park and Boardwalk, Big Cypress, 25.8675841 / -81.1501694; Long Key State Park, Layton, 24.814968 / -80.82018; Dunedin Hammock City Park, Dunedin, 28.0324 / -82.781

COMMON YELLOWTHROAT
Geothlypis trichas

"Common," in this case, is correct: Every wetland, forest pool, river, stream, lake, or bay in Florida has some of these chatty, brightly-colored warblers.

Field marks: Male has tan cap, nape, back, wings, and tail; black mask across eyes to the bill, extending to the throat on either side, with a white upper stripe; dark bill, yellow throat, tan belly and flanks, yellow undertail coverts. Female has tan head, neck, back, wings, tail, and underside; white eye ring, yellow throat and undertail coverts. *Fall plumage:* Male has tan head, back, wings, and tail; brown forehead, nearly black shading along the malars, yellow throat, tan underside, light yellow undertail coverts. Female is similar to male, but without the dark shading along the malar, and with a paler yellow throat.

Size: L: 5", WS: 6.75"

Similar species: Yellow-throated and yellow-rumped warblers have yellow throats, but with black and white heads and bodies. Magnolia warbler has a yellow throat and a black mask, but has a black and white head and body and heavy black streaks on its breast and underside.

Season: Year-round

Habitat: Damp woods and fields, wetlands, streambeds, riparian areas, dunes near beaches, or along brushy roadsides with drainage canals

Food source: Spiders, butterflies, dragonflies, beetles, grasshoppers, some seeds

Nest: Near the ground and concealed by high grasses and other vegetation

Call: A musical phrase with the common mnemonic *witchity, witchity, witchity, witt,* sometimes fast and sometimes slower; also a rapid, staccato trill like a rattlesnake and a generally unmusical chatter

Hot spots: Any stop at a wetland, coastal dunes, woodland edge near water, or a riparian area can yield at least one common yellowthroat. Listen for its song and calls to determine exactly where it might be, and watch for movement—yellowthroats are usually on the move through their habitat as they forage for food. These birds are also well known for responding to spishing, a birder trick to attract a bird's attention.

WILSON'S WARBLER
Cardellina pusilla

This small warbler migrates through Florida in spring and fall; a few individuals stay for the winter.

Field marks: Male has black oval cap, lemon-yellow face, large black eye, small pink bill; yellow throat, breast, belly, and undertail coverts; solid olive back, wings, and tail. Female is more muted, with a smaller cap that may be olive, black, or with elements of each. *Fall plumage:* Black cap may (or may not) have olive feathers in it during fall and winter.

Size: L: 4.75", WS: 7"

Similar species: Yellow warbler has no black cap. Hooded warbler has a black throat and a black cap that extends from forehead to throat. Common yellowthroat has a substantial black mask. Prothonotary warbler has no cap and has blue-gray wings.

Season: Spring and fall migration

Habitat: Woodlands with willow and alder trees and water features, including streams, wetlands, and pools

Food source: Insects, spiders

Nest: On the ground among dense vegetation in a thicket or shrubby area

Call: A two-part series of notes, doubling in speed halfway through: *chi-chi-chi-chi-chichichichichi*; alternately, the song may be just the opposite, with its rapid notes first, slowing to a more languid pace in the middle: *chichichichichi-che-che-che-che-che*. Very high pitched single chip notes are also in the repertoire.

Hot spots: Paynes Prairie Preserve State Park, Bolen Bluff Trail, Gainesville, 29.5587838 / -82.3245401; Spanish River Park, Boca Raton, 26.3829 / -80.0692; Mead Botanical Gardens, Winter Park, 28.5836 / -81.3586; Lake Elberta, Tallahassee, 30.4297796 / -84.3005751

© SHUTTERSTOCK.COM/MTKHALED MAHMUD

SWAINSON'S WARBLER

Limnothlypis swainsonii

The muted colors and skulking behavior of this warbler make it particularly difficult to see.

Field marks: Brown-to-rusty cap, whitish face with black line through black eye, whitish-gray breast and underside; brown back, wings, and tail. Stockier than most other migrating warblers.

Size: L: 5.5"–6", WS 9"

Similar species: Worm-eating warbler has bold black stripes on its head, a buffy face and breast, and a grayish back and wings. Ovenbird has black stripes on its head and bold, black streaks on its breast and underside. Waterthrushes have a strong white eyebrow and streaks on their undersides and breasts.

Season: Spring and fall migration; some individuals remain through the winter in the Panhandle and central Florida

Habitat: In the understory of wooded areas, almost always on the ground

Food source: Insects and spiders that live under leaves and among grasses on the ground

Nest: In a knot of vines or dense twigs and branches, just off the ground

Call: *Ti-tee, tee, tee, we-tee-WHEEoo;* also a simple *cht* call note

Hot spots: Paynes Prairie Preserve State Park, Bolen Bluff Trail, Gainesville, 29.5587838 / -82.3245401; Spanish River Park, Boca Raton, 26.3829 / -80.0692; Mead Botanical Gardens, Winter Park, 28.5836 / -81.3586; Lake Elberta, Tallahassee, 30.4297796 / -84.3005751

© SHUTTERSTOCK.COM/AGAMI PHOTO AGENCY

KENTUCKY WARBLER
Geothlypis formosa

A low-level dweller with a clear, ringing song, this brightly colored bird migrates close to Florida's coastlines.

Field marks: Mottled black cap, bright yellow face with distinctive black crescent from eye to cheek; bright yellow breast and underside, olive back and wings, olive tail. Female lacks the crescent and has an olive patch under the eye from bill to nape.

Size: L: 5"–5.5", WS: 8"–9"

Similar species: Connecticut, Nashville, and mourning warblers have gray heads; Connecticut and Nashville have a white eye ring.

Season: Spring and fall migration, mostly on the state's western coast

Habitat: Forest understory, usually foraging low in shrubs or on the ground

Food source: Insects and spiders

Nest: On or near the ground, sometimes in a shrub with low-growing foliage

Call: *turWEE, turWEE, turWEE, turWEE, turWEE,* loudly and in rapid succession

Hot spots: Elinor Klapp-Phipps Park, Tallahassee, 30.535666 / -84.28821; San Felasco Hammock Preserve State Park, Moonshine Creek Trail, Gainesville, 29.7144357 / -82.460804; Pinecraft Park, Southgate, 27.3189746 / -82.5037765; Key West Tropical Forest and Botanical Gardens, Key West, 24.5734 / -81.7496

TANAGERS AND ALLIED SONGBIRDS

SUMMER TANAGER
Piranga rubra

North America's only totally red bird and its muted yellow mate love to forage at the tops of trees.

Field marks: Male is entirely bright red, with a heavy gray bill. Female is a dull yellow with olive-yellow wings.

Size: L: 7.5"–8", WS: 11"–12"

Similar species: Northern cardinal has a black facial pattern around the bill, and a pronounced crest (female is soft brown with red accents and an orange bill). Scarlet tanager has black wings. Vermilion flycatcher is smaller and has black wings and tail and a black mask.

Season: Spring and fall migration in south Florida; breeding in central and northern Florida

Habitat: Deciduous or mixed forests

Food source: Primarily bees and wasps; also a number of other insects

Nest: On a forked tree branch, usually overhanging a waterway or road

Call: A short phrase of five or six sliding whistles, very like an American robin

Hot spots: Torreya State Park, Bristol, 30.5656 / -84.9468; Elinor Klapp-Phipps Park, Tallahassee, 30.535666 / -84.28821; Newnan's Lake State Forest, East Trail, Gainesville, 29.6611775 / -82.2544858; Clearwater Lake Recreation Area Trailhead, Paisley, 28.97664 / -81.5502; Boyd Hill Nature Park and Lake Maggiore, St. Petersburg, 27.7322367 / -82.6521206

SCARLET TANAGER
Piranga olivacea

The flaming red bird with black wings stands out from any tree it inhabits.

Field marks: Male has red head and body, black wings and tail, gray bill. Female has olive head, back, wings, and tail; black eye, yellow lores and throat, gray bill, olive-yellow underparts. *Fall plumage:* Male has olive head and back, black wings, yellow lores and malars, darker yellow throat and breast, yellow belly, yellow-gray underside and undertail coverts. Female retains the same plumage in nonbreeding season.

Size: L: 7", WS: 11.5"

Similar species: Northern cardinal male has red wings and tail, a pronounced crest, a black face, and a red bill.

Season: Spring and fall migration

Habitat: Deciduous and mixed woodlands, especially those with pine and oak; parks, residential areas

Food source: Insects, fruit, tree leaf and flower buds

Nest: On a tree branch at least 20 feet above the ground

Call: A sweet, burry *cheet-chip-chureet, churrit, chureet, churitt, chureet*; also a more frequent and recognizable *chick-burr* note

Hot spots: St. George Island State Park, Youth Camp Area, Eastpoint, 29.7155 / -84.7535; Paynes Prairie Preserve State Park, Bolen Bluff Trail, Gainesville, 29.5587838 / -82.3245401; Pinecraft Park, Southgate, 27.3189746 / -82.5037765; J. N. Ding Darling National Wildlife Refuge, Sanibel, 26.4540529 / -82.1155071; Evergreen Cemetery, Fort Lauderdale, 26.1061594 / -80.1318741

© SHUTTERSTOCK.COM/JUKKA JANTUNEN

WESTERN SPINDALIS
Spindalis zena

Formerly known as striped-headed tanager, this flamboyantly plumaged bird visits from the Caribbean.

Field marks: Boldly striped black and white head; yellow-orange throat, breast, and nape; brown back, white wings with black outer flight feathers, white underside and flanks, orange rump, black tail with white outer feathers. Female is muted brown with white stripe above and below eye, brown back and wings with black wings and white-edged outer feathers, yellowish wash on breast, lighter white underside, white undertail coverts.

Size: L: 6.5"–7", WS 9"–10"

Similar species: No other Florida bird has this bold facial pattern.

Season: Spring, occasionally in fall

Habitat: Fruit trees, low brush, often in neighborhood yards with shrubs and flowering trees

Food source: Fruit and berries, leaf buds; possibly snails

Nest: High in trees

Call: A long series of very high-pitched *seet-seet-seet* and *sip* notes

Hot spots: There are no reliable places for this vagrant from the Bahamas, but these spots have hosted western spindalis at least twice in the past several years: Crandon Park, Key Biscayne, 25.7089712 / -80.1536322; Lantana Nature Preserve, Lantana, 26.5843827 / -80.0415768; Bill Baggs Cape Florida State Park, Key Biscayne, 25.6733 / -80.1582

NORTHERN CARDINAL
Cardinalis cardinalis

The denizen of backyard feeders and neighborhood parks throughout the eastern states, this local resident is one of the first birds that new birders recognize on sight.

Field marks: Male has bright red head with pronounced crest, black face, red bill, red body and tail with darker red wings. Female has brown body, crest with red wash, black face, bright orange bill, red wings and tail.

Size: L: 8.75", WS: 12"

Similar species: Scarlet tanager has no crest, has black wings and a black tail.

Season: Year-round

Habitat: Deciduous and coniferous woods, residential areas, woodland borders of farm fields and wetlands, parks

Food source: Seeds, insects, fruit, berries

Nest: In a bush or tree with low branches, not more than 5 feet from the ground

Call: Musical and varied, often beginning with a long, plunging pennywhistle note that ends with a *cha-cha-cha-cha-cha* series; or beginning with a *neerEET, neerEET* series and returning to the *cha-cha-cha* notes at the end. Other variations are likely. Also a metallic chip note, often heard just before dusk.

Hot spots: Every neighborhood has several families of cardinals, so you don't need to look far to find them. Draw them into your yard by offering black oil sunflower seed at your feeders, or take a walk in a park or on a converted rail trail to find them just beyond the first trees as you pass. Cardinals perch on the tops of fences or on posts, as well as on low tree branches.

ROSE-BREASTED GROSBEAK
Pheucticus ludovicianus

The black head, white belly, and bright red breast make the male of this species unmistakable.

Field marks: Male has black head, large white bill, bright red breast, white underside, black wings with large white patch, white rump, black tail with white outer tail feathers. Underwings are pink in flight. Female has brown head with white eyebrow and chin stripe, pale pink bill, white throat, white breast with brown streaks, buff flanks streaked with brown, brown back and wings with two white wing bars, whitish undertail coverts, brown tail. Underwings are yellow in flight. *Fall plumage:* Male is brown and white like a female, but with a light orange breast. Female is similar to breeding season, with a buff breast.

Size: L: 8", WS: 12.5"

Similar species: Eastern towhee has a black head, white breast, and rusty orange flanks.

Season: Spring and fall migration

Habitat: Woodlands, farm fields and meadows with wooded edges

Food source: Insects, seeds, fruit

Nest: On the branch of a tree, not far from the ground

Call: A continuous, musical warble, often compared to American robin, but longer and with a burry quality; also a short *turtle-lee* phrase

Hot spots: St. George Island State Park, Eastpoint, 29.7155 / -84.7535; Kanapaha Botanical Gardens, Gainesville, 29.6128267 / -82.4088335; Fort De Soto Park, St. Petersburg, 27.6327266 / -82.718157; Frog Pond Wildlife Management Area, Lucky Hammock, Homestead, 25.396439 / -80.566581; Tall Cypress Natural Area, Coral Springs, 26.2768695 / -80.214057

BLUE GROSBEAK
Passerina caerulea

The largest of the predominantly blue birds in Florida prefers open areas with low brush and few trees.

Field marks: Male is royal blue with darker wings and two rufous wing bars; a large, light gray bill. Female is light brownish gray with darker wings and one rufous wing bar.

Size: L: 6.5"–7", WS: 11"–12"

Similar species: Indigo bunting is smaller and solid blue with no wing bars. Eastern bluebird has an orange breast and a white underside.

Season: Breeding from the Panhandle to central Florida; spring and fall migration along the coasts and in south Florida

Habitat: Shrubby areas with low, dense vegetation, like fallow farm fields, edges of woodlands, power line right-of-way corridors, and other overgrown lots

Food source: Mostly insects, some snails

Nest: Low in a tree, shrub, or tangle of vines

Call: A series of bubbly musical notes like a shortened finch song, usually for about 3 seconds

Hot spots: Sweetwater Wetlands Park, Gainesville, 29.6151026 / -82.3254061; J. R. Alford Greenway, Tallahassee, 30.444382 / -84.1754436; Paynes Prairie Preserve State Park, Bolen Bluff Trail, Gainesville, 29.5587838 / -82.3245401; Hálpata Tastanaki Preserve, Dunnellon, 29.0456464 / -82.3777467; Fort De Soto Park, St. Petersburg, 27.6327266 / -82.718157

INDIGO BUNTING
Passerina cyanea

This gorgeous all-blue bird raises its young near open woodlands, meadows, and farm fields.

Field marks: Male has bright blue head, body, and tail; whitish bill, black wings with blue shoulders. Female has light brown head and body with a white throat, fine brown streaks on its breast, slightly darker brown wings, whitish undertail coverts, and a light brown tail with a bluish hue. *Fall plumage:* Male has mottled blue and brown head and body, with brown wings with a bluish cast, white undertail coverts, and a bluish tail. Female has rosy brown head with white throat, pinkish breast with faint streaks, whitish belly and undertail, rosy brown wings and tail.

Size: L: 5.5"–5.75", WS: 8"–9"

Similar species: Blue grosbeak has dark wings with two rufous wing bars. Eastern bluebird has an orange breast and belly and white undertail coverts. Cerulean warbler has a white throat, breast, and belly and two white wing bars. Black-throated blue warbler has a black throat and white belly.

Season: Summer north of Tampa; winter throughout south Florida and the Keys

Habitat: Scrubby fields, pastures with wooded edges, cleared gaps between woodlands

Food source: Seeds, berries, insects

Nest: Well-concealed in a shrub or small tree, not far from the ground

Call: A musical *pitty-pitty-cheeRAH-chee-chee-peeyu*, with longer and shorter variations. A single sharp *chit*, repeated frequently, is the chip note.

Hot spots: Lake Apopka Wildlife Drive, Apopka, 28.6691082 / -81.5574338; Sweetwater Wetlands Park, Gainesville, 29.6151026 / -82.3254061; J. R. Alford Greenway, Tallahassee, 30.444382 / -84.1754436; Loxahatchee National Wildlife Refuge, Valencia Reserve, 26.4928139 / -80.2168894; Frog Pond Wildlife Management Area, Lucky Hammock, Homestead, 25.396439 / -80.566581

PAINTED BUNTING
Passerina ciris

One of the most beautiful and sought-after birds in North America makes parts of Florida its breeding and overwintering grounds.

Field marks: Male has a purple head with a red eye ring; red throat, breast, underside, and rump; green back and darker wings with a vague red wing bar. Female is olive above and muted yellow below.

Size: L: 5"–6", WS: 8.5"–9"

Similar species: Indigo bunting is solid blue. No other Florida bird has this striking color pattern.

Season: Winter in south Florida and the Keys, migration along both coasts and through central Florida, breeding (summer) along the Atlantic coast north of Titusville.

Habitat: Fields near sparse woods, such as rows of trees between farm fields; roadsides, backyards with feeders

Food source: Seeds, as well as some insects on the ground; also comes to feeders

Nest: In scrub or other dense foliage, 6 feet or higher from the ground

Call: A jumble of rising and falling notes, like a house finch but shorter; also a simple *twik* note

Hot spots: Visitor center feeders at Merritt Island National Wildlife Refuge, Titusville, 28.6411839 / -80.7774067; Huguenot Memorial City Park, Jacksonville, 30.4112444 / -81.4206594; Anastasia State Park, St. Augustine, 29.8661797 / -81.2705122; Bill Baggs Cape Florida State Park, Key Biscayne, 25.6733 / -80.1582; Key West Tropical Forest and Botanical Gardens, Key West, 24.5734 / -81.7496; visitor center feeders at Audubon Corkscrew Swamp Sanctuary, Corkscrew, 26.375442 / -81.6040206

DICKCISSEL
Spiza americana

A Midwestern bird of open grasslands, this sparrowlike visitor puts in regular appearances during spring migration, with some overwintering in central Florida.

Field marks: Male has gray head and nape, white and yellow eyebrow, yellow patch on sides of throat, black V-shaped patch at throat, yellow breast, gray belly and flanks, gray back streaked in black, brown and gray wings with rufous shoulders, gray tail. Female has brownish-gray head with dull yellow eyebrow, darker gray cap, white malar stripe edged in black, whitish throat, yellowish breast, gray flanks and belly, black and gray wings with rufous wing stripe, white undertail coverts, gray tail.

Size: L: 6.25"–7", WS: 9.75"–11"

Similar species: Eastern meadowlark is larger and has a bright yellow throat, breast, and underside. House sparrow is smaller, has no yellow areas, and its black breast patch is not in a V shape.

Season: Spring migration; some winter

Habitat: Open farm fields, especially where grain is grown

Food source: Grain, seeds, insects

Nest: Near the ground among the plant stalks

Call: A clear series of notes followed by a hissing trill: *dick-dick-dick-cissss* or *dick-dick-cis-cis-cis*

Hot spots: Fort Zachary Taylor Historic State Park, Key West, 24.5463 / -81.8106; Garden Key, Dry Tortugas National Park, 24.6276 / -82.8728; Point Ybel Lighthouse Beach Park, Sanibel, 26.4520609 / -82.0151281; Fort De Soto Park, St. Petersburg, 27.6327266 / -82.718157; Paynes Prairie Preserve State Park, La Chua Trail, Gainesville, 29.6068756 / -82.3031116

SPARROWS AND THEIR ALLIES

EASTERN TOWHEE
Pipilo erythrophthalmus

The East's only towhee (formerly known as rufous-sided) prefers to perch atop stalks in open fields near woodlands.

Field marks: Male has black head, breast, back, wings, and tail; red eye, white underside, bright rufous flanks, light orange undertail coverts, white patch at the edge of the primary feathers. Female is identical to the male, but with a brown head, breast, back, wings, and tail instead of black.

Size: L: 7.5"–8.5", WS: 10.5"–11"

Similar species: American robin has a brown head, back, wings, and tail; a rufous underside from breast to belly. Rose-breasted grosbeak has a bright red breast.

Season: Year-round

Habitat: Open woods on the edges of brushy fields, especially among oak trees

Food source: Insects, seeds, berries, acorns

Nest: Under a dense shrub on the ground

Call: Commonly transcribed as *drink-your-TEEEEEEE*, two or three notes followed by a high, musical trill; also a rising *jeWINK* call note

Hot spots: Eastern towhee populates open fields and forest edges across the state, making a choice of just a few hot spots particularly difficult. Visit wildlife refuges, nature centers, and other open spaces with fields of wildflowers—especially native varieties—and listen for the "drink-your-tea" song. This bird will sit right up on a strong stalk and sing, especially during breeding season.

315

© SHUTTERSTOCK.COM/ARCHAEOPTERYX TOURS

BACHMAN'S SPARROW
Peucaea aestivalis

This secretive sparrow's preference for an open understory has made it a relative rarity in Florida and throughout the southeastern states.

Field marks: Light brown face with thin, darker brown line through the eye; darker brown crest, small gray bill, light brown throat, breast, and flanks; whiter underside, brown back, brown wings with rufous streaks, long, rounded brown tail.

Size: L: 5"–6", WS: 7"–7.5"

Similar species: Grasshopper sparrow is smaller; has a flat head (no crest), a thin bill, and no rufous areas.

Season: Year-round

Habitat: Open pine woodland with little or no brushy understory, or where brush has been burned away

Food source: Mostly seeds, some insects

Nest: On the ground, often just under a shrub

Call: A long, high buzz, followed by six to eight rapid *twee* notes

Hot spots: Oscar Scherer State Park, Nokomis, 27.1734149 / -82.466383; Withlacoochee State Forest, Croom Tract, Croom 28.5887423 / -82.2340393; Tosohatchee Wildlife Management Area, Christmas, 28.495247 / -80.9501839; Tall Timbers Research Station, Tallahassee, 30.6567786 / -84.2087889; St. Sebastian River Preserve State Park, Micco, 27.839059 / -80.5438571

FIELD SPARROW
Spizella pusilla

Listen for a song that accelerates like a bouncing Ping-Pong ball to find this bird in an open field or meadow.

Field marks: Rufous and gray crown, gray head, rufous line behind eye, white eye ring, pink bill, buff breast, gray underside with light rufous flanks, rufous and brown wings with black primaries and two thin white wing bars, long gray tail.

Size: L: 5.75", WS: 8"

Similar species: Chipping sparrow has a white eyebrow and a dark bill.

Season: Winter

Habitat: Disused pastures and farm fields, grasslands

Food source: Insects, seeds

Nest: On the ground or very low in a shrub

Call: An extended, accelerating song on one note: *twee, twee, twee, tweetitititititititi*; also a thin, high, sharp chip note

Hot spots: St. Marks National Wildlife Refuge, St. Marks, 30.1515653 / -84.1473314; Watermelon Pond Wildlife and Environmental Area, Newberry, 29.5803805 / -82.6070997; Paynes Prairie Preserve State Park, La Chua Trail, Gainesville, 29.6068756 / -82.3031116; J. R. Alford Greenway, Tallahassee, 30.444382 / -84.1754436; Bald Point State Park, Bald Point, 29.9377826 / -84.3381304

LARK SPARROW
Chondestes grammacus

A rare but regular visitor to Florida's coastlines, this Midwestern sparrow makes its unpredictable appearances during the winter.

Field marks: Rufous cap with white center stripe, wide gray-white eyebrow, black eye line, rufous cheek, white lower eye ring, white malar stripe with black edge, gray throat, clear whitish breast with dark center spot, grayish-white underside, buff flanks, gray wings and tail with white outer tail feathers.

Size: L: 5.75"–6.5", WS: 10.5"–11"

Similar species: Clay-colored sparrow has a similar but browner facial pattern, buff underparts, and no black dot on the breast.

Season: Winter

Habitat: Scrubby areas and dunes along shorelines, open grasslands

Food source: Insects, seeds

Nest: On the ground or very low in a shrub or sapling; midwestern and western United States

Call: A long series of whistles and trills, not unlike a song sparrow; also a very high, thin *tsp* chip note

Hot spots: Lark sparrow very rarely visits the same place in Florida twice, but a few places have enjoyed more than one winter's sighting: Gulf Islands National Seashore, Fort Pickens, Pensacola Beach, 30.3231 / -87.2829; Bald Point State Park, Bald Point, 29.9377826 / -84.3381304; Fort De Soto Park, St. Petersburg, 27.6327266 / -82.718157; Oscar Scherer State Park, Nokomis, 27.1734149 / -82.466383; Okeeheelee Park, West Palm Beach, 26.6527518 / -80.1575804

CLAY-COLORED SPARROW
Spizella pallida

This Midwestern vagrant appears in grassland refuges and in parks along the coasts.

Field marks: Dark cap with wide white middle stripe, wide white eyebrow, black eye line, brown cheek patch, pink bill, white malar stripe edged in black; gray throat, breast, and underside; brown wings with darker primaries and two white wing bars.

Size: L: 5.5", WS: 7.5"

Similar species: Chipping sparrow is more rufous overall and lacks the brown cheek patch. Lark sparrow is larger and has more rufous in its facial pattern.

Season: Winter

Habitat: Open grassland, disused farm fields, prairie-like areas near beaches

Food source: Insects, seeds

Nest: Among the grasses and plants, up to 6 feet off the ground; midwestern United States

Call: Three or more toneless buzzes like an insect, sometimes preceded by a tiny *tsp* note

Hot spots: Big Cypress National Preserve, Oasis Visitor Center, Big Cypress, 25.8588889 / -81.0338889; Frog Pond Wildlife Management Area, Lucky Hammock, Homestead, 25.396439 / -80.566581; Sparrow Fields at C-357 Pump Station, Gold Coast, 25.6039244 / -80.5301929; Sweetwater Wetlands Park, Gainesville, 29.6151026 / -82.3254061

CHIPPING SPARROW
Spizella passerina

Common from backyards to woodland edges, this little sparrow's rusty cap and white eyebrow make it easy to spot as it forages on a lawn.

Field marks: Rufous cap, white eyebrow, black eye line, gray face, white malar stripe, grayish bill; gray throat, breast, and underside; gray nape, brown wings with two white wing bars, long gray tail. *Fall plumage:* Rufous cap fades to brown with buff eyebrow, pink bill.

Size: L: 5.5", WS: 8.5"–9"

Similar species: American tree sparrow is present only in winter; has a dark spot in the middle of its breast.

Season: Summer

Habitat: Woodland edges, parks, gardens, mowed lawns in neighborhoods and commercial areas

Food source: Insects, seeds

Nest: Among a mass of vines, in a brush pile, or low in a shrub

Call: A long, one-note trill; also a high chip note, repeated incessantly

Hot spots: Throughout winter, chipping sparrows gather in small flocks under trees in landscaped gardens, in backyards with feeders, and in parks with arboretums or grassy paths. One of the best places to find them is on the ground on a rail trail, where they forage for seeds and tiny insects in full view of passers-by. They are far more numerous in residential neighborhoods than in wilderness areas, so south Florida's grasslands record few of these otherwise abundant sparrows.

GRASSHOPPER SPARROW
Ammodramus savannarum

A small sparrow of the grasslands, this bird gets its name from its buzzy, insect-like song and its preference for grasshoppers as a steady diet.

Field marks: Brown cap with white middle stripe, gray eyebrow, black eye with white eye ring, buff bill, tan cheek, dark brown ear spot, buff breast and flanks, grayish underside, rufous and black wings, gray tail.

Size: L: 4.5"–5", WS: 7.75"–8.5"

Similar species: Henslow's sparrow has an olive green head and black-streaked breast, belly, and flanks. Nelson's and saltmarsh sparrows have wide gray napes, streaked breasts, and orange and gray facial patterns. Savannah sparrow is browner overall and has a streaked breast with a dark brown center spot. Vesper sparrow is browner overall, has a brown and white facial pattern, and has a white breast streaked with brown.

Season: Winter; year-round in a small area of central Florida

Habitat: Open grassland, abandoned farm fields, active fields with hay or other grain crops

Food source: Insects, especially grasshoppers; worms, spiders, seeds

Nest: Near or on the ground, among tall grasses

Call: Two or three very high notes, followed by a long, buzzy trill: *keep-keep-keep-zeeeeeeeee*; sometimes followed by additional high-pitched chatter

Hot spots: Three Lakes Wildlife Management Area, Osceola County, 27.9312364 / -81.1522293; Kissimmee Prairie Preserve State Park, Basinger, 27.5746341 / -81.0228825; St. Sebastian River Preserve State Park, Micco, 27.839059 / -80.5438571; Babcock-Webb Wildlife Management Area, Punta Gorda, 26.8582653 / -81.9401121; Fran Reich Preserve SFWMD, Parkland, 26.3545316 / -80.2837256

HENSLOW'S SPARROW
Centronyx henslowii

Relatively rare, this secretive sparrow can be identified by its greenish facial coloring, flat head, and dry *ts-lik* note.

Field marks: Black crown stripes with buff median, olive face with yellow lores, yellow malar stripe outlined in black, white throat, brown and white back, rufous wing edges, buff breast streaked in black, rufous flanks with black streaks, white underside, short tail.

Size: L: 5", WS: 6.5"–7"

Similar species: Nelson's and saltmarsh sparrows have wide gray napes, streaked breasts, and orange and gray facial patterns. Savannah sparrow is browner overall and has a streaked breast with a dark brown center spot. Vesper sparrow is browner overall, has a brown and white facial pattern, and has a white breast streaked with brown.

Season: Winter

Habitat: Open grassland

Food source: Insects, seeds, caterpillars

Nest: Near or on the ground, among dry grass

Call: A simple *ts-lick*; sometimes *ts-lee-ik*

Hot spots: Sightings of Henslow's sparrow are few and far between in Florida, but the species has visited these sites more than once in the past several years: Pine Meadows Conservation Area, Eustis, 28.88406 / -81.66308; Prairie Creek Preserve, Lodge Trail, Rochelle, 29.5894494 / -82.2467422; St. Marks National Wildlife Refuge, St. Marks, 30.1515653 / -84.1473314

DOMINIC SHERONY

NELSON'S SPARROW
Ammospiza nelsoni

A secretive bird of grassy coastal marshes, Nelson's nonetheless stands out from the savannah and song sparrows that share its habitat—it's one of only two sparrows in the region with orange facial features.

Field marks: Gray crown stripe, orange eyebrow, black eye line, gray cheek with orange outline, grayish throat, gray bill, buff breast and flanks streaked with gray, white belly; gray nape, back, and tail; gray shoulders streaked with darker gray, brown and black wings.

Size: L: 4.75"–5", WS: 7"–7.25"

Similar species: Saltmarsh sparrow has a nearly identical facial pattern, but its throat is bright white and its breast and belly have black streaks.

Season: Winter

Habitat: Salt marshes with high grasses

Food source: Insects, seeds, marine invertebrates

Nest: Near the ground in dense vegetation

Call: A raspy, insect-like *pssshuh-tuck*; also a tiny, high-pitched *zeet* note

Hot spots: Many salt marshes along the Atlantic and Gulf coasts provide habitat for populations of Nelson's sparrows. These are particularly dependable from one year to the next: St. Marks National Wildlife Refuge, Panacea Unit, Bottoms Road, St. Marks, 30.0241521 / -84.3681856; Fort Island Gulf Beach, Crystal River, 28.908602 / -82.69082; Fort De Soto Park, St. Petersburg, 27.6327266 / -82.718157; Estero Bay Preserve State Park, Winkler Point, Fort Meyers, 26.4800134 / -81.898452; Merritt Island National Wildlife Refuge, Shiloh Marsh Road, Oak Hill, 28.8004574 / -80.8465862; Guana Tolomato Matanzas National Estuarine Research Reserve, St. Augustine, 30.0074 / -81.3325

SALTMARSH SPARROW

Ammospiza caudacuta

Closely related to Nelson's sparrow (they were once considered a single species), the saltmarsh shares the same facial pattern, habitat, nesting habits, and diet.

Field marks: Gray crown stripe, orange eyebrow, black eye line, gray cheek with orange outline, clean white throat, gray bill, buff breast and flanks streaked with black, white belly with some streaking; gray nape, gray back with black and white streaks, gray tail; brown and black wings.

Size: L: 5"–5.25", WS: 7"–7.5"

Similar species: Nelson's sparrow has a shorter bill and more contrast between its buff breast and white belly.

Season: Winter

Habitat: Salt marshes; occasionally in freshwater marshes near the coast

Food source: Insects, seeds, tiny crustaceans

Nest: Near the ground among dense vegetation

Call: A series of buzzy trills separated by *tsk* notes, changeable from one phrase to the next

Hot spots: Fort De Soto Park, St. Petersburg, 27.6327266 / -82.718157; Honeymoon Island State Park, Dunedin, 28.0706 / -82.8314; Estero Bay Preserve State Park, Winkler Point, Fort Meyers, 26.4800134 / -81.898452; Merritt Island National Wildlife Refuge, Shiloh Marsh Road, Oak Hill, 28.8004574 / -80.8465862; Guana Tolomato Matanzas National Estuarine Research Reserve, St. Augustine, 30.0074 / -81.3325

SEASIDE SPARROW
Ammospiza maritima

Another sparrow of coastal marshes, the seaside's mostly gray body and bright white throat set it apart from the others.

Field marks: Dark crown, gray face, yellow lores, dark patches at the cheek and ear, bright white throat and malar stripes; gray breast with buff streaks, gray underside, buff undertail coverts, gray back with pale white streaks, brown wings and tail.

Size: L: 6"–6.5", WS: 7.5"–8.5"

Similar species: Nelson's and saltmarsh sparrows have a distinctive orange pattern on their faces, buff breasts, and white undersides. Savannah sparrow is browner overall with a white breast and underside and reddish or grayish streaks on its breast and flanks.

Season: Year-round on the northern Gulf coast and on the Atlantic Coast of south Florida, as well as in the Everglades. Very localized in winter along the central Gulf coast and the northern Atlantic coast to St. Augustine; sporadic farther south.

Habitat: Coastal salt marshes

Food source: Snails, seeds, insects; some small crustaceans

Nest: Close to the ground in a clump of vegetation; attached to marsh reeds or grasses

Call: A raspy *benni-HAAAAW*, dropping in pitch at the end; also *bip-chaWEEEE*, rising in pitch on the *weee*

Hot spots: Huguenot Memorial City Park, Jacksonville, 30.4112444 / -81.4206594; Guana Tolomato Matanzas National Estuarine Research Reserve, St. Augustine, 30.0074 / -81.3325; Everglades National Park, Mahogany Hammock, 25.322954 / -80.833145; Werner-Boyce Salt Springs State Park, Hudson, 28.3313652 / -82.7073625; Road to Nowhere, Jena, 29.5705764 / -83.3788609

SAVANNAH SPARROW
Passerculus sandwichensis

Common throughout grassland and marsh habitats, this may be the first bird you see perching on a fence post or gritting on the edge of a road when you arrive at its habitat.

Field marks: Brown crown stripe, light brown head with dark brown eye line, yellow lores, white throat outlined in dark brown, buff breast, flanks, and underside streaked with brown; whitish undertail coverts, light brown back and wings streaked with darker brown, brown tail.

Size: L: 5.5"–6.25", WS: 6.75"–8"

Similar species: Vesper sparrow is larger and has a rufous patch at the shoulder. Grasshopper sparrow has a clear breast, gray eyebrow, and is more buff overall.

Season: Winter

Habitat: Grasslands, marshes, open fields and meadows, farms, beach dunes

Food source: Seeds, insects, spiders

Nest: On the ground among tall grasses

Call: Two quick notes followed by a long trill, ending with a lower note: *chip-cheet-laeeeeeee-cheep*; also a thin, high chip note

Hot spots: Every salt marsh or open field you visit will have savannah sparrows. Watch along roadsides or on fences and fence posts for the very vocal, very streaky sparrows with the yellow spot at the base of the bill.

FOX SPARROW
Passerella iliaca

Large and reddish, this sparrow makes an impression when it arrives under a feeder or deep in the woods on its way to its far northern breeding grounds.

Field marks: Rufous crown, gray face with rufous cheek patch, gray and yellow bill, gray nape, white breast and underside with deep reddish streaks, red central breast spot, gray back with reddish streaks, rufous wings and tail.

Size: L: 7", WS: 10.5"

Similar species: Song sparrow is also reddish and streaked, but it is smaller and browner overall.

Season: Winter

Habitat: Forest edges, thickets, brushy overgrowth; sometimes comes to backyard feeders

Food source: Seeds, insects, spiders, berries, small invertebrates

Nest: On the ground or close to it; northern Canada and Alaska region

Call: A series of single, clear notes, with as many as a dozen in the phrase, often with a scratchy buzz in the middle

Hot spots: Sightings of this bird are sporadic and fleeting. These spots have seen visits in more than one year: Tall Timbers Research Station, Tallahassee, 30.6567786 / -84.2087889; Boulware Springs Park, Gainesville, 29.6220792 / -82.3079824; San Felasco Hammock Preserve State Park, Gainesville, 29.7180976 / -82.4636471

VESPER SPARROW
Pooecetes gramineus

The gray, brown, and white sparrow with the lilting song can be found in grasslands and fields left fallow near active farms.

Field marks: Gray-brown streaked head with a brown cheek patch and white forehead patch, heavy gray bill, grayish throat; white breast and flanks delicately streaked with dark gray, white underside, gray back with black streaks, rufous shoulder patch, gray and black wings, long black tail with white outer feathers.

Size: L: 6.25", WS: 10"

Similar species: Savannah sparrow is more buff and browner overall. Grasshopper sparrow is more buff with rufous features and has a clear breast.

Season: Winter

Habitat: Open grassland, farm fields

Food source: Insects, spiders

Nest: In a hollow on the ground, sheltered by tall grass

Call: Four clear notes: *here-here, where-where*, followed by an extended series of whistles and trills

Hot spots: River Road, Live Oak, 30.3341407 / -83.2282135; M&M Dairy, Port Jacksonville Parkway, Jacksonville, 30.4508888 / -81.5630391; Newnan's Lake State Forest, West Trail, Gainesville, 29.6637993 / -82.2523239; Sweetwater Wetlands Park, Gainesville, 29.6151026 / -82.3254061; Watermelon Pond Wildlife and Environmental Area, Newberry, 29.5803805 / -82.6070997

WHITE-THROATED SPARROW
Zonotrichia albicollis

If you don't see this bird at your backyard feeder, look for it on the woodland floor turning over leaves in search of seeds and bugs.

Field marks: Black and white–striped cap, yellow lores, gray face and bill, white throat edged in black, gray breast and underside, brown wings with two thin white wing bars, brown tail. Young lack the bright white cap and throat.

Size: L: 6.75"–7.75", WS: 9"–10"

Similar species: White-crowned sparrow has a gray throat, a pink bill, and no yellow on its face.

Season: Winter

Habitat: Mixed woods with open understory, parks, gardens, backyards

Food source: Maple and oak leaf buds, seeds, insects

Nest: On or just above the ground, in a wooded area or in brush along a roadside or power line right-of-way

Call: Thready, musical song often transcribed as *old-sam-peabody-peabody-peabody*, also a sharp *chik* note

Hot spots: Guana Tolomato Matanzas National Estuarine Research Reserve, St. Augustine, 30.0074 / -81.3325; Sweetwater Wetlands Park, Gainesville, 29.6151026 / -82.3254061; Paynes Prairie Preserve State Park, La Chua Trail, Gainesville, 29.6068756 / -82.3031116; St. Marks National Wildlife Refuge, St. Marks, 30.1515653 / -84.1473314; Lake Woodruff National Wildlife Refuge, Leon Springs, 29.1092685 / -81.3752445

WHITE-CROWNED SPARROW

Zonotrichia leucophrys

Habitat helps distinguish this sparrow from its white-throated cousin: The white-crowned prefers the edges of woods, fields, and marshes, where scrubby brush dominates.

Field marks: Black and white–striped crown, gray face, pink bill; gray throat, breast, and underparts; black and white back, brown and black wings with two thin white wing bars, brownish-gray rump, gray tail.

Size: L: 6.5"–7.5", WS: 9.5"–10"

Similar species: White-throated sparrow has a white throat and yellow lores, and is usually found in different habitat.

Season: Spring and fall migration

Habitat: Brushy grassland edges, dense scrub fields

Food source: Insects, seeds, grass, fruit, leaf buds

Nest: Near the ground or up to 30 feet high in a shrub, scrubby bush, or tree

Call: A descending series of clear notes with a buzzy ending: *Wee-weedle-doo-zee-zee-trzzzzz*

Hot spots: Lake Apopka North Shore, Astatula, 28.6740878 / -81.7059258; Paynes Prairie Preserve State Park, La Chua Trail, Gainesville, 29.6068756 / -82.3031116; Hague Dairy, Gainesville, 29.7785775 / -82.4163169; Tall Timbers Research Station, Tallahassee, 30.6567786 / -84.2087889; Timber Lake Road wetlands, Fort Walton Beach, 30.4804162 / -86.6164497

SONG SPARROW
Melospiza melodia

There are many variations in the song sparrow's appearance across the United States. The dark brown sparrows more commonly found in Florida are of the Eastern race.

Field marks: Dark brown crown with a gray stripe up the middle, which sometimes stands up like a crest; gray eyebrow and cheek, brown eye line and malar stripe, white throat and chest, dark brown streaks on chest and flanks, culminating in a dark breast spot; gray back with brown stripes, brown and rufous wings and tail.

Size: L: 6.25", WS: 8.25"

Similar species: Fox sparrow is larger, plumper, and redder, with more flank streaks. Savannah sparrow has a yellow stripe over the eye, and its bill and tail are shorter. Lincoln's sparrow has finer streaking overall, a lighter-colored back, and a buff wash over its breast.

Season: Winter

Habitat: Woodland edges, brushy fields, stands of thick shrubs, open wetlands, marshes, beach dunes, parks, gardens, backyard feeders

Food source: Seeds, berries, grasses, some insects

Nest: On the ground, usually surrounded by taller grass or weeds

Call: A varied series of rising and falling warbles, usually ending in a trill; also a high-pitched *seet*, sometimes followed by a single, much lower *hup* note

Hot spots: Virtually every open field, forest edge, and neighborhood in northern and central Florida has resident song sparrows. Detectable first by song, they often pop up to stand at the top of a small shrub or on a blade of tall grass and sing, throwing their heads back and pumping out the notes using their entire bodies for emphasis. These sparrows are easy to spot and cooperative in giving birders good looks.

LINCOLN'S SPARROW
Melospiza lincolnii

Wintering in Florida's wetlands and woods, this sparrow heads for its breeding grounds in Canada by late March.

Field marks: Black cap with a slight peak, wide gray eyebrow, thin buff eye ring, black eye line, brown cheek, buff malar stripe with a black edge, grayish throat, buff breast and flanks with fine black streaks, white belly and undertail coverts, gray back with fine black streaks, brown wings and tail.

Size: L: 5.75", WS: 7.5"

Similar species: Song sparrow is browner overall with a large black spot in the middle of the breast. Young swamp sparrow has tawny flanks, rufous wings, and lacks the fine streaking on the breast and flanks. Savannah sparrow has a yellow spot at the lores and a short tail. Vesper sparrow has a wide white eye ring, no gray on its face, and a white breast rather than buff.

Season: Winter

Habitat: Fields with shrubs, forests near the ocean, wetlands with tall grasses and reeds, bogs

Food source: Insects, seeds

Nest: On the ground, hidden by vegetation (not in Florida)

Call: Three notes followed by a musical trill: *chur-chur-chur-cheeeeeeeee*; variations are possible. Call notes are very high-pitched and come in groups of three or four: *tsee-tsee-tsee*.

Hot spots: Myakka River State Park, Myakka City, 27.2405033 / -82.3148167; Tall Timbers Research Station, Tallahassee, 30.6567786 / -84.2087889; Paynes Prairie Preserve State Park, La Chua Trail, Gainesville, 29.6068756 / -82.3031116; Lake Apopka North Shore, Astatula, 28.6740878 / -81.7059258; Frog Pond Wildlife Management Area, Lucky Hammock, Homestead, 25.396439 / -80.566581; Sparrow Fields at C-357 Pump Station, Gold Coast, 25.6039244 / -80.5301929

SWAMP SPARROW
Melospiza georgiana

With its bright rufous cap and a song similar to a chipping sparrow, the swamp sparrow can be easy to confuse with a chipping—but habitat decreases the margin for error.

Field marks: Male has bright rufous cap, gray face, black patch at ear, buff malars, white throat, gray underside with rufous flanks; rufous and black back, wings, and tail. Female is the same except with a dark brown cap.

Size: L: 5.75", WS: 7.25"

Similar species: Lincoln's sparrow has a dark brown cap with a gray central stripe, a buff breast streaked with black. Chipping sparrow is slightly smaller and has a bright white eyebrow, white malars, and a less-rufous back.

Season: Winter

Habitat: Salt- and freshwater wetlands and swamps with tall grasses and reeds

Food source: Grasshoppers, crickets, ants, and other insects; seeds

Nest: Constructed over water in a mass of vegetation

Call: A continuous trill, sometimes quite rapid, sometimes slow and whistled; also a simple *chik* call note

Hot spots: Every salt- and freshwater marsh, swamp, and wetland has its population of swamp sparrows, birds that are relatively easy to find if you're willing to wait. Very vocal, these sparrows compete with marsh wrens for length and volume of song, but they generally make themselves somewhat easier to see. Once you've triangulated the source of the song, stay close—the sparrow will probably pop up shortly.

DARK-EYED JUNCO
Junco hyemalis

If you travel across the country, you'll encounter this bird in as many as six different plumages. Juncos in Florida are the "slate-colored" variety. Northern Florida represents the southern limit of the junco's eastern range.

Field marks: Male is solid slate gray above, with pink bill, white belly, gray rear, white undertail coverts, gray tail with white outer feathers. Female has slate gray head, breast, and back; gray wings with some brown feathers, white belly, gray rear, white undertail coverts, gray tail with white outer feathers.

Size: L: 5.75"–6.25", WS: 9.25"–10"

Similar species: Tufted titmouse has a gray crest, nape, back, and wings; a white throat, breast, and belly; and rosy flanks. Eastern towhee is larger and has a black head, white underside, and bright rust-orange flanks.

Season: Winter

Habitat: Woodland edges, neighborhoods, parks, gardens, fields with adjacent woodlands, roadsides

Food source: Seeds, insects, fruit, berries

Nest: On the ground or just above it, in a shrub or brush pile, or under a log

Call: High, full-bodied, three-second trill, sometimes broken halfway through

Hot spots: Nearly all junco sightings in Florida are in the Panhandle, and the vast majority of these are at bird feeders at private residences. Juncos feed on the ground under bird feeders and on platform feeders filled with sunflower seed. If you don't live in the area and want a junco for your winter trip list, try Wakulla Springs State Park, Wakulla Springs, 30.2335 / -84.3037, or Tall Timbers Research Station, Tallahassee, 30.6567786 / -84.2087889.

MEADOWLARK, BLACKBIRDS, AND ORIOLES

EASTERN MEADOWLARK
Sturnella magna

A large, brightly colored songbird with a high, clear voice, this bird heralds spring when it arrives in local meadows and farm fields.

Field marks: Breeding adult has black and white–striped head, light brown cheek, white malar stripe, gray bill, bright yellow throat, wide black V on breast, yellow breast and underside, buff and black streaks on flanks; scaly brown and buff pattern on wings, back, and tail; white outer tail feathers. In nonbreeding plumage, black on the crown and black breastband fade to gray.

Size: L: 9.5"–11", WS: 14"–17"

Similar species: Western meadowlark (not seen in Florida) is identical except for a white malar stripe on eastern meadowlark's face. Female bobolink has a similar but more muted head pattern, and a buff breast with faint black streaks and no black V. Dickcissel male has a gray head with a single white eye line, yellow malars, and a white throat with a black V patch, but it has rufous shoulders and brown and black–streaked back and wings.

Season: Year-round

Habitat: Farm fields, open meadows, and grasslands

Food source: Insects, berries, seeds

Nest: On the ground and hidden among tall grasses and crops

Call: A whistled *seeyu, SEE-oh-yu*, sometimes with a trill on the last note, sometimes ending with a downward slide; also a chattering call that ends in another *see-yu*

Hot spots: Every large, grassy field or stretch of cultivated farmland in Florida has its share of eastern meadowlarks. Listen for the distinctive, melancholy song and watch for one to pop up on top of a corn stalk or a fence post, where it will pose for pictures and sing for some time.

BOBOLINK
Dolichonyx oryzivorus

A bird of wide-open spaces, this bubbly-voiced blackbird prefers farm fields, marshes, prairies, and grasslands. Large flocks of hundreds of bobolinks often pause in Florida on their way north each spring.

Field marks: Breeding male has black head with bright yellow back and lighter nape, solid black breast and underside, white shoulders, black wings, white rump, black tail. Breeding female has buff head and body with black cap and eye line, light black streaking on flanks, black and buff wings, buff rump, gray tail. *Fall plumage* (both sexes): Black cap, warm buff head and body with black streaks on flanks, buff and black back and wings, buff rump, gray tail.

Size: L: 6.25"–7", WS: 10.5"–12.5"

Similar species: Eastern meadowlark has a black and white–striped head, a bright yellow throat with a wide black V on its breast, and a yellow breast and underside. Brown-headed cowbird has a dark brown head and iridescent blue body. Common grackle has an iridescent blue head, black body, and long, rudder-shaped tail.

Season: Spring and fall migration

Habitat: Open meadows and grasslands, corn fields, marshes

Food source: Insects, seeds

Nest: On the ground, sheltered by tall grasses and stalks

Call: A long, twangy series of rising and falling syllables, like the repeated snapping of a rubber band

Hot spots: Sweetwater Wetlands Park, Gainesville, 29.6151026 / -82.3254061; Lake Apopka North Shore, Astatula, 28.6740878 / -81.7059258; Orlando Wetlands Park, Orlando, 28.5753263 / -80.9966826; River Lakes Conservation Area, Moccasin Island, Melbourne, 28.2299949 / -80.8110523; Harns Marsh, Buckingham, 26.6496729 / -81.6869336

BROWN-HEADED COWBIRD
Molothrus ater

Cowbirds are notorious in the birding world for laying their eggs in the nests of other birds, abandoning their babies for others to raise.

Field marks: Male has brown head, black body with a slightly turquoise sheen. Female is uniformly drab gray-brown, with slightly darker wings.

Size: L: 7.5", WS: 12"

Similar species: Rusty blackbird is uniformly blue-black with a yellow eye. Common grackle has an iridescent blue head, a blackish body, and a very long tail.

Season: Year-round in most of the state; winter south of Fort Myers

Habitat: Edges of wooded areas, farm fields, neighborhoods, parks

Food source: Insects, seeds

Nest: Lays one egg per nest of another bird species. In one season, a single cowbird may lay as many as thirty-six eggs in other birds' nests.

Call: A liquid-sounding burble, ending in a very high squeal: *blug-lug-EET*

Hot spots: Find cowbirds in just about any green space, especially those with open fields adjacent to forest edges. These birds usually move and feed in flocks, so if you discover one cowbird, you are likely to see many more.

DOMINIC SHERONY

BRONZED COWBIRD

Molothrus aeneus

A shorter, heavier cowbird than the much more common brown-headed variety, this one maintains localized populations in and near Miami and Fort Myers.

Field marks: Red eye, black head with thick ruff on back of neck, bronze sheen in reflective light; black body and tail, iridescent dark blue wings. Female is similar but not as iridescent. Juveniles are gray-brown with streaky breast and underside.

Size: L: 8.5"–9", WS: 14"–15"

Similar species: Brown-headed cowbird is slimmer and has a distinctly brown head and a dark blue body. Shiny cowbird is slimmer and is all black with a distinct shininess.

Season: Winter vagrants in central Florida; year-round in Fort Myers/Naples area and in Miami and Homestead.

Habitat: Open areas including grasslands, farmlands, golf courses, airports

Food source: Seeds, some insects

Nest: These birds lay their eggs in other birds' nests and leave their young for the host birds to raise as their own.

Call: A series of whistles, gurgles, and very high-pitched wheezes

Hot spots: Green Cay Wetlands & Nature Center, Boynton Beach, 26.4861584 / -80.1607561; Sem-Chi Rice Mill, Wellington, 26.6668727 / -80.4574621; Cortadito Cowbirds restaurant, Miami, 25.7323915 / -80.3350863; West Kendall Baptist Hospital area, The Hammocks, 25.6826869 / -80.4526034; Homestead General Aviation Airport, Homestead, 25.5017258 / -80.5510082

© SHUTTERSTOCK.COM/FOTO 4440

SHINY COWBIRD
Molothrus bonariensis

This much-sought-after vagrant has made frequent trips up from the Caribbean islands in recent years. Look for it in late spring or early summer.

Field marks: Slender, all-black bird with distinctive glossy sheen. Female is uniformly a warm brown, with or without indistinct streaks of slightly darker brown on its breast and underside.

Size: L: 7"–8", WS: 11"–12"

Similar species: Brown-headed cowbird has a brown head and iridescent black body that can appear green. Bronzed cowbird is larger and heavier, and has a red eye and a pronounced ruff on the back of its neck.

Season: Summer

Habitat: Farm fields and open lands with occasional trees and scrubby edges; also comes to feeders

Food source: Seeds, insects, spiders

Nest: Like other cowbirds, this one is a parasitic nester, laying its eggs in other birds' nests and leaving them for the other birds to hatch and raise.

Call: Long series of various musical notes; also a chattering one-pitch call and a single high-pitched *piiit*

Hot spots: West Kendall Agricultural Area, Miami, 25.650781 / -80.464181; agricultural fields, SW 217th Avenue and SW 384th Street, Florida City, 25.407384 / -80.5472946; Everglades National Park, Flamingo, 25.1416 / -80.9255

RED-WINGED BLACKBIRD
Agelaius phoeniceus

No open field is complete without a colony of these highly visible, always active blackbirds.

Field marks: Male is solid black from head to tail with a red and yellow patch at the shoulder. Female is like a large sparrow, with a brown cap, lighter brown eyebrow and malar stripe, brown cheek, buff underside streaked with dark brown, brown wings with two white wing bars, brown tail.

Size: L: 8.75"–9.5", WS: 13"–14.5"

Similar species: Rusty blackbird, common grackle, European starling, and brown-headed cowbird have no wing patch. Female rose-breasted grosbeak has a more vivid facial pattern than female red-winged blackbird, and has more finely streaked underparts and a yellow patch under each wing.

Season: Year-round

Habitat: Open fields, farmlands, meadows, wetlands of all varieties, beach dunes, woodland edges, neighborhoods

Food source: Insects, seeds, fruit, marine invertebrates, crop grains; also come to backyard feeders

Nest: Firmly attached to reeds or other canes in grassy marshes or other wetlands

Call: A familiar three-note *onk-or-REE*; also a piercing, descending whistle and a deeper descending trill

Hot spots: Any plot of land with tall grasses contains red-winged blackbirds, whether it's in an agricultural area, a wildlife refuge, a creek near a shopping mall, along a drainage ditch on a roadside, or alongside a schoolyard. Red-wings perch on top of cattails and phragmites, hop through low shrubs and the lowest branches of trees on woodland edges, and show up at backyard feeders when natural food sources become scarce.

RUSTY BLACKBIRD
Euphagus carolinus

This uncommon blackbird gets its name from its nonbreeding plumage, which adds a rufous edge to its feathers.

Field marks: Breeding male is solid black with a greenish hue from head to tail, with a black bill and a bright yellow eye. Breeding female is drab brown overall with a lighter throat, black bill, yellow eye, and darker brown wings and tail. Nonbreeding male is black overall with rusty streaks, especially on head and wings. Nonbreeding female has mottled rufous and buff body and wings, with a dark eye line and paler areas on face.

Size: L: 9"–9.75", WS: 14"–15"

Similar species: Common grackle has an iridescent blue-black head, dark brown-black body, and a very long tail. Red-winged blackbird has a red and yellow patch on its shoulders. Brown-headed cowbird has a brown head and a glossy blue-black body.

Season: Spring and fall migration

Habitat: Wooded edges along roadsides, meadows, shrubby areas near water, beaver ponds

Food source: Insects, seeds, small fish, post-harvest grains

Nest: In a tree or shrub, not far from water

Call: A rattling, squeaky *quira-LEEK-LEEK*, like a rusty hinge; also a series of clucks and whistles as an alarm call

Hot spots: Sweetwater Wetlands Park, Gainesville, 29.6151026 / -82.3254061; Magnolia Parke, Gainesville, 29.6916411 / -82.3945212; M&M Dairy, Port Jacksonville Parkway, Jacksonville, 30.4508888 / -81.5630391; St. Marks National Wildlife Refuge, St. Marks, 30.1515653 / -84.1473314; Lake Henrietta, Tallahassee, 30.4036824 / -84.3079448

BREWER'S BLACKBIRD
Euphagus cyanocephalus

All black with a yellow eye, this blackbird stands out from similar birds in its limited range on the Panhandle.

Field marks: Solid, glossy black from head to tail, with a yellow eye and a short bill; long tail. Female is dull grayish brown with a black eye.

Size: L: 9", WS 15"–16"

Similar species: Rusty blackbird is similar in size and shape but is not shiny. Red-winged blackbird has red and yellow shoulder stripes.

Season: Winter

Habitat: Marshes and grassy areas near small bodies of water

Food source: Seeds, insects in summer

Nest: In colonies in shrubs or low trees, usually near water

Call: A sharp, rising *pit-TWEEEE*, followed by a single *cht*

Hot spots: Fred Myers Williams III Memorial Fish Pond, Monticello, 30.3598622 / -83.9899685; Rabon Road pond, Monticello, 30.500898 / -83.913198; St. Marks National Wildlife Refuge, St. Marks, 30.1515653 / -84.1473314

COMMON GRACKLE
Quiscalus quiscula

This grackle's long, rudder-shaped tail makes it easy to differentiate from the straight tails of cowbirds and blackbirds.

Field marks: Blue-black, iridescent head and breast, yellow eye, large black bill, uniformly brown-black body, long tail with flat, triangular end. Juvenile (pictured right) is browner and lacks the iridescence.

Size: L: 12.5"–13.5", WS: 17"–18.5"

Similar species: Rusty blackbird is blue-black all over and has a shorter tail. Red-winged blackbird is smaller, has a red and yellow patch on its wings, and has a shorter tail. European starling is much smaller and has a short tail. Boat-tailed grackle has a much longer and larger tail.

Season: Year-round

Habitat: City streets, parks, and neighborhoods; meadows, farm fields, beaches, dunes, shrubby areas

Food source: Insects, seeds, fish, fruit, eggs and nestlings in other birds' nests

Nest: In a tree or tall shrub, up to 12 feet off the ground

Call: An unmusical *chaa-ak, chaa-REE*, like the creak of metal against metal

Hot spots: All it takes to find a common grackle is a walk down any city or suburban street, a stroll through a beach parking lot or along a shopping center's edges, or a scan of the trees near an open field. Grackles often crowd other birds off backyard feeders (especially the platform variety), and they have been known to peck the head of a house sparrow until the smaller bird relinquishes a prime feeder perch.

BOAT-TAILED GRACKLE
Quiscalus major

The long, paddle-like tail distinguishes this grackle from the smaller one with which it shares the region.

Field marks: Dark blue with iridescent green sheen from head to tail, yellow eye, dark gray bill, very long tail with wide fan, black legs and feet. Female is smaller and warm reddish brown with darker wings and a similar but slightly smaller tail.

Size: L: 16"–17", WS: 23" (male); L: 14"–15", WS: 17"–18" (female)

Similar species: Common grackle is smaller with a shorter and less-fanned tail. Great-tailed grackle is very similar but is not found in Florida.

Season: Year-round

Habitat: Fresh- and saltwater marshes, also cities and other places with human habitation

Food source: Crustaceans and other water animals, reptiles, amphibians, seeds, grain, fruit, other birds

Nest: In cattails, reeds, and other vegetation in marshes, usually 2 feet or more above the water

Call: Series of long, raspy *sheeb-sheeb-sheeb* sounds, followed by clicks and one or two contrasting, musical squeaks. This song should be familiar to Florida residents, as these birds chatter constantly.

Hot spots: Any lake, natural pond, river, canal, drainage ditch, retention pond, marsh, or seashore has its population of boat-tailed grackles, as does any picnic area, park, or shopping center parking lot. You will have no trouble spotting these birds walking on the ground or sitting on fences and wires.

© SHUTTERSTOCK.COM.LUIS MARQUEZ

SPOT-BREASTED ORIOLE
Icterus pectoralis

The black facial pattern on this naturalized oriole from Central America is unique among Florida's orioles.

Field marks: Orange head and body, black face from eye to bill, black throat with black spots on breast, black wings with white edges on tertial feathers, black tail. Female is similar.

Size: L: 9"–10", WS: 12.5"–13"

Similar species: Baltimore oriole has a black head and bright white wing bars on black wings. Orchard oriole is a darker orange and also has a black head.

Season: Year-round

Habitat: Parks with large trees in residential neighborhoods in and around Fort Lauderdale and Miami

Food source: Nectar, fruit, insects

Nest: An elongated pouch hanging from a tree branch

Call: A series of languid notes very like a human whistling: *pheer, pheer, fo-FEE-pheer, fo-pheer-pheer FEE-pheer*

Hot spots: Plantation Preserve, Plantation, 26.1156777 / -80.2391624; Spanish River Park, Boca Raton, 26.3829 / -80.0692; Markham Park, Sunrise, 26.1279694 / -80.3596902; Pine Woods Park, Kendall, 25.647447 / -80.356726; Brewer Park, Miller Drive Roost, South Miami, 25.7178837 / -80.2961969

BALTIMORE ORIOLE
Icterus galbula

Perhaps the most hoped-for backyard bird, this stunningly orange and black creature comes readily to feeders that offer oranges and grape jelly.

Field marks: Male has black head, throat, and back; orange breast and underside, black wings with orange patches at shoulder and one white wing bar, orange lower back and rump, black tail with orange outer feathers. Female has yellow-orange head and body with patchy black pattern on head, white throat, black wings with white wing bars, paler yellow flanks, yellow-orange rump and tail. Nonbreeding male has dull yellow head; bright yellow-orange throat, breast, underside, undertail coverts, and tail; pale flanks, black wings with white wing bars.

Size: L: 8.75", WS: 11.5"

Similar species: American robin has a brown head, white eye ring, brown back and wings, reddish-orange breast, and white undertail coverts. Eastern towhee has a black head and white breast and underside, with dark orange streaks on flanks. Orchard oriole is similar but with a darker, burnt-orange body.

Season: Winter throughout most of Florida; migration in the Panhandle

Habitat: Wooded areas, parks, gardens, suburban backyards with mature trees

Food source: Caterpillars, moths, other insects, fruit, flower nectar; also hummingbird nectar, oranges, and grape jelly from backyard feeders

Nest: In a tree in a woven basket nest, usually more than 20 feet from the ground

Call: A syrupy, musical series of clearly defined, whistled notes: *hee-doo-HEE-dee-doo-dee-hoo* and variations of this; also a simple *peep* note, followed by a descending whistle (like a pennywhistle)

Hot spots: Just about any park with large trees may attract Baltimore orioles, but if you're striking out, try one of these near-certain spots in late winter or early spring: Paynes Prairie Preserve State Park, Bolen Bluff Trail, Gainesville, 29.5587838 / -82.3245401; Mead Botanical Gardens, Winter Park, 28.5836 / -81.3586; Circle B Bar Reserve, Lakeland, 27.9959173 / -81.8652327; Fort De Soto Park, St. Petersburg, 27.6327266 / -82.718157; Lantana Nature Preserve, Lantana, 26.5843827 / -80.0415768

ORCHARD ORIOLE

Icterus spurius

Smaller and darker than its Baltimore cousin, this less-common oriole shares much of the same habitat.

Field marks: Male has black head, throat, upper back, wings, and tail; black eye, sharp black bill, dark orange breast and underside, dark orange patch on upper wing, one white wing bar, orange lower back and rump. Female has yellow head and body with darker wash on head, black eye, gray bill, dark gray wings with two white wing bars, yellow-green tail, white patches on underwings. First-summer male is similar to female, but with a black eye ring and throat.

Size: L: 7.25"–7.75", WS: 9.25"–10.5"

Similar species: Baltimore oriole is a brighter orange. American robin has a brown head, back, wings, and tail; a white eye ring, and white undertail coverts.

Season: Summer

Habitat: Woodlands, orchards, arboretums, neighborhoods with mature trees, parks

Food source: Insects, fruit, flower nectar, feeders with oranges and grape jelly, hummingbird nectar

Nest: In a tree or bush, usually well above the ground

Call: A musical series of whistles, faster and more numerous than a Baltimore oriole: *wee-WHOO-purwee-HOO-teewee-ta-dee-pur-dee*, and so on.

Hot spots: J. R. Alford Greenway, Tallahassee, 30.444382 / -84.1754436; Kanapaha Botanical Gardens, Gainesville, 29.6128267 / -82.4088335; Lake Apopka North Shore, Astatula, 28.6740878 / -81.7059258; Everglades National Park, Flamingo, 25.1416 / -80.9255; Point Ybel Lighthouse Beach Park, Sanibel, 26.4520609 / -82.0151281

FINCHES

PURPLE FINCH
Haemorhous purpureus

A welcome winter sight in the few coniferous woodlands of northern Florida, this bright pink finch looks as if it has been dipped in raspberry juice.

Field marks: Male has bright pink head, throat, breast, flanks, and back; brown cheek patch, small gray bill, brown wings with pinkish cast and two pink wing bars, white belly and undertail, pink tail with brownish end. Female has brown cap, white eyebrow, brown cheek patch, black and white–striped malars and throat; white breast and underside with short brown streaks throughout; white undertail, brown back with black streaks, brown wings and tail.

Size: L: 5.5"–6.25", WS: 10"–10.5"

Similar species: House finch has a bright pink or red face, head, and breast, but its back, wings, and underside have no pink.

Season: Winter

Habitat: Mixed woodlands, conifers, neighborhoods with conifers, parks, arboretums, gardens

Food source: Seeds, fruit, buds

Nest: In a coniferous tree, usually many feet from the ground

Call: Continuous, often lengthy series of warbles, whistles, trills, and chatter

Hot spots: Ichetucknee Springs State Park, north entrance, Fort White, 29.985055 / -82.7624606; San Felasco Hammock Preserve State Park, Yellow Trail, Gainesville, 29.7180976 / -82.4636471; Wakulla Springs State Park, Wakulla Springs, 30.2335 / -84.3037

HOUSE FINCH
Haemorhous mexicanus

This small, long-tailed finch came from the western United States and found its way east through New York City pet stores in the 1940s. Today it is widespread in northern and central Florida, and is working its way south.

Field marks: Male has red forehead, face, throat, breast, and rump; pale gray nape, white underside with gray streaks and a pink wash, black wings with thin white wing bars, long dark tail. Female has drab gray-brown head, throat, and back; light gray breast and underside with darker gray streaks, dark wings with two slim white wing bars, gray tail.

Size: L: 6", WS: 9.5"–10"

Similar species: Purple finch is more uniformly pink overall. White-winged and red crossbills are a deeper red from head to tail.

Season: Year-round

Habitat: Neighborhoods, cities, parks, gardens, arboretums, backyards with feeders

Food source: Seeds, fruit

Nest: In a tree cavity, deep in a shrub, or in a crack or hole in a building

Call: Continuous, often lengthy series of warbles, whistles, trills, and chatter

Hot spots: Every neighborhood has at least a small flock of house finches, especially if some of the residents keep their seed feeders stocked. House finches are particularly easy to see from late summer through winter, when they bring their fledglings to feeders and birdbaths. They often flock together in a single large shrub a short distance from a ready food source.

PINE SISKIN
Spinus pinus

Pine siskins can be plentiful in open coniferous woods, but they also spend much of their winter visiting feeders in suburban and rural areas.

Field marks: Male has brown head and back, thin gray bill, white breast with dark brown streaks, black wings with bright yellow stripes, short yellow tail with black tip. Female has a browner breast and underside and has white wing bars instead of yellow stripes.

Size: L: 4.5"–5", WS: 8.5"–9"

Similar species: Female house and purple finches are grayer overall and have no yellow. Female purple finch has buffy flanks.

Season: Winter in northern Florida

Habitat: Forests and woodlands, parks, neighborhoods, farm fields with wooded edges; generally at higher latitudes

Food source: Seeds, insects, spiders, road salt; seeds at feeders during winter months

Nest: On the branch of a conifer well above the ground

Call: A long, continuous warble with occasional buzzy notes

Hot spots: Tall Timbers Research Station, Tallahassee, 30.6567786 / -84.2087889; Harriman Circle Park, Tallahassee, 30.4745686 / -84.2529586; McCord Park, Tallahassee, 30.4730144 / -84.2623043; Chinsegut Wildlife and Environmental Area, Headquarters Tract, Brooksville, 28.6297296 / -82.3522282

AMERICAN GOLDFINCH
Spinus tristis

The only all-yellow bird with black wings in the United States, this goldfinch is a regular visitor to backyards, gardens, and parks in every season.

Field marks: Male has black forehead; yellow head, back, upper wings, throat, breast, and underside; pink bill, black wings with one white wing bar, white rump, black tail. Female has olive-gray head, yellow eye ring, yellow throat, dull yellow breast and flanks with indistinct olive-gray streaks, olive-gray back, black wings with one white and one buff wing bar, white patch under the wing, white undertail and rump, black tail. *Fall plumage:* Male has gray head, back, and underside; yellow patch around eye, gray bill, yellow throat, yellow shoulders, black wings with one whitish wing bar, black tail. Female is uniformly drab brownish gray with black wings, one brownish wing bar, white undertail, black tail with whitish edges.

Size: L: 5", WS: 9"

Similar species: Yellow warbler is yellow overall with red streaks on its breast and flanks. Prothonotary warbler is uniformly golden-yellow with gray-blue wings.

Season: Winter

Habitat: Open grassland, farm fields, marshes, thickets, woodland edges, neighborhoods, parks, gardens

Food source: Seeds, particularly from flower heads; nyjer and sunflower seed at feeders

Nest: In a shrub or young tree, not far from the ground

Call: A simple, lilting *twee-twee-twee-twee-twee*; also a rising *per-WEE* alarm call and a descending *DEE-dee-dee-dee* in flight

Hot spots: Goldfinches are one of the most common winter birds in Florida, found in virtually every grassy area, from the vacant lot behind a shopping center to national wildlife refuges. They are frequent visitors to feeders, often commandeering a nyjer feeder and feeding in small flocks from every port. In summer, watch fields of wildflowers for perching goldfinches pulling seeds from the flower heads.

OLD WORLD (WEAVER) FINCH

HOUSE SPARROW
Passer domesticus

No household is complete without a dozen or so of these in the backyard. This introduced species from England can be found anywhere that humans frequent, from front porches to city centers.

Field marks: Male has gray cap, wide brown stripe from eye to back, gray cheek; black eye, bill, throat, and breast; white collar, gray belly and flanks, brown back, brown and black wings, white patch on wing, gray tail. Female is drab grayish tan overall with small yellow bill, thin white eye line, brown and gray wings with thin white wing bar, brown tail.

Size: L: 6.25", WS: 9.5"

Similar species: No other Florida bird has the facial pattern of a male house sparrow.

Season: Year-round

Habitat: Cities, towns, parks, neighborhoods, backyards with bird feeders

Food source: Seeds, fruit, crumbs from human discards, some insects

Nest: In a tree cavity, a hole in a building, a bowl created by a man-made sign, or a man-made nest box. House sparrows are known to evict eastern bluebirds from nest boxes and take them over for their own broods.

Call: A simple, fairly dry *cheep* from a male and a chattier series of *cheeps* from a female are familiar sounds in most neighborhoods.

Hot spots: This ubiquitous sparrow is found in every backyard, park, garden, beach, city street, outdoor restaurant, and even inside big-box stores and malls, where they plunder the crumbs humans leave behind in food courts. No hot spot is required to find a house sparrow; chances are you can see one outside your window as you read this.

APPENDIX A: SPECIES BY COLOR

Birds with Pink or Red Plumage

- [ ] American flamingo
- [ ] Canvasback
- [ ] Hermit thrush
- [ ] House finch
- [ ] Magnificent frigatebird (male)
- [ ] Northern cardinal
- [ ] Painted bunting
- [ ] Pileated woodpecker
- [ ] Purple finch
- [ ] Red-bellied woodpecker
- [ ] Redhead
- [ ] Red-headed woodpecker
- [ ] Red-whiskered bulbul
- [ ] Red-winged blackbird
- [ ] Roseate spoonbill
- [ ] Rose-breasted grosbeak
- [ ] Ruby-crowned kinglet
- [ ] Ruby-throated hummingbird
- [ ] Scarlet tanager
- [ ] Summer tanager
- [ ] Vermilion flycatcher
- [ ] Yellow-bellied sapsucker

Birds with Orange or Rufous Plumage

- [ ] American kestrel
- [ ] American redstart
- [ ] American robin
- [ ] Baltimore oriole
- [ ] Barn swallow
- [ ] Bay-breasted warbler
- [ ] Black-bellied whistling duck
- [ ] Blackburnian warbler
- [ ] Brown thrasher
- [ ] Chestnut-sided warbler
- [ ] Cinnamon teal
- [ ] Clapper rail
- [ ] Cooper's hawk

- [ ] Eastern bluebird
- [ ] Eastern towhee
- [ ] Fox sparrow
- [ ] Fulvous whistling duck
- [ ] Great-crested flycatcher
- [ ] Green heron
- [ ] Horned grebe
- [ ] Hudsonian godwit
- [ ] King rail
- [ ] Nelson's sparrow
- [ ] Northern shoveler
- [ ] Orchard oriole
- [ ] Red knot
- [ ] Red-breasted merganser
- [ ] Reddish egret
- [ ] Red-tailed hawk
- [ ] Ruddy duck
- [ ] Ruddy turnstone
- [ ] Saltmarsh sparrow
- [ ] Song sparrow
- [ ] Spot-breasted oriole
- [ ] Virginia rail
- [ ] Wood thrush

Birds with Yellow Plumage

- [ ] American goldfinch
- [ ] American redstart (female)
- [ ] Baltimore oriole (female)
- [ ] Blackburnian warbler (female)
- [ ] Black-throated green warbler
- [ ] Blue-winged warbler
- [ ] Cape May warbler
- [ ] Chestnut-sided warbler
- [ ] Common yellowthroat
- [ ] Connecticut warbler
- [ ] Dickcissel
- [ ] Eastern meadowlark
- [ ] Great-crested flycatcher

- [ ] Hooded warbler
- [ ] Horned lark
- [ ] Kentucky warbler
- [ ] Magnolia warbler
- [ ] Nashville warbler
- [ ] Northern parula
- [ ] Orchard oriole (female)
- [ ] Palm warbler
- [ ] Pine warbler
- [ ] Prairie warbler
- [ ] Prothonotary warbler
- [ ] Scarlet tanager (female)
- [ ] Wilson's warbler
- [ ] Yellow warbler
- [ ] Yellow-breasted chat
- [ ] Yellow-rumped warbler
- [ ] Yellow-throated vireo
- [ ] Yellow-throated warbler

Birds with Green or Olive Plumage

- [ ] American wigeon
- [ ] Black-throated green warbler
- [ ] Black-whiskered vireo
- [ ] Blue-headed vireo
- [ ] Common goldeneye
- [ ] Golden-crowned kinglet
- [ ] Greater scaup
- [ ] Green heron
- [ ] Green-winged teal
- [ ] Indian peafowl (female)
- [ ] Mallard
- [ ] Monk parakeet
- [ ] Mourning warbler
- [ ] Nanday parakeet
- [ ] Nashville warbler
- [ ] Northern shoveler
- [ ] Orange-crowned warbler
- [ ] Pine warbler
- [ ] Prairie warbler

❒ Red-breasted merganser
❒ Red-eyed vireo
❒ Ruby-crowned kinglet
❒ Ruby-throated hummingbird
❒ Scarlet tanager (female)
❒ Tennessee warbler
❒ White-eyed vireo
❒ White-winged parakeet
❒ Wood duck
❒ Yellow-throated vireo

Birds with Blue or Iridescent Plumage
❒ Barn swallow
❒ Belted kingfisher
❒ Black-throated blue warbler
❒ Blue grosbeak
❒ Blue jay
❒ Blue-gray gnatcatcher
❒ Blue-headed vireo
❒ Blue-winged teal
❒ Blue-winged warbler
❒ Cave swallow
❒ Cerulean warbler
❒ Cliff swallow
❒ Common grackle
❒ Common ground dove
❒ Eastern bluebird
❒ European starling
❒ Florida scrub-jay
❒ Indian peafowl (male)
❒ Indigo bunting
❒ Painted bunting
❒ Prothonotary warbler
❒ Purple martin
❒ Ruddy duck (blue bill in breeding plumage)
❒ Shiny cowbird
❒ Snow goose, "blue" phase
❒ Tree swallow

Birds with Purple Plumage
❒ Common grackle
❒ European starling
❒ Glossy ibis
❒ Gray-headed swamphen

❒ Lesser scaup
❒ Purple gallinule
❒ Purple martin
❒ White-faced ibis

Birds with Predominantly Brown Plumage
❒ American bittern
❒ American black duck
❒ American golden-plover
❒ American oystercatcher
❒ American pipit
❒ American robin
❒ American wigeon (female)
❒ American woodcock
❒ Antillean nighthawk
❒ Ash-throated flycatcher
❒ Bachman's sparrow
❒ Bald eagle
❒ Bank swallow
❒ Barred owl
❒ Black scoter (female)
❒ Black-bellied plover (winter)
❒ Blue-winged teal (female)
❒ Bobolink (female)
❒ Broad-winged hawk
❒ Bronzed cowbird
❒ Brown booby
❒ Brown creeper
❒ Brown noddy
❒ Brown pelican
❒ Brown thrasher
❒ Brown-headed cowbird
❒ Brown-headed nuthatch
❒ Buff-breasted sandpiper
❒ Bufflehead (female)
❒ Burrowing owl
❒ Canada goose
❒ Canvasback (female)
❒ Carolina wren
❒ Cedar waxwing
❒ Chipping sparrow
❒ Chuck-Will's-widow
❒ Clapper rail
❒ Clay-colored sparrow
❒ Common eider (female)

❒ Common gallinule
❒ Common goldeneye (female)
❒ Common nighthawk
❒ Dickcissel
❒ Dunlin
❒ Eastern meadowlark
❒ Eastern towhee (female)
❒ Eastern whip-poor-will
❒ Field sparrow
❒ Fox sparrow
❒ Gadwall (female)
❒ Grasshopper sparrow
❒ Gray-cheeked thrush
❒ Great horned owl
❒ Greater scaup (female)
❒ Green-winged teal (female)
❒ Henslow's sparrow
❒ Hermit thrush
❒ Hooded merganser (female)
❒ Horned grebe
❒ House wren
❒ Hudsonian godwit
❒ Killdeer
❒ King rail
❒ Lark sparrow
❒ Least bittern
❒ Least sandpiper
❒ Lesser nighthawk
❒ Lesser scaup (female)
❒ Limpkin
❒ Lincoln's sparrow
❒ Long-billed dowitcher
❒ Louisiana waterthrush
❒ Mallard (female)
❒ Mangrove cuckoo
❒ Marbled godwit
❒ Marsh wren
❒ Merlin (female)
❒ Mourning dove
❒ Nelson's sparrow
❒ Northern bobwhite
❒ Northern cardinal (female)
❒ Northern flicker
❒ Northern harrier (female)

- [ ] Northern rough-winged swallow
- [ ] Northern shoveler (female)
- [ ] Northern waterthrush
- [ ] Osprey
- [ ] Ovenbird
- [ ] Pectoral sandpiper
- [ ] Pied-billed grebe
- [ ] Pine siskin
- [ ] Piping plover
- [ ] Red knot
- [ ] Redhead (female)
- [ ] Red-shouldered hawk
- [ ] Red-tailed hawk
- [ ] Red-whiskered bulbul
- [ ] Ring-necked duck (female)
- [ ] Rose-breasted grosbeak (female)
- [ ] Ruddy duck (female)
- [ ] Ruddy turnstone (winter)
- [ ] Ruff
- [ ] Saltmarsh sparrow
- [ ] Sanderling
- [ ] Sandhill crane
- [ ] Seaside sparrow
- [ ] Sedge wren
- [ ] Semipalmated plover
- [ ] Semipalmated sandpiper
- [ ] Short-billed dowitcher
- [ ] Short-tailed hawk
- [ ] Snail kite
- [ ] Song sparrow
- [ ] Sora
- [ ] Spotted sandpiper
- [ ] Stilt sandpiper
- [ ] Surf scoter (female)
- [ ] Swainson's thrush
- [ ] Swainson's warbler
- [ ] Swamp sparrow
- [ ] Turkey vulture
- [ ] Upland sandpiper
- [ ] Veery
- [ ] Vesper sparrow
- [ ] Virginia rail
- [ ] Western sandpiper
- [ ] Western spindalis

- [ ] Whimbrel
- [ ] White-crowned sparrow
- [ ] White-rumped sandpiper
- [ ] White-throated sparrow
- [ ] White-winged dove
- [ ] White-winged scoter (female)
- [ ] Wild turkey
- [ ] Winter wren
- [ ] Wood duck (female)
- [ ] Worm-eating warbler
- [ ] Yellow-billed cuckoo
- [ ] Yellow-breasted chat

Birds with Predominantly Black Plumage

- [ ] American avocet
- [ ] American coot
- [ ] American crow
- [ ] American golden-plover
- [ ] American redstart
- [ ] Anhinga
- [ ] Black scoter
- [ ] Black skimmer
- [ ] Black tern
- [ ] Black vulture
- [ ] Black-and-white warbler
- [ ] Black-bellied plover
- [ ] Blackburnian warbler
- [ ] Black-crowned night-heron
- [ ] Black-necked stilt
- [ ] Blackpoll warbler
- [ ] Boat-tailed grackle
- [ ] Brewer's blackbird
- [ ] Brown-headed cowbird
- [ ] Chimney swift
- [ ] Common eider
- [ ] Common goldeneye
- [ ] Common grackle
- [ ] Common loon
- [ ] Common myna
- [ ] Crested caracara
- [ ] Double-crested cormorant
- [ ] Downy woodpecker
- [ ] Eastern kingbird
- [ ] Eastern towhee

- [ ] European starling
- [ ] Fish crow
- [ ] Great black-backed gull
- [ ] Groove-billed ani
- [ ] Hairy woodpecker
- [ ] Hooded merganser
- [ ] Lesser black-backed gull
- [ ] Long-tailed duck
- [ ] Magnificent frigatebird
- [ ] Muscovy duck
- [ ] Parasitic jaeger
- [ ] Pileated woodpecker
- [ ] Pomarine jaeger
- [ ] Red-bellied woodpecker
- [ ] Red-cockaded woodpecker
- [ ] Red-headed woodpecker
- [ ] Red-winged blackbird
- [ ] Ring-necked duck
- [ ] Rose-breasted grosbeak
- [ ] Rusty blackbird
- [ ] Smooth-billed ani
- [ ] Surf scoter
- [ ] White-winged scoter
- [ ] Wilson's storm-petrel
- [ ] Yellow-bellied sapsucker

Birds with Predominantly Gray Plumage

- [ ] Acadian flycatcher
- [ ] Alder flycatcher
- [ ] Audubon's shearwater
- [ ] Bahama mockingbird
- [ ] Baird's sandpiper (winter)
- [ ] Black-crowned night-heron
- [ ] Bonaparte's gull
- [ ] Canvasback
- [ ] Carolina chickadee
- [ ] Common tern
- [ ] Connecticut warbler
- [ ] Cooper's hawk
- [ ] Dark-eyed junco
- [ ] Dunlin (winter)
- [ ] Eastern phoebe
- [ ] Eastern screech-owl
- [ ] Eastern wood-pewee
- [ ] Egyptian goose

- ❒ Eurasian collared dove
- ❒ Forster's tern
- ❒ Gadwall
- ❒ Golden-winged warbler
- ❒ Gray catbird
- ❒ Gray kingbird
- ❒ Greater scaup
- ❒ Greater white-fronted goose
- ❒ Greater yellowlegs
- ❒ Green-winged teal
- ❒ Herring gull
- ❒ Hooded merganser (female)
- ❒ Laughing gull
- ❒ Least flycatcher
- ❒ Least sandpiper (winter)
- ❒ Least tern
- ❒ Lesser scaup
- ❒ Lesser yellowlegs
- ❒ Loggerhead shrike
- ❒ Magnolia warbler
- ❒ Merlin
- ❒ Mississippi kite
- ❒ Northern harrier
- ❒ Northern mockingbird
- ❒ Northern parula
- ❒ Peregrine falcon
- ❒ Red-breasted merganser (female)
- ❒ Red-breasted nuthatch
- ❒ Redhead
- ❒ Ring-billed gull

- ❒ Rock pigeon
- ❒ Roseate tern
- ❒ Sanderling (winter)
- ❒ Scissor-tailed flycatcher
- ❒ Seaside sparrow
- ❒ Semipalmated sandpiper (winter)
- ❒ Sharp-shinned hawk
- ❒ Stilt sandpiper
- ❒ Tropical kingbird
- ❒ Tufted titmouse
- ❒ Western kingbird
- ❒ Western sandpiper (winter)
- ❒ White-breasted nuthatch
- ❒ White-crowned pigeon
- ❒ White-rumped sandpiper (winter)
- ❒ White-tailed kite
- ❒ Willet
- ❒ Willow flycatcher
- ❒ Wilson's phalarope
- ❒ Wilson's plover
- ❒ Wood stork
- ❒ Yellow-crowned night-heron
- ❒ Yellow-rumped warbler
- ❒ Yellow-throated warbler

Birds with Predominantly White Plumage
- ❒ American avocet
- ❒ American white pelican

- ❒ Barn owl
- ❒ Black-necked stilt
- ❒ Bridled tern
- ❒ Bufflehead
- ❒ Caspian tern
- ❒ Common eider
- ❒ Common goldeneye
- ❒ Common tern
- ❒ Crested caracara
- ❒ Forster's tern
- ❒ Great black-backed gull
- ❒ Great egret
- ❒ Gull-billed tern
- ❒ Herring gull
- ❒ Least tern
- ❒ Lesser black-backed gull
- ❒ Masked booby
- ❒ Mute swan
- ❒ Northern gannet
- ❒ Ring-billed gull
- ❒ Roseate tern
- ❒ Royal tern
- ❒ Sandwich tern
- ❒ Snail kite
- ❒ Snow goose
- ❒ Snowy egret
- ❒ Snowy plover
- ❒ Swallow-tailed kite
- ❒ Trumpeter swan
- ❒ White ibis
- ❒ White-tailed kite
- ❒ Whooping crane

APPENDIX B: A REALISTIC CHECKLIST OF THE BIRDS OF FLORIDA

The following checklist is compiled from official bird checklists of Florida. The original checklists each included rare species that are not seen regularly in Florida, as well as accidentals—birds very far from their native habitat, brought here by storms or other forces of nature—and species that are extirpated from the region or believed to be extinct. We have omitted these accidental and extirpated birds to help you set realistic expectations for the birds you are most likely to see on an average day in the proper habitat, season, and time of day. Should some surprising birds make an appearance, there's room at the end to write in these unusual sightings. (* = Exotic or Introduced species)

Loons
❏ Common loon

Grebes
❏ Horned grebe
❏ Pied-billed grebe

Shearwater & Storm-Petrel
❏ Audubon's shearwater
❏ Wilson's storm-petrel

Boobies and Gannet
❏ Brown booby
❏ Masked booby
❏ Northern gannet

Jaegers
❏ Parasitic jaeger
❏ Pomarine jaeger

Pelicans
❏ American white pelican
❏ Brown pelican

Cormorant/Anhinga
❏ Double-crested cormorant
❏ Anhinga

Herons, Egrets, and Bitterns
❏ American bittern
❏ Least bittern
❏ Great egret
❏ Snowy egret
❏ Green heron
❏ Cattle egret
❏ Reddish egret
❏ Great blue heron
❏ Tricolored heron
❏ Little blue heron
❏ Black-crowned night-heron
❏ Yellow-crowned night-heron

Ibises
❏ Glossy ibis
❏ White ibis
❏ White-faced ibis
❏ Roseate spoonbill

Stork
❏ Wood stork

Swans and Geese
❏ Black-bellied whistling duck
❏ Fulvous whistling duck
❏ Greater white-fronted goose
❏ Snow goose
❏ Canada goose
❏ Egyptian goose*
❏ Mute swan
❏ Trumpeter swan

Ducks
❏ Wood duck
❏ Mallard
❏ American black duck
❏ Muscovy duck*
❏ Gadwall
❏ Northern pintail
❏ American wigeon
❏ Northern shoveler
❏ Blue-winged teal
❏ Cinnamon teal
❏ Green-winged teal
❏ Canvasback
❏ Redhead
❏ Ring-necked duck
❏ Greater scaup
❏ Lesser scaup
❏ Common eider
❏ Long-tailed duck
❏ Surf scoter
❏ Black scoter
❏ White-winged scoter

❒ Common goldeneye
❒ Hooded merganser
❒ Red-breasted merganser
❒ Ruddy duck

Duck-like Birds
❒ Common gallinule
❒ Purple gallinule
❒ Gray-headed swamphen*
❒ American coot

Vultures
❒ Black vulture
❒ Turkey vulture

Hawks, Kites, and Eagle
❒ Osprey
❒ Swallow-tailed kite
❒ Snail kite
❒ Mississippi kite
❒ White-tailed kite
❒ Bald eagle
❒ Northern harrier
❒ Sharp-shinned hawk
❒ Cooper's hawk
❒ Red-shouldered hawk
❒ Broad-winged hawk
❒ Short-tailed hawk
❒ Red-tailed hawk
❒ Crested caracara
❒ Merlin
❒ American kestrel
❒ Peregrine falcon

Quail, Peafowl, and Turkey
❒ Northern bobwhite
❒ Indian peafowl*
❒ Wild turkey

Rails
❒ Sora
❒ Virginia rail
❒ King rail
❒ Clapper rail

Cranes
❒ Sandhill crane
❒ Whooping crane

Stilt and Avocet
❒ Black-necked stilt
❒ American avocet

Plovers
❒ Black-bellied plover
❒ American golden-plover
❒ Piping plover
❒ Semipalmated plover
❒ Wilson's plover
❒ Snowy plover
❒ Killdeer

Oystercatcher
❒ American oystercatcher

Sandpipers
❒ Lesser yellowlegs
❒ Greater yellowlegs
❒ Solitary sandpiper
❒ Spotted sandpiper
❒ Upland sandpiper
❒ Willet
❒ Whimbrel
❒ Long-billed curlew
❒ Hudsonian godwit
❒ Marbled godwit
❒ Ruddy turnstone
❒ Red knot
❒ Sanderling
❒ Semipalmated sandpiper
❒ Western sandpiper
❒ Least sandpiper
❒ White-rumped sandpiper
❒ Pectoral sandpiper
❒ Dunlin
❒ Stilt sandpiper
❒ Buff-breasted sandpiper
❒ Ruff
❒ Short-billed dowitcher
❒ Long-billed dowitcher
❒ American woodcock
❒ Wilson's snipe
❒ Wilson's phalarope

Gulls and Terns
❒ Laughing gull
❒ Bonaparte's gull

❒ Ring-billed gull
❒ Herring gull
❒ Lesser black-backed gull
❒ Great black-backed gull
❒ Gull-billed tern
❒ Caspian tern
❒ Royal tern
❒ Sandwich tern
❒ Roseate tern
❒ Common tern
❒ Forster's tern
❒ Least tern
❒ Bridled tern
❒ Sooty tern
❒ Black tern
❒ Brown noddy
❒ Black noddy
❒ Black skimmer

Doves and Pigeons
❒ Rock pigeon*
❒ White-crowned pigeon
❒ Eurasian collared dove*
❒ White-winged dove
❒ Mourning dove
❒ Common ground dove

Parrots and Parakeets
❒ Nanday parakeet*
❒ Monk parakeet*
❒ White-winged parakeet*

Cuckoos and Anis
❒ Yellow-billed cuckoo
❒ Mangrove cuckoo
❒ Smooth-billed ani
❒ Groove-billed ani

Owls
❒ Barn owl
❒ Eastern screech-owl
❒ Great horned owl
❒ Burrowing owl
❒ Barred owl

Nightjars
❒ Lesser nighthawk
❒ Antillean nighthawk

❐ Common nighthawk
❐ Eastern whip-poor-will
❐ Chuck-Will's-widow

Swift
❐ Chimney swift

Hummingbird
❐ Ruby-throated hummingbird

Kingfisher
❐ Belted kingfisher

Woodpeckers
❐ Red-headed woodpecker
❐ Red-bellied woodpecker
❐ Yellow-bellied sapsucker
❐ Downy woodpecker
❐ Hairy woodpecker
❐ Red-cockaded woodpecker
❐ Northern flicker
❐ Pileated woodpecker

Flycatchers
❐ Olive-sided flycatcher
❐ Eastern wood-pewee
❐ Acadian flycatcher
❐ Alder flycatcher
❐ Willow flycatcher
❐ Least flycatcher
❐ Eastern phoebe
❐ Vermilion flycatcher
❐ Ash-throated flycatcher
❐ Great-crested flycatcher
❐ Eastern kingbird
❐ Tropical kingbird
❐ Western kingbird
❐ Gray kingbird
❐ Scissor-tailed flycatcher

Shrike
❐ Loggerhead shrike

Vireos
❐ White-eyed vireo
❐ Yellow-throated vireo
❐ Blue-headed vireo
❐ Red-eyed vireo
❐ Black-whiskered vireo

Jays and Crows
❐ Blue jay
❐ Florida scrub-jay
❐ American crow
❐ Fish crow

Swallows
❐ Purple martin
❐ Tree swallow
❐ Northern rough-winged swallow
❐ Bank swallow
❐ Cliff swallow
❐ Cave swallow
❐ Barn swallow

Titmouse and Chickadee
❐ Tufted titmouse
❐ Carolina chickadee

Nuthatches and Creeper
❐ Red-breasted nuthatch
❐ White-breasted nuthatch
❐ Brown-headed nuthatch
❐ Brown creeper

Wrens
❐ Carolina wren
❐ House wren
❐ Winter wren
❐ Marsh wren
❐ Sedge wren

Bulbul
❐ Red-whiskered bulbul*

Kinglets and Gnatcatcher
❐ Golden-crowned kinglet
❐ Ruby-crowned kinglet
❐ Blue-gray gnatcatcher

Thrushes
❐ Eastern bluebird
❐ Veery
❐ Gray-cheeked thrush
❐ Swainson's thrush
❐ Hermit thrush
❐ Wood thrush
❐ American robin

Mimic Thrushes
❐ Gray catbird
❐ Northern mockingbird
❐ Bahama mockingbird
❐ Brown thrasher

Starling, Pipit, and Myna
❐ European starling*
❐ American pipit
❐ Common myna*

Waxwing
❐ Cedar waxwing

Warblers
❐ Blue-winged warbler
❐ Golden-winged warbler
❐ Tennessee warbler
❐ Orange-crowned warbler
❐ Nashville warbler
❐ Northern parula
❐ Yellow warbler
❐ Chestnut-sided warbler
❐ Magnolia warbler
❐ Cape May warbler
❐ Black-throated blue warbler
❐ Yellow-rumped warbler
❐ Black-throated green warbler
❐ Blackburnian warbler
❐ Yellow-throated warbler
❐ Palm warbler
❐ Pine warbler
❐ Prairie warbler
❐ Bay-breasted warbler
❐ Blackpoll warbler
❐ Cerulean warbler
❐ Black-and-white warbler
❐ American redstart
❐ Prothonotary warbler
❐ Worm-eating warbler
❐ Swainson's warbler
❐ Ovenbird
❐ Northern waterthrush
❐ Louisiana waterthrush
❐ Kentucky warbler
❐ Connecticut warbler

❒ Common yellowthroat
❒ Hooded warbler
❒ Wilson's warbler
❒ Canada warbler
❒ Yellow-breasted chat
❒ Tanagers
❒ Scarlet tanager
❒ Summer tanager
❒ Western spindalis

Sparrows

❒ Bachman's sparrow
❒ Chipping sparrow
❒ Clay-colored sparrow
❒ Field sparrow
❒ Vesper sparrow
❒ Lark sparrow
❒ Savannah sparrow
❒ Grasshopper sparrow
❒ Henslow's sparrow
❒ Nelson's sparrow
❒ Saltmarsh sparrow
❒ Seaside sparrow
❒ Fox sparrow
❒ Song sparrow
❒ Lincoln's sparrow
❒ Swamp sparrow
❒ White-throated sparrow
❒ White-crowned sparrow

Blackbirds and Orioles

❒ Bobolink
❒ Red-winged blackbird
❒ Eastern meadowlark
❒ Yellow-headed blackbird
❒ Rusty blackbird
❒ Brewer's blackbird
❒ Common grackle
❒ Boat-tailed grackle
❒ Shiny cowbird
❒ Bronzed cowbird
❒ Brown-headed cowbird
❒ Baltimore oriole
❒ Orchard oriole
❒ Spot-breasted oriole*

Finches and Allies

❒ Purple finch
❒ House finch
❒ Pine siskin
❒ American goldfinch
❒ Northern cardinal
❒ Rose-breasted grosbeak
❒ Blue grosbeak
❒ Indigo bunting
❒ Painted bunting
❒ Dickcissel
❒ Dark-eyed junco

Old World (Weaver) Finch

❒ House sparrow*

Accidentals

_____
_____
_____
_____
_____
_____
_____
_____
_____
_____
_____
_____
_____
_____
_____
_____
_____
_____
_____
_____
_____

APPENDIX C: RESOURCES

"All About Birds." Cornell Laboratory of Ornithology, allaboutbirds.org.

"Audubon of Florida Checklist of Florida Birds." February 2006 revision. https://fl.audubon
.org/sites/default/files/birds_checklist.pdf.

"Birds of North America." Cornell Laboratory of Ornithology, birdsna.org/Species-
Account/bna/home.

"Climate Change." Audubon Florida, fl.audubon.org/conservation/climate.

Common, James. "Birders Behaving Badly." James Common, September 21, 2017.
commonbynature.co.uk/2017/09/21/birders-behaving-badly.

Dunn, Jon L., and Jonathan Alderfer. *Field Guide to the Birds of North America*. Seventh
edition. Washington, DC: National Geographic Society, September 12, 2017.

eBird (globally crowdsourced content). Cornell Laboratory of Ornithology, ebird.org.

"Official Florida State Bird List." Florida Ornithological Society, December 31, 2018. fos
birds.org/florida-bird-list.html.

Peterson, Roger Tory. *A Field Guide to the Birds: A Complete New Guide to All the Birds
of Eastern and Central North America*. Sixth edition. Boston: Houghton Mifflin Har-
court, 2010.

Sibley, David Allen. *The Sibley Guide to Birds*. First edition. New York: Alfred A. Knopf,
October 3, 2000.

INDEX BY HOT SPOT

INDEX BY SPECIES

ABOUT THE AUTHOR AND PHOTOGRAPHER

Avid birders for many decades, bestselling author-photographer team **Randi** and **Nic Minetor** have produced more than forty books for FalconGuides and its parent company, Globe Pequot, including *Birding New England*, *Best Easy Birding Guide: Acadia National Park*, *Best Easy Birding Guide: Cape Cod*, *The New England Bird Lover's Garden*, and *Backyard Birding: A Guide to Attracting and Identifying Birds*. Their work includes guides to a number of national parks and historic cities, as well as *Hiking Waterfalls in New York State*, *Hiking the Lower Hudson River Valley*, and *Hiking Through History New York*. Nic's photography also appears in eight foldout "Quick Reference Guides" to the birds, trees, and wildflowers of New York City and New York State, and the trees and wildflowers of the Mid-Atlantic region. Randi is the author of six books that tell the true stories of people who have died in national and state parks: *Death in Rocky Mountain National Park*, *Death on Mount Washington*, *Death on Katahdin*, *Death in Acadia National Park*, *Death in Glacier National Park,* and *Death in Zion National Park.*

When not in the field, Nic is the resident lighting designer for Eastman Opera Theatre and the Memorial Art Gallery at the University of Rochester, and for theatrical productions at Rochester Institute of Technology and the National Technical Institute for the Deaf. Randi writes for a number of trade and medical magazines and serves as a ghostwriter for executives and entrepreneurs in a wide range of fields.